Languag

The issue of sexist language has been hotly debated within feminist circles since the 1960s. Previous books have tended to regard sexism in language as easy to identify and have suggested solutions to overcome and counter sexism. Sara Mills takes a fresh and more critical look at sexism in language, and argues that even in feminist circles it has become a problematic concept. Drawing on conversational and textual data collected over the past ten years, and with reference to recent research carried out in a range of different academic disciplines, Mills suggests that there are two forms of sexism – overt and indirect. Overt sexism is clear and unambiguous, while indirect sexism can only be understood contextually in relation to the interpretation of surrounding utterances. Indirect sexism is extremely common and we therefore need new ways to challenge and analyse its usage in language.

SARA MILLS is a Research Professor in Linguistics in the English Department at Sheffield Hallam University. Her recent publications include *Gender and Colonial Space* (2004) and *Gender and Politeness* (2003).

Language and Sexism

Sara Mills

Sheffield Hallam University

CAMBRIDGE UNIVERSITY PRESS
Cambridge, New York, Melbourne, Madrid, Cape Town, Singapore, São Paulo, Delhi

Cambridge University Press
The Edinburgh Building, Cambridge CB2 8RU, UK

Published in the United States of America by Cambridge University Press, New York

www.cambridge.org
Information on this title: www.cambridge.org/9780521001748

First published 2008

Printed in the United Kingdom at the University Press, Cambridge

A catalogue record for this publication is available from the British Library

Library of Congress cataloguing-in-Publication Data

Mills, Sara, 1954–
Language and sexism / Sara Mills.
    p.   cm.
Includes bibliographical references and index.
ISBN 978-0-521-80711-1 (hardback)
1. Sexism in language.   I. Title.
P120.S48M555   2008
408.2 – dc22   2008019588

ISBN 978-0-521-80711-1 hardback
ISBN 978-0-521-00174-8 paperback

To Francis and Gabriel,
who have challenged me
(mostly constructively) on
everything I have ever
thought about sexism.

Contents

Acknowledgements

I would like to thank the following people with whom I have discussed ideas about sexism, some of whom have commented on sections of this book or on papers I have given related to the topics in this book: Barbara MacMahon, Alice Bell, Jane Sunderland, June Luchjenbroers, Jill LeBihan, Lynne Pearce, Carol Shepherd, Angie Sandhu, Valeria Schirru, Anna Esch, Sarah Durling, Yonatan Shemmer and Simeon Yates. The management group of the Linguistic Politeness Research Group: Chris Christie, Sandra Harris, Louise Mullany, Bethan Davies, Karen Grainger and Andrew Merrison, have all contributed to discussion of some of the issues in this book. I would also like to thank the many people who responded to the questionnaires I sent out on anti-sexist language policies, and on name changing. Students in my Language and Gender course and also the course I co-teach with Barbara MacMahon: Language Power and Identity, at Sheffield Hallam University have been a constant source of inspiration, as have PhD students Leigh Wetherall, Sam Pitchforth, Sarah Gormley, Diane Wright, Abdurrahman Hamza, Mitra Memarzia, Alison Kinneavy and Erica Brown. Thanks also to Bonnie McElhinny and Jose Santaemilia. I would like to thank the members of the International Gender and Language Association for keeping me on my toes. Lucy Jones set up the Gender and Language reading group in 2007 which has proved an excellent forum for debating ideas about sexism. I am grateful to the two anonymous reviewers who made constructive comments on my book and also to Olga Castro Vazquez who painstakingly read through the manuscript and discussed the ideas in the book on many occasions. I benefited greatly from these discussions and her comments helped in the process of revision. Andrew Winnard has been, as always, a very supportive and insightful editor. And finally, I would like to thank the dyed-in-the-wool sexists whom I have met or whose work I have read who have greatly clarified my thoughts on this issue and who have inspired me to write this book.

1   Introduction

Since the 1960s, the issue of sexist language has been keenly debated within feminist circles. The concern to change language which discriminated against women and which seemed to belittle and trivialise those activities associated with women was a key concern for feminist theorists and activists, trying to change the way that women were represented in advertisements, newspapers and magazines, and also the way that they were named and addressed in texts and in interaction. The debate has widened within recent years, so that 'sexism' and the more problematic 'political correctness' are no longer terms which only have currency within feminist theory but which are used by people outside the university context. However, both these terms 'sexism' and 'political correctness' are now used in ways which are often very different from their original feminist usage.[1]

Whilst there are many definitions of sexism, one which is often cited is 'the practices whereby someone foregrounds gender when it is not the most salient feature' (Vetterling-Braggin, 1981). In this book, I interrogate this definition, since it seems to be based on a liberal-feminist notion that sexism is based on an error made by the speaker or writer which can be rectified when brought to their notice. It assumes a position of objectivity from which statements can be judged as sexist and from which gender can be seen to be not in fact 'the most salient feature'. Throughout this book, I question this view that sexism is simply an individual mistake or slip caused by thoughtlessness or lack of awareness (although it is, of course, sometimes the result of these factors) which can be rectified by simply pointing out the error and suggesting alternative usages. Rather than assuming an individual basis for sexism, I will be foregrounding the view that sexism, just like racism and other discriminatory forms of language, stems from larger societal forces, wider institutionalised inequalities of power and ultimately, therefore, conflict over who has rights to certain positions and resources. Whilst not assuming that all men have power over all women, as

---

[1] It is debatable whether the term 'political correctness' was in fact developed by feminists. Some have argued that it was from the start a term of irony or abuse, used by political campaigners to mock over-zealous colleagues (see Dunant, 1994).

many earlier feminist texts on this subject have (for example, Spender, 1980; Lakoff, 1975), I will nevertheless document the ways in which sexism is an index of ongoing conflict between men and women, particularly within the public sphere (Cameron, 1998a; 2006). Instead of seeing language as a neutral vehicle which represents reality, I will rather describe language as a tool which is drawn on strategically by both sexists and feminist campaigners, and as a site of struggle over word-meaning, which is also often a struggle over who has the right to be in certain environments, speak in certain ways and hold certain jobs.

Sexism is not just about statements which seem to excessively focus on gender when it is not relevant, and whilst I will analyse such statements, I will also focus on other contexts where listeners or readers might consider other factors contributing to a text being judged as sexist. For example, statements may be considered to be sexist if they rely on stereotypical and outdated beliefs, when referring to a particular woman (i.e. 'Look at you crying over this film – women are so emotional'). Here, it is assumed that the woman referred to is exhibiting behaviour which is typical of feminine women and therefore she is being classified less as a person in her own right, with her own feelings, but rather as simply an anonymous member of a social group, experiencing an emotion due to membership of that group. A further factor in statements being considered sexist is when they imply that men's experience is human experience (to give an example from a textbook: 'Circumcision was common amongst Americans in the 1950s' – where it is only male circumcision which is, in fact, being referred to). Another factor in the judgement of statements as sexist is when they are based on the presupposition that any activity associated with women is necessarily trivial or secondary in relation to male activities (for example, 'Women tennis players get lower prize money at Wimbledon because the game is less exciting'). These beliefs are ones which are affirmed in some measure by conservative and stereotypical beliefs, some of which have been institutionalised and which form part of a background common sense which it is assumed that speakers and writers can draw on.

As an example of some of these stereotypical beliefs which underpin sexist statements I would like to consider the lyrics of a pop song. Although I am not arguing that all pop songs are sexist, because there are many songs, such as those by American singer Pink, which challenge sexist beliefs about women, there are nevertheless a large number of songs which objectify and portray women as sexual objects. I shall take as emblematic of these types of beliefs a song by Calvin Harris entitled 'The Girls' (2007). In the chorus, Harris sings: 'I got all the girls, I got all the girls' (repeated throughout the chorus).[2] In

---

[2] This is a version of the words of the song which I have reproduced from memory. Unfortunately because of the nature of this book, it would be extremely unlikely that I would be granted permission to quote from this song. In past publications, publishers have refused to grant me permission to use advertisements or poems in my work (Mills, 1995b; 1996a).

the verse, Harris chants 'I love them white girls, I love them Black girls, I love them Asian girls, I love them skinny girls, I love them fat girls, I love them carrying a little bit of weight girls' and other varieties of girls who are categorised largely in terms of their appearance, weight or nationality/ethnicity. This song is presumably seen as a testament to the degree to which Harris adores women since he says he 'loves' all of them. However, we might ask ourselves whether it is possible to 'love' women in general without being sexist, since the women's individuality is erased. Harris suggests here that he does not care what women look like, and by implication, since he only lists their physical attributes, we can assume that he is not interested in their personalities or their intellect. In the chorus, Harris sings that he has 'got' all the girls, almost as if he is scoring the number of women he has 'had', which seems to be based on a very stereotypical masculinist view of male sexual drive. In the chorus, he has 'got' women and in the verse he 'loves' women; the juxtaposition of these two elements suggests that for Harris 'getting' women and 'loving' them are the same, so that love is indistinguishable from lust. Further objectification can be observed when he states that he loves all 'them girls', rather than, for example, 'you ... girls'; here the listener is forced to ask herself who Harris is addressing. In short, these lyrics seem to exemplify a sexist and objectifying attitude towards women. However, we need not see this as a point of view developed solely by Harris himself, but rather he is drawing on stereotypical discourses about women, men and the relations between the sexes.

I shall be arguing for a more social and institutional view of sexism, but I shall not be arguing that sexism resides in certain words or phrases which can be objectively exposed by feminist linguistics. As we can see from the examples given above, none of the words in the sentence 'Women tennis players get lower prize money at Wimbledon because the game is less exciting' are in themselves sexist; and neither is the juxtaposition of 'getting' and 'loving' women in the song by Calvin Harris intrinsically sexist. It is, in fact, the belief systems which are articulated which are sexist, ones which see women as inevitably different and inferior to men. As Cameron (2006: 16) puts it:

If we take it that no expression has a meaning independent of its linguistic and non-linguistic context, we can plausibly explain the sexism of language by saying that all speech events in patriarchal cultures have as part of their context the power relations that hold between women and men ... This varied and heterogeneous context is what makes expressions and utterances liable to sexist interpretation.

Therefore, I will be discussing not only the language elements of sexism, but also the beliefs or discourses about women and men which are represented in and mediated through language.[3] Although there are certain words and grammatical choices which have a history of usage which seems to indicate

---

[3] I discuss this discourse view in more detail later in this chapter.

particular sexist attitudes and which have been associated in past usage with certain types of meanings, this is not to say that these words will always in every context be interpreted as sexist by readers or hearers. In a sense, what I am arguing for is, at one and the same time, a much more social model of sexism (to describe discriminatory attitudes which develop within institutionalised contexts where there are conflicts about access and power) and also a more localised model of sexism (how this particular word or phrase is or is not interpreted as sexist within this particular context by particular readers or hearers). This does not mean that these two levels of analysis are entirely distinct, as it is clear that institutional sexism develops at least in part from individual usages within particular contexts, and interaction between individuals is informed and takes issue with institutional norms. Thus, I will not be assuming an inherent sexism to words, but I will be arguing for a much more fluid and pragmatic, context-dependent view of sexism. As I will demonstrate in this book, this focus on the importance of context runs the risk of challenging any generalisation about sexist language which I make, but I feel it is in the nature of feminist linguistic analysis at the present time to attempt both to challenge and to hold onto the possibility of generalisation about language and gender (see Eckert and McConnell-Ginet, 2006; Holmes and Meyerhoff, 2003).

The move against generalisation within language and gender research has stemmed from a dissatisfaction with simplistic notions of men's and women's language. As I will discuss more fully later, within feminist thinking there has been a tendency to dismiss what is deemed essentialist thinking, that is, any theoretical or analytical work which is based on the notion of a stable binary opposition of male and female, masculine and feminine (Fuss, 1989; Butler, 1990). However, this has led to a difficulty in arguing that there are any gender differences in language, or that certain language is discriminatory because it refers exclusively to women in stereotypical terms. Holmes and Meyerhoff (2003: 14–15) in particular think that we should make generalisations about data and draw on these findings to argue for the need for change in society; they note:

We should never cease to engage actively with and challenge assumptions about gender norms, and loudly draw attention to the way power, privilege and social authority interact with and are naturalised as properties of independent social categories . . . Such stances of committed engagement may distance us from younger women, or from those widespread contemporary attitudes which valorise diversity and individual expression . . . it may be useful if those working in language and gender research resolved to avoid using terms such as 'essentialist' to dismiss research which focuses on the big picture, research which attempts to identify regularities and make generalisations about global patterns observable in the relationship between language and gender.

For Holmes and Meyerhoff, it is important that we recognise that not all thinking about gender which discusses men and women or generalises about the language associated with women or men should be assumed to be essentialist.[4] It is possible to generalise about gender without making simplistic assumptions about gender difference. However, I would modify this argument slightly. The assumption which has held sway from the 1960s until now that feminists can only make political statements when we can generalise about women's conditions needs to be interrogated. Page (2005: 44) comments:

Various writers have argued that when theoretical arguments and paradigms are divorced from their actual contexts, then a discussion of feminist principles has the potential to become apolitical. Once the discussion shifts from the particular into the abstract, it becomes difficult to ask vital feminist questions, such as to whom the differences of gender matter and what might be done about them.

Thus, the focus on the particular instance allows a more focused interrogation of the way gender is being deployed. Page is arguing that focus on the particular context can in fact enable us to make political statements about the way that women are treated within particular contexts and propose action to change that particular problem, whilst at the same time being aware that the particular instance occurs in relation to other wider instances of discrimination.

1.   Problems with research on sexism

When I have discussed writing a book on sexism with other colleagues and at conferences, many people have looked slightly askance at the thought of working on such a topic. In recent years, campaigns about sexism have been the focus of a great deal of humour and ridicule in the media and have been the subject of verbal play and irony. The term which has been generally adopted by the popular press in discussions about sexism has been 'political correctness' which suggests an over-punctilious concern with the 'trivial' issue of language, rather than serious questions of equal opportunities and discrimination against women, as I will show in more detail in Chapter 4. Thus, feminist, disability and race-awareness campaigns within universities and local councils have been reported as being concerned with whether to use the term 'manhole cover' or 'personhole cover', and whether it is acceptable to talk about 'black coffee' and 'blackboards'. Jokes on the lines of 'vertically challenged' and 'follically challenged' have proliferated. Despite the fact that the examples which are given are almost always invented by the media, these parodies of campaigns against discriminatory language have had a major impact on the way that people, both within institutions and outside them, think about the issues of sexism, racism and other forms of linguistic discrimination.

---

[4] Perhaps also we need to be more aware of the negative evaluation assumed by the use of the term 'essentialist'.

Even within feminist circles, the use of the term 'sexism' is problematic. When it is used, it often has a slightly jaded and anachronistic feel about it. Sexist usage and the English language as a whole are clearly changing so much that, for example, each year when I teach an undergraduate course on Language and Gender, which has a session on sexism, I have to change my examples, as it is generally the case that one or more of them has fallen out of usage. For example, several years ago, I would discuss the distinction between such terms as 'courtier' and 'courtesan' (with 'courtier' referring simply to a male who works in the court, whereas a 'courtesan' is someone who has a sexual relationship with a member of the royal family or the aristocracy). Such examples now have a very dated feel to them and do not seem to be part of the vocabulary that is of interest to or in use by women and men of university age. This may be partly because the recognition of language items which are considered to be discriminatory was researched and the subject of popular discussion during the 1970s and 1980s, due to the work of feminists such as Dale Spender and Robyn Lakoff (Lakoff, 1975; Spender, 1980). However, now that the sexist attitudes of these terms has become apparent to many people, there is an assumption that overt forms of sexism will simply fall out of usage. Other sexist usages are assumed to be easily recognised and thus easily challenged and reformed. However, as Cameron has shown, linguistic reform is not so readily achieved, and language-reform measures may be used in problematic ways by both individuals and institutions to mask fundamental discriminatory practices (Cameron, 1998c). The very notion of reforming language has come under increased scrutiny, being categorised by Cameron (1995) as 'verbal hygiene', that is, the attempt to change language because of fears about incorrect, irritating or offensive usages. Cameron argues, in addition, that 'many people care deeply about linguistic matters; they do not merely speak their language, they also speak copiously and passionately *about* it' (Cameron, 1995: ix). Cameron includes in her analysis of verbal hygiene the historical debates about grammar and style and discussions about political correctness. I would take issue with this analysis, since I see feminist anti-discrimination campaigns as being of a different order to debates about grammatical correctness. The sexist statements made about women which have been objected to by feminists since the 1980s contributed to and were emblematic of wider discriminatory practices in the workplace and within relationships with men.[5]

---

[5] Another problematic aspect to the concept of sexism is that feminist concern with linguistic sexism often had a heterosexual bias, which it was assumed could be simply rectified by having homophobic terms 'added on' to the list of terms which are problematic for straight women. This is clearly not the case and homophobic terms need to be part and parcel of our consideration of sexism as a whole. Thus, what is defined as sexist is in need of a thorough re-examination and reformulation, taking on board the research which has been undertaken within Queer theory and gay and lesbian studies (Kulick, 2000; Cameron and Kulick, 2003).

Many feminists are no longer interested in sexist language. It is assumed that identifying examples of sexism is, in a sense, too easy. Toolan (1996: 4) notes that it is now no longer enough to accuse texts of being coercive and describing ways in which they manipulate the reader; it is necessary to 'include a clear sense of how a particular control-revealing, hegemony eliciting, manipulative text might have been constructed, so as to more nearly attain the status of being a non-manipulative and non-hegemonic text'. He argues that we need to move to analysing 'the subtle and hence more insidious discriminatory and exclusionary discourses that abound'. This is one of the main aims of the book, i.e. moving from a simple analysis of overt sexism, which I feel we need to do, since examples of overt sexism still abound, to an analysis of indirect sexism, that more subtle form of contextualised sexism. Conventional linguistics alone will not equip us with the tools to analyse discrimination, since if sexism is more socially determined and only locally made meaningful, we will need a model of analysis which can do more than analyse phrases in isolation. I have argued in *Feminist Stylistics* (1995b) that we need to look above the level of the sentence to the level of discourse. Drawing on Foucault's (1972; 1978; 1981) work, I see discourse as the 'practices that systemically form the objects of which they speak' (Foucault, 1972: 49). To explain this assertion by Foucault, I argue in *Discourse* (2004: 14) that:

A discourse is something which produces something else (an utterance, a concept, an effect), rather than something which exists in and of itself and which can be analysed in isolation. A discursive structure can be detected because of the systematicity of the ideas, opinions, concepts, ways of thinking and behaving which are formed within a particular context, and because of the effects of those ways of thinking and behaving. Thus we can assume that there is a set of discourses of masculinity and femininity, because women and men behave within a certain range of parameters when defining themselves as gendered subjects. These discursive frameworks demarcate the boundaries within which we can negotiate what it means to be gendered.

Discourses can be seen as the 'rules' and 'guidelines' which we produce and which are produced for us in order to construct ourselves as individuals and to interact with others.

Sunderland (2004: 203), from a similar position, argues that we need therefore to approach sexist belief systems at the level of discourse; she states: 'intervention in *discourse* . . . needs to be distinguished from the feminist "non-sexist language" linguistic activism . . . of the 1970s and 80s' (original emphasis). Whilst I would agree that we cannot describe and combat discoursal sexism by focusing on individual words alone, I feel it is important to focus on the linguistic *and* the wider discourse level. She argues that discourses are those collections of statements which seem to group together to form particular views of men and women, such as the 'neat girls' discourse, the 'girls as good language learners' discourse, the 'father as bumbling parent' discourse. In her book *Gendered Discourses*, she aims to categorise discourse structures around gender and provide ways of intervening at this discursive level. She suggests that we can use six different strategies:

1) meta-discoursal critique [that is, commenting openly on someone's use of a particular gendered discourse]
2) principled non-use of discourses seen as damaging [therefore we simply refuse to use such discourses in our own speech and writing]
3) principled non-confrontational use of discourses seen as non-damaging [so we choose to use progressive discourses about women and men without drawing attention to the fact that we are doing so]
4) principled confrontational use of discourse seen as non-damaging [here we draw attention to our use of progressive discourses about women and men]
5) facilitated group intervention by people other than feminists and linguists [we encourage others to comment on gendered discourse use]
6) rediscursivation [we construct new, more progressive discourses]

(Sunderland, 2004: 203)

We can avoid or affirm certain views of women and men by drawing on certain discursive resources. However, this is often not easy; since, if friends or colleagues begin to use one of the discourses which Sunderland identifies, a discourse of 'fathers as bumblers', stressing the fact that they have had difficulty looking after their children, it is much easier (in English at least), to simply contribute to the discourse by offering examples from one's own experience, than providing counter-examples from more progressive discourses about male parenting. However, what Sunderland has isolated is that, whilst it may be a more difficult option, there is no compulsion to contribute to gendered discourses. We can comment on their use explicitly and simply reframe the comments so that they are positioned within another discursive structure. For example, we could link the discussion of paternal incompetence to an anecdote about fathers who enjoyed looking after their children or we could comment pointedly on the fact that not all fathers are incompetent. In this way, we can begin even in a small way the process of rediscursivation, that is, the process whereby we redraw the boundaries of discourses and begin to develop discourses which are more productive for women and men.

Toolan (1996: 9) suggests that we can integrate a concern with the discourse level with the more local linguistic level; he argues that:

while language is never a code, it is apparent that most individuals become habituated to a code-like predictability of usage, forms and meanings . . . Part of the human response to finiteness and normativity is the tireless schematising that we evidently undertake, the sorting of past experiences into remembered scripts, activities and stereotyped situations. It is through this shifting multidimensional mental network of scripts, situations and styles that we undertake the making of contextualized sense of particular episodes of linguistic interaction.

Thus, for Toolan, we become habituated to certain ways of talking, writing and interpreting which spring from institutionalised settings, from our interactions with others, which we then adopt and use more or less unthinkingly. Schultz (1990: 130) argues that 'analysis of language tells us a great deal about the interests, achievements, obsessions, hopes, fears and prejudices of the people who created the language'. Whilst this is broadly accurate, it is important to take issue with this notion that there were people who 'created' the language – a view which seemed to be prevalent amongst Second Wave feminists such as Schultz and Spender (1980). We need to see language evolving in a very gradual way with certain meanings and usages being kept in play for long periods of time whilst other usages and meanings fall out of circulation fairly rapidly (Deutscher, 2005). No-one in the past 'created' the language wholesale; rather it developed out of a series of struggles and crises over whose views should be represented and which groups were in a dominant position.

Language does indeed reveal to us the values of groups and institutions within our culture in the past who were instrumental in encoding their own perspectives within the language. However, the language as it is used at present and the resources available within it, reveal to us the struggles, both political and moral, over whose voices should be represented and mediated. Thus, sexist usages are still available but they are more stigmatised than they were in the past. Feminist alternatives to sexism are available for usage, but some of them also pose difficulties for usage, since, for some people, they appear to be marked forms, seeming odd or difficult to use. Sexism, in this view, is an ever changing resource which is available to people to use in their own writing, thinking and speaking, which is more or less institutionalised, affirmed or contested by particular influential bodies, and challenged and contested by feminists.

Part of the reason that the study of sexism sometimes feels outdated and archaic is that the model of language which it presupposes is itself outdated, assuming that meanings reside in words and that words are stable in their meaning and unaffected by their localised and contextualised usage. A more adequate view of sexism would see sexism as a judgement made about particular language usages, with certain facts and linguistic and social histories being used to justify that judgement. It is important to analyse these judgements about language, as they are also judgements about us as individuals. If we adopt constructionist positions on the relation between identity and language, that is, that the self is constructed through language, then analysis of sexism is still important as it affects how we think about our identity as women. Benwell and Stokoe (2006: 4) argue:

There is no such thing as an absolute self, lurking behind discourse. A constructionist approach examines people's own understandings of identity . . . Although discourse is not all there is in the world, we understand who we are to each other in this public and accountable realm.

...l feel that, since discourse plays such an important role in the
...d negotiation of identities, despite this anachronistic feel to a
...sexism, discursive structures which are available as a resource
...d trivialise those activities associated with women, must still be

1.1.   Overt sexism and indirect sexism

Sexist language is a term used to denote a wide range of very different elements, from the use of such items as generic pronouns such as 'he' (when used to refer to both males and females); word endings such as '-ette' used to refer to women (for example 'usherette'), nouns referring to men and women (such as 'landlord' and 'landlady', 'manager' and 'manageress', which seem to have a different range of meanings), insult terms which seem to differ for men and women, the names we are given and those which are used for parts of our bodies, and so on. The term sexism is, however, also used to categorise a set of stereotypical beliefs about women which cannot be directly related to a certain set of linguistic usages or features. Take this example from a humorous magazine entitled *The Joy of Sexism*, which is presented in the format of a newspaper report on world records:

Car Parking: The smallest kerbside space successfully reversed into by a woman was one of 19.36m, 63ft 2ins, equivalent to three standard parking spaces by Mrs Elizabeth Simpkins (GB) driving an unmodified Vauxhall Nova 'Swing' on the 12th October 1993. She started the manoeuvre in Ropergate, Pontefract and successfully parked within three feet of the pavement 8 hours and 14 mins later. There was slight damage to the bumpers and wings of her own and the two adjoining cars, as well as a shop frontage and two lamp posts. (Donald, n.d.: 6)

This is followed by another world record report entitled 'Incorrect Driving' which states:

The longest journey completed with the handbrake on was one of 504 km 313 miles from Stranraer to Holyhead by Dr Julie Thorn (GB) at the wheel of a Saab 900 . . . The journey also holds the records for the longest completed with the choke out and the right indicator flashing. (Donald, n.d.: 6)

These 'humorous' reports are based on the assumption that women are bad drivers, an assertion which can be classified as sexist for most people, since it seems to be asserting that gender is an important element in driving ability. Because this is a stereotypical view of women's driving, it is available for use by individual speakers and writers. However, it is important to note, as I will be making clear later in this book, that stereotypical statements do not go unchallenged, and part of the discursive framework within which statements such as this are made, are feminist interventions about sexism. This often makes the sexist statement itself one which might be mediated, for example, by humour, nervous laughter and hesitation. Cameron (2006: 3) notes in her work on sexual politics that we need to analyse the 'contending forces that are active around gender relations': the sexism, the feminist responses and the anti-feminist discourses.

However, it is practically impossible to categorise these jokes about women's driving as sexist linguistically (as would be the case with certain pronouns or word endings) and it seems that we need to be able to distinguish between those statements which can be categorised as sexist (on the basis of the stereotypical knowledge or gendered discourses that they seem to be based on) and those linguistic features which seem to be indicative of sexist beliefs in most contexts. Within each context, we will always have to analyse the cues that could lead us to consider a statement to be sexist. Cameron (1990: 14) argues that:

'sexist language' cannot be regarded as simply the 'naming' of the world from one, masculinist perspective; it is better conceptualised as a multifaceted phenomenon occurring in a number of quite complex systems of representation, all with their places in historical traditions.

Cameron suggests that this multifaceted nature of sexism makes it difficult to analyse, as the feminist linguist is often dealing with many different linguistic and non-linguistic elements in any one analysis. But this should not make it impossible to isolate sexism; what we can analyse is the process whereby certain items become associated with sexist or discriminatory opinions, the history of their usage, their affirmation or contestation by institutions, the use that is made of them by individuals, the challenges that feminism makes to them and the judgements which are made about those usages.

What I shall be distinguishing between in this book is overt sexism and indirect sexism. Overt or direct sexism is the type of usage which can be straightforwardly identified through the use of linguistic markers, or through the analysis of presupposition, which has historically been associated with the expression of discriminatory opinions about women, which signals to hearers that women are seen as an inferior group in relation to males. This is the type of language usage which has been most contested by feminists and which has, as a result, become stigmatised by most language users. Hearers have the option of ignoring this type of language use but they may draw attention to the fact that this type of language use is sexist and hence will draw attention to the fact that they consider the person who has used these terms conservative or chauvinist.[6] This type of overt sexism still exists but it is seen by many as anachronistic and signalling very conservative views of women, which are at odds with current views of gender relations. Feminist reforms have led to changes in the way

---

[6] Just as sexist statements made in conversation have an impact on the community of practice within which they are uttered, so does feminist critique which draws attention to sexism. Sexist statements and anti-sexist statements alike may well be made in order to affect the dynamics of the community of practice in particular ways.

that people refer to women and have also led to changes in the way that people feel about articulating sexist beliefs. 'Political correctness' is a direct response to this unease with feminist interventions. Another direct response to feminist interventions is indirect sexism. I will argue later in Chapter 5, that because overt sexism is more difficult to articulate these days, a more indirect or discourse level of sexism has developed which manages to express sexism whilst at the same time denying responsibility for it.[7] For example, sexist terms are now often used in newspapers, and on certain radio and television programmes, whilst at the same time being undercut by humour or irony, signalled by, for example, exaggerated or marked intonation or stress. This indirect sexism is largely associated with young men, as Benwell (2006) has shown, and with publications and programmes associated with them. For example, Chris Moyles, a UK BBC Radio 1 DJ, regularly insults female colleagues and female listeners with terms such as 'stupid cow' and 'daft slapper'. He also makes assertions about females which can only be classified as sexist and stereotypical (women are no good at football; any sport associated with women, for example netball and hockey, are stupid games and men who play them are emasculated and gay, and so on). When listeners complain about these views and the terms of abuse that Moyles uses on his show, it is asserted that Moyles does not believe these views himself; they are used for humorous effect and they constitute part of a public persona which Moyles has constructed. When recently Moyles used the term 'gay' to mean 'rubbish' (as in 'That's so gay'), the BBC responded to complaints about this by stating that 'gay was widely used by young people to mean "rubbish"' (Cashmore, 2006: 34). Thus, for the BBC, Moyles is not individually responsible for the meaning of this term, but is simply using a term which is current amongst his audience, a strategic response which is often used to deny homophobia (Leap, 1997). Thus, Moyles can use sexist and homophobic terms but, because they are widely used, he can deny responsibility for the offence that they caused. However, this type of indirect sexism is not restricted to the speech of young men and, as I will show in Chapter 5, there is evidence of indirect sexism in many other contexts.

1.2.   *Responses to sexism*

Accusations of sexism can be problematic: when the term sexism is used to accuse someone of having made a stereotypical comment about women in

---

[7] My focus is largely on English in this book, although I will be giving examples from other languages. However, whilst it is clear that overt sexism is more difficult to articulate in natural-gender languages such as English, and in other languages overtly misogynistic terms may be in decline, in languages which have grammatical gender (that is where gender is assigned not only to males and females but also to all objects) overt sexism is very much foregrounded in the way that these grammatical distinctions are handled, as I show in Chapter 2.

conversation, it can often be seen as a way of attacking someone's beliefs and standing within a group. Accusations of sexism can be seen as confrontational and may be interpreted as the taking of a moral stand. On a personal level, such judgements may be difficult to accept.

Furthermore, we should not imagine that sexism is easy to categorise. Some women play with stereotypical beliefs. I recently saw a woman driving a car which had a sticker in the rear window which said in pink 'Dippy Tart' and which featured a cartoon illustration of a doll-like girl. Both 'dippy' and 'tart' are terms which have been associated with overt sexist beliefs in that both of them have been largely restricted to reference to women, stereotypically asserting that women lack intelligence and competence, and that if they are sexually active or are seen to dress in a way which is interpreted as sexually provocative, they should be viewed negatively. In a similar way, I saw a woman carrying an umbrella recently which had a picture of a cow on it with the phrase 'Stroppy Cow'. Obviously, these women are unashamedly embracing these terms to describe themselves ironically or jokingly. This strategy of appropriating negative and stereotypical terms about yourself as a woman has a long history within feminist activism and theorising; for example, lesbians often refer to themselves as 'dykes', which was originally an insult term; 'virago' was originally used to refer to troublesome women, but was then used as the name of a women's publishing press. Mary Daly suggests that this should be a strategy which can help to subvert some of the negative words which have been used about women (Daly, 1981). Judith Butler equally sees the ironic usage of insult terms as a way of combating racist and sexist language (Butler, 1997). Jane Mills argues (1989: xvi) that:

There are many problems about the attempt to reform language. I might for example wish to impart a positive sense when using the word 'cunt' but if this meaning is not understood by my reader then we're back to square one: in the minds of sexists, language can always be sexist. But this is not to believe that there can be no change in either language or society. For me, one of the reasons for studying the history of word meaning, as well as to analyse the way in which patriarchal society defines and thus controls women, was to draw attention to the past and present masculinist bias of conventional usage. Definitions are not static and closed, they are subjects for rational discourse. With almost every word we utter, we have a choice.

Women have a range of options when responding to statements or texts which they consider to be sexist. And this multiplicity of response to sexism also poses problems for any simple notion of reform. Sunderland discusses an incident in a workplace, where a poster was made of a woman colleague and e-mailed to others. It was the woman's birthday and the picture showed the woman's head superimposed on a naked body. One of the woman's female colleagues protested about this image as degrading to women but the woman who was figured e-mailed everyone, saying 'I would like to take this opportunity to say thank you to all my friends and colleagues who made me feel very special on my 40th birthday' (Sunderland, 2004: 195). In this case, the colleague who complained felt that, if there was potential damage to one woman in this image, it was in some ways damaging to all women, as Sunderland (2004: 196) argues: 'the damaging potential of a given discourse must be relevant to more than just an individual'. However, Sunderland also argues that this multiplicity of response to sexism, whilst making reform difficult, may have positive effects: 'whereas some individuals may be damaged by sexist discourse, others will recognise it for what it is, resist it, laugh at it and/or become empowered in the process' (Sunderland, 2004: 194). We might want to question whether the process of laughing at a sexist joke directed at oneself is always empowering, however. We may feel, as perhaps in the case just mentioned, that we have to laugh at sexist jokes in order not to lose face, in order to appear to be 'one of the boys'. Admitting that we recognise a joke as sexist can put us in a difficult interactional fix, classifying ourselves as a victim of sexism, which might clash with our professional status.

There are a number of ways of responding to sexism, which do not involve anger and condemnation but rather draw on irony and humour. In this book I analyse the effectiveness of these responses.

1.3.   Problems of reform

As I mentioned above, the model which up until now has been used to describe sexism has assumed that sexism resides in individual words and phrases and that the solution to the problem of sexism is to reform the word, that is, to propose an alternative non-sexist usage. In certain cases, that is the most effective strategy, for example when the generic pronoun 'he' is replaced by 's/he' or 'they' (as in 'the patient or his carer must complete this form' which can be rephrased as 'Patients or their carers must complete this form' or the more long-winded 'The patient and her/his carer must complete this form'). Here, simply replacing the pronoun with another one which signals its inclusive reference and signals an awareness of the problematic nature of sexism for both women and men, has a major impact on a workplace or institution and has an impact on the way that some women see their relation to institutions (for a fuller discussion, see Chapter 2). However, for some nouns which appear to be problematic, a simple replacing of the noun with another seeming non-sexist one is not always possible. If, for example, the term 'spaceman' seems to be a male-specific noun which is used generically to refer to all astronauts, then one strategy would be to replace that word with a truly generic noun such as 'astronaut'. However, as Cameron (1990) has argued, what if, because of the highly specialised and military nature of much space training which has resulted in most astronauts being male, the term 'astronaut' itself is used as a term which refers to males only and females in the profession are then termed 'female astronauts'? Similarly, how can we believe that reform is a viable option when the non-sexist word that has been developed to replace a sexist term, for example 'chairperson', is then largely used to refer to women? Although 'chair' and 'chairperson' have been adopted fairly widely throughout institutions, it seems that the lower-status term 'chairperson' is used to refer to women and low-status men (Sunderland, 2006). Furthermore, how can feminist linguists deal with those who adopt these reformist measures at a superficial level and mark their superficial acceptance of these terms by intonation or stress? For example, from my own experience, at a primary school governors' meeting where the chair was female, several governors asked the elderly treasurer (a renowned sexist and conservative) if he would mind referring to the chair as 'chair' or 'chairwoman', rather than calling her 'chairman' or, worse, 'madam chairman'. Since there was general acceptance in the meeting that this was something which many of the women and men present approved of, he grudgingly agreed to change his usage. However, each time he thereafter referred to the chair he took a very audible intake of breath and pronounced 'chair' with a great deal of aspiration, which seemed like a sigh of despair at the inanity of this type of 'political correctness'. On the surface, at least, he could not be criticised, as he had acceded to our demands by using the term 'chair'. However, he made it abundantly clear by his facial expressions and by his pronunciation of the term that he was only doing so at a very superficial level and his beliefs about women and about language reform were entirely unchanged.

A further problem with reform can be illustrated by examining the case of Italian where feminists have argued that professional women should not have to refer to themselves using names referring to men. Thus, a female lawyer in the past would have to refer to herself as 'avvocato', a female minister as 'ministro' and a female mayor as 'sindaco', the 'o' ending here signifying a male referent. Because of feminist campaigns, it has become possible for women to refer to themselves as 'avvocatessa', 'ministra' or 'sindachessa', using newly developed feminine endings. However, these terms have not been widely adopted, because, it is argued, they sound very 'forced'. This is a common strategy to adopt in relation to words which have been introduced to refer to women. All words which are introduced in this way feel 'forced' and cause resentment, these especially since they are seen to have been introduced because of political pressure. In addition, they seem to emphasise the fact that the referent is a woman, rather than stressing her professional status. Added to this is the problem that there are no feminine terms in Italian as yet for certain professions, for example for engineer and architect ('engeneer' and 'architetto'). Thus, the proposed language reforms have not been widely adopted and have been widely characterised as 'ridiculous' (V. Schirru, pers. com., 2007).

In Spanish there are similar difficulties. The suffix '-ista' is neuter in Spanish, that is it does not signify masculine or feminine ('una artista': a female artist; 'un artista': a male artist). This should be the case for all neuters, but there are some notable exceptions; for example 'un modista': a male fashion designer and 'una modista': a female fashion designer. Because male fashion designers wish to ensure that they are referred to with a prestige term, they have started to use 'un modisto': a male fashion designer (using an explicitly masculine ending), in order to differentiate themselves from women tailors and dressmakers. Paradoxically, there are now some women in the fashion industry who refer to themselves as 'una modisto', using the feminine determiner with a masculine noun form, to emphasise that they are in the high fashion industry and not mere dressmakers. This example highlights the extent to which what is usually characterised as a simple grammatical choice, is in fact determined by questions of power and males wishing to set themselves apart from women (O. Castro, pers. com., 2007).

A further example from Spanish illustrates the complexity of grammatical gender and also illustrates the fact that when feminine forms are changed to masculine ones, they are not considered to be 'forced' or 'too difficult to pronounce' as the changes from masculine to feminine are. The most common way of referring to nurses in Spanish used to be 'las enfermeras' which is a feminine form grammatically. Doctors were referred to as 'los médicos' or 'los doctores', both of which are masculine. As more men entered the nursing profession, the masculine form 'los enfermeros' began to be used both for them individually and as a general term to refer to all nurses. And as more women became doctors, 'las médicas' and 'las doctoras', the feminine forms, began to be used, but this time, only in relation to individual female doctors and not generically. At the present time, women nurses are still in the majority; however, the generic masculine is currently used to refer to nurses in general. Two examples illustrate this point: the first was stated by an announcer when covering the demonstrations of Spanish nurses on the TV news: 'los enfermeros continúan con sus protestas para mejorar sus condiciones laborales' ('Nurses [masc.] continue their protests to improve their working conditions').[8] This announcement was made whilst an image of a crowd of largely female nurses was shown demonstrating. A further instance of the use of 'nurses' with a masculine determiner can be seen in the following example from the free Madrid newspaper *Que! Edición Madrid* (June 2006):

!No estamos para servir café al jefe! Una juez de Valencia prohíbe utilizar a los sub-alternos para servir agua, leche o refrescos. Las secretarias no son camereras, los enfermeros no son limpiadores. (We are not here to serve the boss coffee! A judge in

---

[8] This example comes from *Telediario* TVE1, the news on Spain's main public TV channel, on 13 June 2006 and was provided by Olga Castro (pers. com., 2007).

Valencia has forbidden the use of subordinates to serve water, milk or refreshm

Secretaries [fem.] are not waitresses, nurses [masc.] are not cleaners [masc.].)

Here the term for nurses is the masculine form. Even though this change from the feminine 'las enfermeras' to the masculine 'los enfermeros' has been relatively recent, there have not been protests against the 'forced' and 'ridiculous' nature of this change (O. Castro, pers. com., 2007).

Whilst, in the 1980s, feminists hoped that it would be possible to reform language and, as I show in Chapter 3, the reforming strategies of feminists in a range of different countries have proved very effective in changing certain types of linguistic sexism, reform of sexist statements is now seen to be more difficult to achieve and more fraught with problems (see Pauwels, 1998; 2001). Cameron (1998a) argues that for reform to be effective, it is necessary to have it accepted by the gatekeepers of language, that is the dictionary compilers, the newspapers, and editors who provide guidance on writing style for publishers and so on. Reform can only be effective if it is accepted and promoted by those in positions of influence. In fact, the alternative terms suggested by feminists *have* been largely adopted by these gatekeepers, since publishers, trade unions and universities have generally adopted policies in relation to sexist and racist language. However, Sunderland reports on an anti-sexist language policy which was issued at the Lancashire Polytechnic, UK in 1987; critics of the policy argued that it displayed 'cultural dictatorship' and these critics claimed that it had been written by 'frustrated spinsters' (Sunderland, 2006: 11). Other institutions, such as right-wing newspapers, have ridiculed the proposed alternatives as 'politically correct' and they have therefore not been adopted. Others have revelled in their sexism, terming it 'politically incorrect'.

In considering the effectiveness of reform, we need to ask whether sexism is a reflection of social oppression or a mediation and factor in oppression. If it is a simple reflection of discriminatory social practices, then changing the social system will lead to sexism disappearing, and simply changing the language items themselves will have no impact whatsoever – those who are sexists will simply find other ways to be sexist. If sexism is a mediation of or a factor in oppression, that is, if the way that language is used systematically represents women as secondary to men, then perhaps if the language is changed, it will change the commonsense assumptions that people have about women. In turn, social discrimination will diminish. I would argue that in some ways these two positions on language, which have often been polarised in the past by feminist linguists, should be seen as both true, since language does change when social systems and structures change,[9] and equally changes in language, especially when they are affirmed by institutions, can have an impact on the

---

[9] However, I do not see language as simply reflecting social structures. There is a much more complex relation between language and culture.

re considered and treated. Thus, language is neither simply
vehicle for social values, nor solely a catalyst for social
e of its role in the construction of identity and roles for both
ups within society, it should be seen as a resource which
at people think about their positions in society. Linguistic
as an impact on the way people feel that they can express
thers, as I discuss in more detail in Chapter 3, but it also has
an impact on wider social values by leading the way in enabling challenges to
stereotypical thinking.

1.4.   Changing nature of feminist impact

In recent years it has become clear that there has been a major change in the
role of feminism (Gormley, 2008). There has been much discussion of the fact
that for many women, feminism is not a term that they would use to refer to
themselves, even though they would probably agree largely with a feminist
agenda. In the university system, there are now few Women's Studies courses
available either at undergraduate or postgraduate level.[10] In the 1980s and
1990s I regularly sat on interview panels within the institutions in which I then
worked as the obligatory female representative, as it was deemed important
to foreground gender issues within the interviewing process (as if the mere
presence of a woman on the panel would solve problems of discrimination).
This is no longer standard practice. Furthermore, on many of the committees
which I attended in the 1980s and 1990s, 'Equal Opportunities' was frequently
a standard item on the agenda, and under this topic we would discuss the
implications of what had been decided at the meeting for equal opportunities.
Whilst there are still equal opportunities officers within institutions, this focus
on equal opportunities as an integral part of everyday business has changed in
universities (but perhaps not in other institutions and organisations). However,
despite this decrease in the status of feminism within the academy, there are still
strong professional bodies associated with the study of feminism (for example,
the International Gender and Language Association) and there are numerous
feminist journals (for example, *Gender and Language*, *Journal of Gender Studies*, *Feminist Review*, *Gender and History* and so on). For Cameron, however,

---

[10] When I first started working at Sheffield Hallam University in 1995, there were BA and MA
courses in Women's Studies. Now those courses no longer run; there are still, however, many
courses which are explicitly drawing on feminist theory. Most of these courses concern themselves with gender issues at some level whilst not using 'gender' or 'women' in their titles. In
the past ten years, the term 'gender' has been much more commonly used as a term to refer to
both men and women and this reflects the integration of feminist theory and women's issues
into the curriculum. In other countries, the situation is much worse; for example in Japanese
institutions, feminist theory and women's studies are negatively viewed and colleagues who
work on these subjects find promotion difficult (H. Kumagai, pers. com., 2006).

'though feminism remains strong in the academy, its cultural influence outside academic circles has declined along with the organised women's movement and that has also changed the academic conversation' (Cameron 2006: 8). This changing relation of academic feminism to a wider public and to institutions has had a great impact on the way in which sexism is thought about. Whereas in the past, there was a popular Women's Movement outside the academy, which campaigned against pornography, protested against nuclear weapons at Greenham Common, and 'reclaimed the night', it is difficult to discern a clear women's movement now. Some of these protests have become institutionalised, for example most European governments have established Equal Opportunities Commissions and Ministers for Women; and there are a great number of highly efficient and professional feminist campaigning groups, such as, in the UK, the Women's Environmental Network and the Fawcett Society. However, for many people, there is no longer a popular feminist movement, since feminism has achieved its goals of equal opportunities and discouraging discrimination. We are, in short, for these people, in a post-feminist era. Popular feminism seems for some to have lost its edge and vigour; as Gauntlett argues: it appears like a 'radio friendly remix of a multi-layered song with the most exciting bits sampled and some of the dense stuff left out' (Gauntlett, 2002, cited in Gill, 2007: 2).

1.5. Changing status of women

Since the 1970s and 1980s, women's position in British society has changed immeasurably, most notably the proportion of women in the workplace and in full-time work. This has made a major impact on the way that women are viewed, but it has also posed a threat to those men who have stereotypical views of women and who contest the access which women now have to careers and promotion. It has also made a major impact on the way that women behave and the way that they view themselves. Because of increased financial independence and status within the workplace, women are less likely to tolerate sexist comments and discrimination. But this does not mean that women are treated as equals to men. Gill (2007: 1) notes that there is a curious schizophrenia about women:

Confident expressions of 'girl power' sit alongside reports of 'epidemic' levels of anorexia and body dysmorphism; graphic tabloid reports of rape are placed cheek by jowl with adverts for lap-dancing clubs and telephone sex lines; lad magazines declare the 'sex war' over, while reinstating beauty contests and championing new, ironic modes of sexism; and there are regular moral panics about the impact on men of the new idealised male body imagery, while the re-sexualisation of women's bodies in public space goes virtually unremarked upon. Everywhere, it seems feminist ideas have become a kind of common sense, yet feminism has never been more bitterly repudiated.

Levy also comments on the rise of what she terms 'raunch culture', in contemporary society, where those forms of sexual behaviour which Second Wave feminists condemned as exploiting women are now embraced as part of women's empowerment: 'this new Raunch culture didn't mark the death of feminism [friends] told me; it was evidence that the feminist project had already been achieved' (2005: 3). So empowered are women that they can enjoy going to strip clubs and lap-dancing. For Levy, 'raunch culture is a litmus test of female uptightness' (2005: 40). She adds: 'embracing raunch culture is a way for young women to thumb our noses at the intense fervour of 2nd wave feminists' (2005: 74).

Men and women have changed, because of the impact of feminism and the changes which have come in the wake of women's integration into the workforce. Talbot (1998: 191) argues that changes in institutions result in changes in the way individuals see their roles:

masculine and feminine identities are effects of discursive practices. Masculinity is not an individual property or attribute; it is formed within institutions and is historically constituted. Like femininity it is discursively produced and its articulation spans institutions.

Men have had to change their roles and attitudes and for some this has been difficult. Some have welcomed the changes, but often these new, more progressive roles have been mocked. For example, the New Man has been much derided. Goodwin has described the New Man as 'the toxic waste of feminism'; she goes on to argue that: 'The worst of it is that these men are so unappealing, so unaesthetic, so unsexy. Once you see through the dubious charms of someone "who really understands women" what you're left with is a man . . . who is so busy trying to be supportive that he has probably forgotten what an erection is for' (Goodwin, 1993, cited in Gill, 2007: 210).

The integration of women into the public sphere has not been achieved without conflict and resistance from men. It is clear that women are not treated equally even now, but the sheer visibility of women in all sectors of the public sphere has changed the type of language which it is possible to use. It is no longer possible to address a departmental meeting at a university by saying 'Gentlemen, shall we start, now?' (something which happened to me in the 1980s when I was the only female in a department). There have also been institutional and legal changes which make many types of sexist statements appear aberrant, and which have conferred on women, in theory though not in practice, the same legal status as men (the Equal Pay Act, the Sex Discrimination Act and the reforms of the divorce legislation in Britain). Finally, there have been feminist campaigns in most Western European countries and America which drew attention to the problems associated with sexist language; many of these campaigns received support from institutions, such as trades unions, publishing houses and universities. Thus quasi-legalistic measures were taken by institutions to reform language use and, whilst these reforms are not without their difficulties, they have meant that individuals have a certain amount of institutional support when challenging the use of overt sexism. All of these factors together have resulted in a fundamental change in the nature of overt sexism and the way that sexism operates in Britain, Australasia and North America today. It could be argued that these changes have meant that overt sexism has been 'driven underground' and that other more subtle forms of expression which are equally pernicious and discriminatory have been used instead.

It has also become clear that, given the more sophisticated models of gender and language use that are currently being deployed in language and gender research (see for example Holmes and Meyerhoff, 2003; Eckert and McConnell-Ginet, 2003), it is no longer possible to speak about sexism in the simplistic way that many feminists did in the 1980s and 1990s (Miller and Swift, 1982/1989). The term sexism implied a model of the relation between the sexes which is necessarily antagonistic: all women pitted against all men in the 'battle of the sexes'. Women were presented as the victims of male aggression, fear and hatred. Sexism was seen to be determined by patriarchy – a social system which privileged men at the expense of women. Whilst being keenly aware of the persistence of structural inequalities between men and women, and emphasising the notion of institutional sexism, the notion of a global homogeneous patriarchy is simplistic. Lazar suggests that we see patriarchy as 'an ideological system that interacts in complex ways with . . . corporatist and consumerist ideologies' (2005: 1). Thus, we need a much more complex notion of male power and the way it is buttressed by other forces. Sexism is better understood as a set of discursive practices and stereotypical knowledge which changes over time and which can be challenged, rather than as the reflection of a fixed and unchanging patriarchy.

Furthermore, rather than assuming that all men are contemptuous of women, we need to be able to see sexism as a resource available to men but which not all men draw on. Working with more complex models of the differences within gender categories and trying to integrate models of gender with factors of race, age, education and sexual orientation, have led many feminists working on language and gender to move away from a concern with sexist language, precisely because of these problems of essentialism. So, whilst in this book I will be drawing on analyses of sexist language which show that overt sexism is still prevalent, I will not be assuming that all women will interpret an utterance which seems to be sexist in the same way, nor will I assume that all women are affected in the same way. I will instead analyse the range of meanings that statements may have and the way that meaning is not always clearly defined – misunderstanding and conflict over meaning are more common than clarity in this area (Pauwels, 1998; Wodak, 1998). In fact, the conflict over resources, the conflict over women working in the public sphere and antagonism to feminism have often led to a strategy of using language items which cannot be seen to be openly sexist but which can be interpreted as functioning as sexist at the level of implicature (Cameron, 1998b). Interpretation is one of the key elements here, as is the assessment of what we assume someone's intentions are.

2.   My theoretical position

2.1.   Third Wave feminism

I will be distinguishing in this book between two types of feminist analysis, Second Wave and Third Wave feminist analysis. Broadly speaking, Second Wave feminism focuses on the language of women as a subordinated group and Third Wave feminism challenges the homogeneity of women as a group, focusing instead on localised studies.[11] I would like to challenge the notion that these forms of analysis are simply chronological so that Third Wave feminism supersedes and supplants Second Wave feminism; rather I argue that Third Wave feminism is best seen as a development from Second Wave feminism which nevertheless depends on the basic framework of Second Wave feminism for its theoretical integrity. The term Third Wave feminism is one over which there is a great deal of debate. In the UK it is generally used to refer to those feminists who are trying to work with more constructionist models of gender, that is, who see gender difference and gender identity as socially constructed rather than as originating in biological difference. These feminists are trying to move beyond the notion of a simple binary sex difference. However, in the US, the difference between Second and Third Wave feminism is characterised less as a theoretical issue but rather as a generational conflict between younger and older more established feminists (see Gillis *et al.*, 2004; Gormley, 2008). In order to contrast the way in which these two approaches work and to demonstrate that each tendency can be put to work in particular contexts, I examine the difficulties which each approach finds with the analysis of sexism.

The term Third Wave feminism has developed relatively recently to describe a form of analysis which is critical of Second Wave feminism. Whilst the term Second Wave feminism is fairly uncontentious, referring to the largely liberal and radical feminism of the 1960s onwards which argued for the equality of women, the term Third Wave feminism is more contentious. A conference at Exeter University (2002) on the subject of Third Wave feminism together

---

[11] This section is a substantially revised version of papers given at the International Gender and Language Association Conference, Lancaster University, 2002, and at the Third Wave Feminism Conference, Exeter University, 2002. An earlier, longer version of this section has been published as Mills (2004b).

with the work of Mary Bucholtz (1999; 2000) and Janine Liladhar (2000) have convinced me that Third Wave feminism is a term preferable to post-feminism (which assumes implicitly that the aims of feminism have been achieved and that therefore feminism is largely irrelevant) and post-modern feminism (which, whilst theoretically more complex, has difficulty formulating any notion of a political programme).

Third Wave feminism seems to be part of a wider post-modernist-influenced theoretical position where 'big stories are bad, little stories are good', but, unlike some other forms of analysis, such as post-feminism, it locates itself within a feminist trajectory (Holmes and Meyerhoff, 2003; Potter, 1996). Second Wave feminism has achieved a great deal: feminist campaigning and consciousness-raising in the 1960s and onwards have changed attitudes to the role of women and have resulted, in Western Europe and the US, in equal opportunities legislation, greater access to work within the public sphere, access to childcare, and reproductive rights. However, this campaigning was largely focused on the needs of heterosexual white middle-class women.[12] Third Wave feminist linguistics has largely been concerned with analysing women's speech without assuming that women are a homogeneous grouping. For example, Penelope Eckert (2000) analyses the differences between the language use of different groups of girls in a high school in America, drawing on the categories and groupings that they themselves use, such as 'jocks' and 'burnouts'. Mary Bucholtz (1996) and Nancy Henley (1995) analyse the way that black American women's speech does not necessarily accord with the type of speech patterns described by earlier feminist linguists Lakoff and Spender, since there are different linguistic resources available, signalling potentially different affiliations. The essays in the collections edited by Bergvall *et al.* (1996) and Coates and Cameron (1988) all stress the way in which women's language differs according to context and factors such as class, ethnic and regional affiliation.

Even the notion of the status of the variable 'gender' itself has been questioned; for example, Mary Bucholtz has argued that in Second Wave feminism 'locally defined groupings based on ongoing activities and concerns were rarely given scholarly attention; if they were, members were assigned to large scale categories of gender, race and ethnicity and class' (Bucholtz, 1999: 208). In contrast, in Third Wave feminism, these large-scale categories are now questioned, so that rather than gender being seen as a stable unified variable, to be considered in addition to race or class, gender is now considered as a variable constrained and constituted by them and in turn defining them in the context of

---

[12] We need to question the homogeneity of our current characterisation of Second Wave feminism. Susan Stryker (2002) argues that Second Wave feminism was more diverse than most feminists acknowledge; there was a great deal of dissent and alternative accounts of gender – for example, see work by Angela Davis and Chela Sandoval (extracts of these writers' works can be found in Lewis and Mills, 2004).

local conditions. Indeed, feminist linguistics now seems to have turned away from these more established identity categories to an analysis which focuses on, as Swann (2002: 49) puts it, 'a whole set of identity features (being a manager, someone's mother, a sensible person)' which might be potentially relevant. Furthermore, identities are now seen as plural and potentially conflicting, even within a specific individual in a particular interaction (Benwell and Stokoe, 2006). Third Wave feminist linguistics does not make global statements about women's language or the language used about women but rather focuses on a more *punctual* analysis, that is, one which can analyse the way that one's interpretation of statements about women can vary from context to context. However, Swann (2002: 48) has argued that this contextual focus in relation to variables has almost invalidated the notion of the variable; she argues:

if gender identity is something that is done in context, this begs the question of how an analyst is able to interpret any utterance in terms of masculinity (or working class, white, heterosexual masculinity). How does an analyst assess whether a speaker is doing gender, or another aspect of identity?

What Swann goes on to argue is that rather than seeing Third Wave (or as she terms it Post-modern) feminism as a simple reaction to Second Wave feminist linguistics, we need instead to see the way in which Third Wave feminism depends on early feminism; the contextualised studies are interesting 'partly because they qualify, or complexify, or introduce counter-examples' (Swann, 2002: 60). Thus, the localised studies should be seen against the background of the earlier global (and problematised) claims of Second Wave feminism, which they can perhaps help to modify and temper.

Much Third Wave feminist linguistics draws on the work of Judith Butler, particularly the notion of performativity (Butler, 1990; 1993; 1997).[13] Gender within this type of analysis is viewed as a verb, something which you do in interaction, rather than something which you possess (Crawford, 1995). Gender is constructed through the repetition of gendered acts and varies according to the context. In many readings of Butler's work, gender is seen almost like a set of clothes that one puts on – the individual chooses the type of identity they would like to have and simply performs that role. However, it is clear that institutional and contextual constraints determine the type and form of identity and linguistic routines which an individual considers possible within an interaction and which others feel are available. Second Wave feminist linguistics assumed that gender pre-existed the interaction and affected the way that the interaction developed, and gender was seen as something which pre-existed texts and was drawn on by producer and reader in their interpretation of the

---

[13] This is rather curious because many of the linguists who draw on Butler's work would be critical of the use of Speech Act Theory from which the notion of the performative is drawn.

text. In contrast, Third Wave feminists focus on the way that participants in conversation bring about their gendered identity, thus seeing gendering as a process; in the process of construction and interpretation of texts, gender is one of the elements which is forged from ideological knowledge which it is assumed is accepted or challenged. This focus on the orienting of participants to gender is clearly influenced by heated debates between Conversation Analysis and Critical Discourse Analysis about whether extra-textual factors such as gender and race can be considered if they are not specifically addressed by participants (Schegloff, 1997; Wodak and Meyer, 2001; Mills, 2003b). However, it could be argued this more process-oriented feminism still has a very clear notion of what gender is, bringing that pre-constructed notion to their analyses of the way that participants orient to gender within interactions (Mills, 2003b; Swann, 2002). This is of crucial import for the analysis of sexism, since, as Holmes and Meyerhoff (2003: 9) argue: 'No matter what we say about the inadequacy or invidiousness of essentialised, dichotomous conceptions of gender, no matter how justifiable such comments may be, in everyday life, it really is often the case, that gender is "essential".' They go on to argue that 'gender as a social category *matters*' (2003: 9). Sexism is a particular case where in interaction or in texts gender is drawn attention to and where it makes a difference for participants.

It is difficult for Third Wave feminism, focusing as it does on the local, to make its feminist agenda explicit. Cameron (2006: 2) comments on this:

I would not define research as 'feminist' primarily on the grounds that it adopts a constructionist view of gender in which the categories 'men' and 'women' are treated as unstable, variable and thus non-natural. I do not disagree with this view of gender but proclaiming it . . . is neither a defining feature of a feminist approach nor the most important task for feminist scholarship. For me what defines feminism is not its theory of gender but its critique of *gender relations*. [Original emphasis]

Thus, at the same time as working out a model of sexism, it is necessary to formulate a model of feminism which can function at the local and the more global level.

2.1.1. Meaning Second Wave feminist linguistics was concerned with analysing the inherent meanings of words and often made statements about the abstract meanings of words, constructing dictionaries of sexist language and advising on the avoidance of certain words (Kramarae and Treichler, 1985; Miller and Swift, 1982/1989). After Cameron *et al.*'s (1988) work on the multifunctionality of tag-questions and Michael Toolan's (1996) analysis of the difficulty of assigning clear functions to specific formal features, the notion that there was a clear link to be made between power, gender and language items was made more problematic (for a discussion, see Thornborrow, 2002).

Third Wave feminist linguistics focuses on the way that words are made to mean in specific ways and function to achieve certain purposes in particular contexts (Christie, 2001). Thus, rather than discussing oppressive global social structures such as patriarchy, Third Wave feminists analyse the way that gender and conflict are managed by women at a local level (Cameron, 1998c). It is still possible to refer to structural inequality and to highlight instances of discrimination, but Third Wave feminist linguistics is more concerned with variability and resistance than on making global statements about the condition of women in relation to language use. Thus, whilst a Second Wave analysis might focus on the use of the generic pronoun 'he' to refer to both men and women, or derogatory terms used to describe women such as 'bitch' or 'slag', a Third Wave feminist analysis might focus on the variable ways in which terms such as 'bitch' might be used and the way that hearers may draw on certain inferences in order to disambiguate meaning: for example, knowledge of someone's beliefs about women, or someone's verbal dexterity. Rather than assuming that 'bitch' is by its very nature always sexist, a Third Wave feminist analysis might focus on the factors which lead to a hearer or reader considering the term to be offensive to women, or personally offensive to you as a woman, and those contextual factors which lead to it being considered ironic or funny. For example, as I show in Chapter 2, 'bitch' used in gangsta rap songs has a very different function to the way it is used if I jokingly call a friend a 'bitch' who has said something playfully sarcastic about me. Similarly 'bitch' functions differently when it is used in contexts where the speaker is angry. However, whilst this local focus helps women to describe practices which discriminate against them, Third Wave feminists find it difficult to refer to global, structural and systematic forms of discrimination (Eckert and McConnell-Ginet, 2006).

Rather than meanings being imposed on women, Third Wave feminists consider meanings to be co-constructed: that is, within particular contexts, women and men jointly engage in the contestation and affirmation of particular types of practices and interpretations. What something means in a particular context is the result of the actions of all of the individuals concerned, negotiating with the institutional constraints of status and institutionalised linguistic routines. For example, Thornborrow (2002) analyses an interview between a woman and two police officers, where the woman claims that she has been raped and the police try to throw doubt on the veracity of her claim, by suggesting that she is mentally ill. Thornborrow draws attention to the way that the woman plays an active role in contesting their assertions. A Second Wave feminist analysis would analyse this interaction as the police oppressing and silencing the woman; however, this woman seems to have accrued to herself a certain amount of what I have termed 'interactional power', that is, she has drawn on linguistic resources which were available within that particular context, using questions and rebuttals to challenge her characterisation by the police as an untrustworthy person (Mills, 2003b). Ultimately, however, the police officers' version of events seems to be the one which holds sway, even though the woman's interventions are important in defining the way that the interview takes shape – the institutional status of the police officers plays a crucial role in their version being seen as the 'truth' (see also Potter, 1996). We cannot see this woman as simply powerless as a Second Wave feminist analysis might have done. However, what perhaps Third Wave feminism needs to draw from Second Wave feminist analysis is a campaigning edge whereby we would argue for a change in the way police interviews are carried out, or call for training for police officers in the type of language which it is appropriate to use with rape victims. What is necessary is to integrate the campaigning zeal of Second Wave feminism which would bring about material changes in women's lives, with Third Wave feminism's theoretical sophistication and contextualised focus.

2.1.2. Power Most Third Wave feminists have been influenced by Michel Foucault's theorisation of power (Foucault, 1978; 1981). Power is seen as a net or web of relations not as a possession; thus power is enacted and contested in every interaction (Thornborrow, 2002). Power becomes a much more mundane, material and everyday element rather than something abstract and intangible which is imposed from above. Thus, there is now a concern with the local management of power relations, the way that individuals negotiate with the status which they and others have been allotted or which they have managed to achieve. They can contest or affirm this local status within particular contexts, through their use of language and through their behaviour. Many feminist theorists draw a distinction between institutional status (that is, the status that you are allocated through your position within an institution) and local or interactional status (that is, the position that you manage to negotiate because of your verbal skill, confidence, concern for others, 'niceness' and so on) and whilst these two positions are clearly interconnected, it is now often the local status which is focused on by Third Wave feminist theorists (Manke, 1997; Diamond, 1996; Thornborrow, 2002). This is important in the analysis of sexism, since very often it was assumed, by Second Wave feminists, that those in power were able to make derogatory comments about women, simply because of their institutional status. However, in a Third Wave feminist analysis, we can see that sexism may be deployed to address a perception of local status – to try in a particular environment to foreground someone's status as a woman where femininity is not valued, rather than to foreground her status as, say, a manager. Because of this local focus, it is also clear that such attempts to foreground gender can equally be contested locally.

This move away from the analysis of institutional rank to that of local status, whilst important in challenging the characterisation of women as the simple recipients of discriminatory language, means that feminists no longer concern themselves so much with the way that institutional rank and gender relate, and the way that the basis on which local rank is negotiated may be heavily determined by stereotypes of gender and gendered practices. Thus, the analysis of sexism is generally conducted only at the local level and analysts do not consider the way that particular styles are authorised with reference to factors outside the local context. In that the institutional rank is that with which it is most difficult to negotiate, and since institutional status also has a major impact on the parameters of negotiation within your local rank, it seems important to analyse both the more stable institutional factors and the negotiation of what is deemed appropriate at the local level. Thus, in this book, I examine sexism at the institutional and the local level.

   2.1.3. The relation between the individual and the social For many Third Wave feminist linguists, the notion of the 'community of practice' has been important in terms of trying to describe the way that group values affect the individual and their notion of what is linguistically appropriate (Eckert and McConnell-Ginet, 1998; 1999; 2006). A community of practice is a group of people who are brought together in a joint engagement on a task and who therefore jointly construct a range of values and appropriate behaviours. For example, a community of practice might be a group of people who meet to plan an event, or a group of people who go out drinking together. In the process of focusing on a group task, they develop a set of speech styles, ways of interacting, shared meanings. These more or less shared linguistic repertoires serve to consolidate them as a group. Thus, rather than focusing on the role of an oppressive social system, ideology or patriarchy in relation to individual linguistic production and reception, Third Wave feminists often focus on the interaction at the level of the community of practice. Individuals hypothesise what is appropriate within the community of practice and, in speaking, affirm or contest the community's sense of appropriate behaviour. In this sense, one's choice of words and one's speech style can be seen as defining one's position within a group or community of practice, and can contribute to the ongoing development of notions of appropriateness for the community of practice as a whole.
   Bourdieu's notion of 'habitus' has also been extensively drawn on by Third Wave feminist linguists: 'habitus' is the set of dispositions which one draws upon and engages with in order to perform one's identity through discourse (Bourdieu, 1991). This set of attitudes or practices which are seen as constituting a norm by individuals are then discursively negotiated by individuals in terms of their own perception of what is acceptable for their own behaviour within a particular community of practice. Eelen (2001: 223), drawing on Bourdieu's work, argues that we assume that there is a common world, that is, a set of

beliefs which exist somewhere in the social world and which are accepted by everyone, which we as individuals need to agree with or contest. He states:

On the one hand, collective history creates a 'common' world in which each individual is embedded. On the other hand, each individual also has a unique individual history and experiences the 'common' world from this unique position. The common world is thus never identical for everyone. It is essentially fragmented, distributed over a constellation of unique positions and unique perspectives.

Thus, this view of the relation between individuals and others moves us significantly away from notions of society as a whole influencing the linguistic behaviour of individuals to an analysis of the way that, at a local level, individuals decide on what type of language and speech style is appropriate. This local focus of Third Wave feminism is one of its benefits, but it does make it extremely difficult, as I mentioned earlier, to discuss the impact of the values and pressures of the wider society. Talking about society above the level of the community of practice is almost impossible, and it is clear that the wider society as a whole needs to be discussed in terms of the impact it has on practices within communities of practice. Eckert and McConnell-Ginet (2006) attempt to address this issue by arguing that we need to analyse the relations between different communities of practice, but this still does not address the notion of wider social and institutional norms.

Third Wave feminist linguistics tries to maintain a balance between a focus on the local and an awareness of the negotiations at the local level with structures which are largely imposed. Bucholtz (1999: 220) characterises Third Wave feminism as concerned with the following themes:

that language users' identities are not essential to their natures but are produced through contingent social interactions; that those identities are inflected by ideologies of gender and other social constructs; that speakers, writers and signers respond to these ideologies through practices that sometimes challenge and sometimes reproduce dominant beliefs; and that as new social resources become available, language users enact and produce new identities, themselves temporary and historical, that assign new meanings to gender.

However, perhaps this quotation draws our attention to the difficulties encountered by Third Wave feminist linguistics, since it does not seem possible to maintain both a focus on contingent social interactions and wider societal notions such as ideologies of gender, without some fundamental rethinking of our models of language and gender. Eckert and McConnell-Ginet (2006) have argued that in fact it is very important not to focus on communities of practice in isolation, since the norms which are negotiated within these communities derive from perceptions of wider social norms, as well as the rules perceived to be in force in other communities of practice. Thus, we need to hold onto the local level in order to be able to analyse the pragmatic force of utterances and texts, but we also need to be aware of the institutional and wider social norms which influence that local context.

Because of this move away from the top-down model of Second Wave feminism, Third Wave feminism finds it difficult to discuss sexism, since sexism as a concept is based on the idea that discrimination against women is systematic and sexism is imposed on women by those in positions of power, it is ingrained in social structures and works to the benefit of all men (patriarchy). However, as I have argued in this introduction, it is not necessary to focus on the global nature of women's oppression and to view sexism as homogeneous; instead we can analyse the local context where sexism is interpreted and still retain a sense of the wider social and institutional norms which inform local usage. It is possible to see language as a site where challenges to the status quo through challenges to sexism can take place and these changes at the local level may lead to changes in the overall meanings of words and also wider changes at a societal level.

We might consider the case of languages where gender is much more sedimented grammatically than it is in English and examine how Third Wave feminism might deal with this social and cultural problem. For those languages with a grammatical-gender system, where gender is a morphological feature of the language, such as French, German and Arabic, sexism is much more embedded than it is in English.[14] In French, it is much more difficult to refer to a female minister, since the word for minister is masculine, 'le ministre'. Furthermore, the rule in these languages that you use a masculine pronoun and noun ending for plural nouns if there is a masculine and a feminine referent together is one which causes great difficulty for feminist speakers. There are similar problems with highly gender-inflected languages such as Arabic and Berber, as Sadiqi has shown (Sadiqi, 2003). The masculine is used for general commands to males and females; for example road traffic signs signalling 'STOP' in Arabic use the singular masculine form 'qaf' (قف) but are taken by convention to apply to women as well (N. Laamrani, pers. com., 2005).

Hellinger and Bussmann (2001) also draw attention to the way that what they term 'gender languages' (what I have been referring to as 'grammatical-gender languages') such as Arabic deal with gender on a grammatical level.[15] A gender language is one where there is not only natural gender (i.e. women are referred to with a different form of the pronoun to men) but also objects are categorised

---

[14] In grammatical-gender languages, it is not simply women and men who are referred to by the use of gender-differentiated forms such as '*une* femme' – '*un* homme', but also objects are classified according to their grammatical gender (for example '*une* table', '*un* café' etc.).

[15] English is a 'natural-gender language', that is, only males and females are referred to using grammatical gender; for example 'he' refers to males and 'she' refers to females and is not used to refer to objects. Objects are referred to with the neuter form 'it' (apart from reference to countries and ships in conservative usage).

as masculine and feminine (and sometimes neuter) and the pronouns used to refer to them differ accordingly. This could make us think that the relation between grammatical gender and sexism is tenuous because there seems to be no relation between sex and grammatical gender. However, when the referent is a person, grammatical gender does refer to the sex of the person, using the feminine for women and the masculine for men (O. Castro, pers. com., 2007). Hellinger and Bussmann (2001) point to the way that agreement between nouns and adjectives can demonstrate the embedding of sexism. They give the example from Arabic of:

Lab u   bnat- u   ?yyan-in
Father [masc. sing.]   daughters [fem. pl.] his   tired [masc. pl.]
The father and his daughters are tired.

In Arabic the general rule is that there is agreement at a lexical level between adjective and nouns, so if you use a masculine noun you will need to use a masculine ending for the adjective, and a feminine ending for the adjective if you have used a feminine noun. If males and females are referred to, the adjective will need to be masculine, as in the above example, where there is a father and his daughters, but the adjective 'tired' needs to take the masculine form (-in), despite the fact that there are more females than males. Similarly, Hachimi (2001) demonstrates that in Arabic there are often separate terms for male and female occupations, for example male and female lawyers: 'muhamiy-in' (masc. pl.) and muhamiy-at (fem. pl.). However, when male and female lawyers are referred to together, 'muhamiy-in', the masculine form, will always be used and not the feminine form. An invented example from Spanish might illustrate this even more starkly:

Dos milliones de mujeres y un ratón fueron atropellados por un camion. (Two million women and a mouse [masc.] were run over [masc.] by a lorry.)

Here, the fact that the mouse is masculine determines that it is considered to be more valuable than two million women and therefore the verb form referring to both the women and the mouse must be masculine and not feminine (O. Castro, pers. com., 2007). One could argue that this is simply a grammatical convention and does not have any impact in relation to the representation of or thinking concerning males and females, but Hellinger and Bussmann (2001: 15) argue that:

Underlying such syntactic conventions may be a gender hierarchy which defines the masculine as the 'most worthy gender'. As a result, masculine nouns are highly visible in grammatical gender languages and carry considerably more weight and emphasis than feminine nouns.

However, as Pauwels argues (1998), changes are taking place in all Western European languages at a morphological level (that is, in the way that the form of the words changes), rather than just at the level of semantics (that is, at the level of meaning or reference). This type of sedimented sexism in grammatical-gender languages can only be contested using a Second Wave feminist analysis, and, contrary to some Third Wave feminist assertions that reform of sexism is impossible, although change is difficult and slow it *is* possible. In 'natural-gender' languages such as English where gender is not marked in the same way, a combination of Second and Third Wave analysis is necessary.

Feminist analysis and activity have changed in relation to sexism, from a concern with trying to ban or reform terms which seemed to be intrinsically sexist, as much work in the 1970s and 1980s seemed to do, towards a type of research which examines the way that a variety of terms may function within particular circumstances to operate as sexist. This more pragmatic concern with sexism operating within particular contexts, rather than being intrinsic to particular words, has changed the role of the feminist linguist working on sexism.

2.2.   Critical Discourse Analysis

It seems to me that a combination of a modified Critical Discourse Analysis (CDA) and feminist linguistics can help to develop a position from which a Third Wave feminist linguistics might be able to analyse sexism (see Lazar, 2005; Page, 2005; Baxter, 2003; 2006). Feminism and CDA both have a clearly articulated political position and a motivation for analysis, in that they wish to bring about change (although not all feminists believe that sexism is still an issue, nor do they agree on what strategies to take in relation to sexism). Rajagopalan argues that CDA, unlike some other forms of linguistic analysis, wears its ethical and political commitment on its sleeve, and he suggests that Critical Discourse analysts have 'unflinching faith in the truth of one existential proposition, namely that things do not have to be the way they currently are' (Rajagopalan, 2004: 262). Sometimes, however, whilst clear on the need for changes in linguistic usage and in representation, some CDA theorists do not seem willing or able to articulate the range of possible positions of interpretation that there may be of particular statements and phrases, assuming that there are certain meanings inherent in words (however, see Wodak, 1998).

In recent work in CDA, however, there does seem to have been a move towards an awareness of multiple interpretations of words within certain parameters and there have been attempts to chart the range of those interpretations (Ainsworth and Hardy, 2004). It is because CDA has drawn on research on discourse that it is of use to a feminist linguistics analysing sexism. Rather than seeing sexist language as simply words which convey sexist attitudes, Ainsworth and Hardy (2004: 237) argue that:

Discourse does not transparently reflect the thoughts, attitudes and identities of separate selves but is a shared social resource that constructs identity as individuals lay claim to various recognisable social and shared identities.

However, this does not capture the way that individuals and their relations to others are constructed in discourse. Sexism is a set of resources which individuals assume to be available to them, which are socially approved of by certain institutions and groups, but which, within particular communities of practice and institutions, may be contested. Thus, the use of sexism by individuals may be a way of associating oneself with particular people within a group or distancing oneself from other people in a group and associating oneself with groups and values outside the group. As Ainsworth and Hardy (2004: 237) go on to argue:

Individual identity is constructed from social resources and . . . far from being unitary and pre-existent, the individual is a fragmented and ambiguous construction, dependent on context and relationships with others for its self-definition and meaning.

Thus a form of CDA which is able to capture this fluidity and the localised working out of identity will be of use to a Third Wave feminist linguistic analysis of sexism.

3. Structure of the book

I have structured the book to reflect the way that I feel sexism has developed. Chapter 2 considers overt sexism and focuses on such elements as so-called generic pronouns and nouns, the semantic derogation of women, and the use of surnames and titles for women. This is the type of sexism which Second Wave feminism analysed and which many of the campaigns about discriminatory language targeted. In Chapter 3, I describe these anti-discriminatory language campaigns and discuss the validity of attempting to reform language. Rather than reform consisting simply of replacing problematic terms with more acceptable, less offensive terms, I describe the different strategies that anti-homophobic and anti-sexist campaigners developed. In this chapter I also discuss the impact that these anti-discriminatory language campaigns have had and the responses that there have been. For me, there have been two responses to feminist campaigns and these form the basis of the next two chapters. In Chapter 4, I describe 'political correctness', which I see as a media response to feminist campaigns on language. 'Political correctness' was developed as a means of undermining or trivialising the campaigns for those who were arguing for gender-fair and anti-homophobic language. 'Political correctness' is generally viewed negatively, to the point that 'political incorrectness' is generally characterised in a positive way as something quite risky and daring, challenging those who are seen to be trying to limit freedom of expression. In Chapter 5, I describe the second response to feminist campaigns against sexism, and this is 'indirect sexism'. Because of institutional support for anti-sexist policies, those who wish to discriminate against women have had to find other means to do so. Indirect sexism is that sexism which is masked by humour and irony and is consequently quite difficult to classify as sexism. It is also difficult to reform using the tools developed by Second Wave feminism described in Chapter 3. For this reason, it is important to analyse indirect sexism from the perspective of Third Wave feminism, which is aware of the general resources of sexism which make sexist values and expressions available to speakers of a language. However, Third Wave feminism is also concerned with the local manifestations of sexism; we need to maintain this constant dual perspective on the local and the global.

To sum up, this book aims to develop a Third Wave feminist analysis of sexism which still retains some of the features and benefits of Second Wave feminist analysis. Whilst global generalisations about the meanings of words and phrases judged to be sexist are more complex now, it is still essential to hold onto the notion of the possibility of generalising about language and gender and to analyse the influence of wider social structures. Local contextualised analyses eschew all preconceptions about gender and instead analyse very critically the way that gender is drawn upon within a particular context, but they need to be aware of the way that wider ideological forces inform the resources which are available to participants in particular contexts. Rather than seeing sexism as something upon which everyone can agree, I will be trying in this book to demonstrate that sexism is an issue of contestation, which it is essential that feminists engage with, in order to shape the way that women and men are represented and treated.

2   Overt sexism

As I stated in the Introduction, it is difficult to analyse sexism in the way that Second Wave feminists did in the past, because of changes in gender relations and in sexism itself. However, it is nevertheless important to be able to describe the forms that overt sexism takes, since it is clear that sexism does make an impact on the lives of women and men. There have been changes in the way that people use language in the public sphere so that sexist language and other discriminatory forms of language are no longer tolerated, or at least are less tolerated than they were.[1] However, it seems as if it is no longer possible to agree on what constitutes overt sexism, even when it is clear to the hearer/reader that sexism was intended. Pauwels (1998: 67) notes:

The alleged existence of a male bias in language use and its discriminatory and detrimental effect on women as language users are not (at all) unanimously acknowledged or accepted by the speech community at large.

Whilst people still use language to be sexist, they perhaps do not always do so using the terms which have been used in the past and they may use these terms ironically or humorously to deflect the responsibility for sexism (see Chapter 5). Most models of sexism in the past have assumed that sexism is intentional; as Zwicky (1997: 25) argues: 'By their choice of words, people are actively negotiating conceptualisations as personal and political acts.' It is essential to maintain a balance between recognising the institutional nature of sexism and recognising that individuals can intervene in the way that sexism develops. If we characterise language as 'a sort of triffid: an organic growth that develops a life and will of its own', then it will not be possible to describe the human

---

[1] For example, in the UK, homophobic abuse is something which is treated much more seriously by the police than before, and some police forces (for example Greater Manchester Police Authority) have issued guidelines and protocols on how to deal with such language, which it labels clearly as 'hate speech'. They have also clarified the police's role in defending the victims of homophobic abuse. The UK government has tried to introduce legislation about racist abuse and has thus given an institutional basis for anyone complaining about racism. Racist abuse of football players is now something which the British football regulatory body FIFA acts upon, by imposing financial penalties on clubs who do not act against racism and whose fans abuse players using racist terminology.

agents at work in perpetuating sexist ideas, and sexist elements within the language will be seen as unchallengeable by human intervention (Cameron, 1990: 18). If however sexist language is viewed as the result of human intervention in negotiation with discursive norms, it may be possible to bring about change.

Sexism is still a form of language use which affects conversations, one's views of other people and one's own place within society. However, we need to ask ourselves what is it we are claiming about the force of sexist language and what actions feminists are proposing to counter sexism. As Butler asks:

When we claim to have been injured by language, what kind of claim do we make? We ascribe an agency to language, a power to injure, and position ourselves as the objects of its injurious trajectory. We claim that language acts and acts against us and the claim we make is a further instance of language, one which seeks to arrest the force of the prior instance. Thus we exercise the force of language even as we seek to counter its force, caught up in a bind that no act of censorship can undo. (Butler, 1997: 1)

However, surely it needs to be understood that when we make accusations of sexism we are not simply claiming to be 'injured by language'. What we are injured by is a system which seems to condone such discrimination, and viewing this particular instance of sexism as indicative of wider social discrimination. Butler seems here to be arguing that any attempt to challenge sexism is simply 'a further instance of language' which will not change the way that language is used or the way people behave. And yet, feminist campaigns about language have done more than 'arrest the force of the prior instance'; they have, in fact, challenged the conventionalised thinking which informs such utterances and those discursive structures within society which condone sexist statements. Feminist interventions call not only for a change of usage but also they call for critical thinking about gender relations, and as such they should be seen as more than an attempt to ban certain usages. Thus, I would disagree with Butler that we are simply caught up in language if we attempt to call for reform or change of usage; our interventions are calling for more than language change.

In the introduction, I mentioned Sunderland's (2004) notion of 'damaging discourses'. Rather than assuming that individual language items injure an individual, she focuses on the effect of discourses which are potentially damaging both to the individual and to the group who are being maligned. However, she stresses that 'even if a word is agreed to be sexist in a particular context – for example a derogatory term intended to be abusive by a speaker and taken as abusive by a hearer – "damage" may not be a result' (Sunderland, 2004: 192). Instead, she insists that we consider the way that the individual abusive term must be seen in the context of the discourses within the society as a whole which either affirm or contest sexism: 'any potential "damage" from a given gendered discourse within the nexus must be seen in the light of these discoursal relations' (Sunderland, 2004: 194). So damage cannot accrue from one usage but will only happen in the light of the combined effect of links between discourses and the position of institutions in relation to those discourses.

Sexist statements categorise you as belonging to a group which you do not associate yourself with or associate you with a set of values which you do not value and which you recognise as negatively evaluated, for example when an insult term such as 'slag' is used about you which positions you in a role which you do not recognise. Butler (1997: 4) argues:

> To be injured by speech is to suffer a loss of context, that is, not to know where you are. Indeed, it may be that what is unanticipated about the injurious speech act is what constitutes its injury, the sense of putting its addressee out of control.

This sense of sexism or racism 'putting [you] out of control' is important as you are not defining yourself but being defined. However, it is clear that, although the unexpectedness of sexist comments is crucial (for example, one does not expect sexual comments in the workplace), I would take issue with Butler that this means that the addressee '[does not] know where you are'. In a sense, this is precisely the problem, because you know *exactly* the position to which you are being relegated, but this position is not one that you recognise for yourself – you do not identify with this position.

Butler argues that we are constituted in language and we rely upon interpellation (that is, the process whereby we are incessantly called upon by language to recognise ourselves as a particular type of person) in order to be an individual. Sexism and racism have an impact on us since we are 'dependent on the address of the Other in order to be' (Butler, 1997: 26).[2] However, this view of interpellation, whereby we are called into existence by the address of the Other, in strict Althusserian terms, does not capture the complexity of our constitution as subjects and individuals. The role of discourse in the process of the constitution of the subject is not a simple one and what Althusser (1984) and Butler have not considered is the way that we are constituted by different discourses. Feminism, anti-racism, gay and lesbian campaigns and disability rights discourses have all played a role in the constitution of our identity and what we think is permissible to say. The discourses of sexism, racism and homophobia are all in conflict with these more progressive discourses. We negotiate with

---

[2] For Butler, the notion of the Other, that is, a being almost diametrically opposed to yourself against whom you define yourself, is very important. The Other was developed within psychoanalytic theory to describe the process whereby the Self developed in relation to this Other. However, although it is difficult to engage with such concepts briefly, I would argue that it is not a useful concept, since the self is clearly constructed from a range of experiences with many different types of other individuals, some of whom are characterised as similar to oneself and some of whom are seen as different, some of whom are important for one's development and some of whom have little impact.

those discourses, challenging some and affirming others, but rarely simply taking discourses on board wholesale (Benwell and Stokoe, 2006). Intervention by activists to change language is productive social action. Sunderland (2004: 199) argues: 'If gendered discourses can and do damage, the feminist project entails attempting to redress this. Feminism recognises the possibility of change and strives for it, including through explicit contestation of the existing social order *through language*' (original emphasis). Thus, feminist anti-sexist interventions should not be seen as trivial tinkering with language, but as political action.

In the 1970s and 1980s, it seemed very clear to many feminists what sexism was. Sexism was defined as language which discriminated against women by representing them negatively or which seemed to implicitly assume that activities primarily associated with women were necessarily trivial (Vetterling-Braggin, 1981). The aim of feminists therefore was to call attention to the way in which the use of certain language items seemed to systematically discriminate against and cause offence to women, by compiling lists of such language items in dictionaries and calling for people and institutions to avoid such language use (Kramarae and Treichler, 1985; Doyle, 1994; Miller and Swift, 1982/1989; Mills, 1989; Mills, 1995b; Schultz, 1990; Graham, 1975/2006). That lexicographical work has been important in calling attention to overt sexist language, but perhaps it needs to be made more complex, so that overt sexism is seen as only one type of sexism, meaning that we need to analyse the other types of sexism which have arisen more recently in response to these feminist campaigns.

1.   Hate speech and sexism

Within North America the term 'hate speech' is used more frequently than it is in the UK. This term refers to speech which is considered in itself as an incitement to violence and which is offensive enough to constitute violence in its own right. Thus, if a racist demonstrator had a placard on which was written 'Death to all Blacks' or a sign was written outside a Muslim American's house which incited violence against that particular family or against all Muslims, then there is the possibility that a prosecution would take place. A similar move has taken place within Britain to prosecute speech which could be considered an incitement to racial hatred, and in 2006 the British Labour government under Tony Blair tried to bring in legislation to tighten up the laws around such language. This was largely due to public and media unease about political demonstrations where extreme anti-Muslim statements and anti-American statements were clearly seen on placards. However, the passage of this legislation has been extremely slow, simply because of the difficulty of defining 'incitement to racial hatred' tightly enough, so that it does not result in, for example, comedians

who are critical of extremism being prosecuted for racial hatred. There wa
a surprising public and political opposition to such laws as they were often
portrayed as a limitation to freedom of speech (which, of course, is not protected
constitutionally in the UK, as it is in the US). Even in the US, where the
notion of 'hate speech' has some legal status, there has been some difficulty
in bringing prosecutions under the current legislation because it needs to be
proved beyond reasonable doubt that the speech in question constituted an
incitement to violence (Butler, 1997).[3]

It is debatable whether sexism can be seen as a type of hate speech. In
some senses it shares certain characteristics with hate speech in that, in certain
cases (for example the use of lyrics such as 'smack my bitch up' in some
gangsta rap, which I discuss later in this chapter), it may be construed as
an incitement to violence against women in general, or as affirming violence
against women as normal. However, that is not to say that it can be easily
proven to have been intended as inciting violence. Sexism seems, even in its
most violent misogynistic manifestations, to be fundamentally different to hate
speech (such as homophobia, anti-Semitism and racism). It could be argued
that this is because of the very different relationship between women and men
within society and the other groups which are subject to discrimination. Racists,
anti-Semites and homophobes generally hate all members of a particular group
and they aim to separate them from the wider society and avoid contact with
them, sometimes to the point of wishing to injure or kill members of the group.
By contrast, society as a whole is based on the notion of the female–male
heterosexual couple who live together in an intimate relationship. That is not
to say that relations between women and men are equal within heterosexual
relationships, because it is clear that in many contexts women are abused and
oppressed within these seemingly intimate relations with men. For example,
recently in the British press there has been great debate about the murder
of an Iraqi Kurdish woman by her family who disapproved of her choice of
boyfriend; sexual violence and murder within heterosexual relationships are
far more common than violence and murder of women outside those relations.
However, it is impossible to imagine that hatred of women as a group would
result in genocide, as it did in the Holocaust, or an apartheid system, as in
South Africa, where women would be exiled to a separate 'homeland'. Because
of the intimate relations which hold between heterosexual women and men,
misogynistic statements against women are usually made about sub-groups of
women, that is, those who are not behaving in a sufficiently feminine way (those
who are behaving in a strong, self-determining, non-deferent way) or those who
are considered to be behaving in an excessively feminine way (those who are
seen to be overly passive, or overly concerned with their appearance). Thus,

---

[3] I discuss the issue of hate speech further in Chapter 6.

book, I will be discussing hate speech and sexism as separate
lthough they both discriminate against groups of people, their
effects of such speech are different.

2.   Contexts of sexism

It is clear that it is often confident women in the public sphere who tend to
be attacked through sexist language, where their sexuality or attractiveness is
drawn attention to, as if this disqualifies them from claiming a place in the public
sphere. For example, Ann Widdecombe, a former member of the Tory Shadow
Cabinet in Britain, is often discussed less in terms of her forthright opinions
and more in relation to her appearance and the fact that she is unmarried. In
a similar way, as Walsh (2001) has shown, newspaper reports suggested that
senior Labour Party member Margaret Beckett's supposed lack of photogenic
qualities ruled her out of the Labour Party leadership elections. Page (2005)
has analysed the way that Cherie Booth/Blair and Hillary Rodham Clinton
have been described in ways that focus on crises in their personal lives rather
than on their professional careers and achievements. It seems as if in order
to attack particular women who have gained prominence within the public
sphere, newspapers can refer to a set of negative characteristics stereotypically
associated with women as a group, such as concern with attractiveness or
emotional crises, in order to undermine them politically or professionally (see
also Chapter 5).

Reference to these stereotypical characteristics has the effect of categorising
the particular woman as only a member of a minority group which does not
belong in the public sphere. To give an example of the way that sexist discourses
are used in this way: two female friends of mine worked as bus drivers for
several years, and both of them left their jobs because of the incessant reference
to supposed incompetence in driving, a quality stereotypically associated with
women as a group, as I mentioned in Chapter 1. Both of these women are
extremely competent drivers, but they stated that the constant jokes about and
reference to such problems in driving ended by undermining their confidence.
For example, on one occasion when a conductor was getting onto the bus that
one of my friends was going to drive, a workmate called out to the conductor,
'Oh, you're on with her, watch yourself,' implying that she might crash the bus.
This is not an overtly sexist statement as such but it does draw on stereotypical
beliefs about women. For both of these women bus drivers, it was the repetitive
and tedious nature of these comments, by both workmates and the general
public, which contributed to their decision to leave. What both of them remarked
upon was the fact that, because the assertions were made with reference to
women as a group, it was not possible to respond to the assertions about their

own driving skills or to counter the claims that women are bad drivers.[4] These jobs are primarily male jobs and they are seen to be devalued when women take them. This may explain the hostility to women which is expressed in stereotypically sexist comments about women drivers.

We can see current sexism as, in some measure, a response to feminism. For many males (and females as well), feminism is seen as disrupting the status quo and overturning the conventional views of how women and men should behave. Thus, sexist comments may well be a way of asserting an older set of values which do not seem to have common currency. McCrum, Cran and MacNeil argue that 'people tend to fasten their anxieties about the changing world on to words' (McCrum *et al.*, 1986: 6). People use lexical choice, where there are alternatives available, as a way of signalling their views about the position of women in society. We need therefore to ask ourselves what motivates sexism and what discursive purposes it serves, as it clearly has effects on those who use sexist language, as well as on those to whom it is directed. When Wetherell and Potter (1992: 3) examined the racist language of Pakeha (white) New Zealanders, they were interested in emphasising 'the ways in which a society gives voice to racism and how forms of discourse institute and solidify, change, create and reproduce social formations'. Thus, we might see that in giving voice to sexist language, people may be aligning themselves with particular conservative models of social formation. What needs to be examined is the way that sexism is made to seem acceptable to many people and for this we need to examine the institutional supports which are given to such views. Only then can we examine the reasons that people are sexist and what 'pay-offs' there are for them. It is not adequate to suggest that sexism is only motivated by fear and hatred, since it is clear that there are a range of motivations and interests at work, such as conflict and competition over resources and status, and a view of women's 'natural' role which is at odds with women's actual roles in contemporary society.

3.   Types of overt sexism

It is necessary to give some detail of the forms of overt sexism, because it is clear that there are some forms which can be generalised about linguistically, and which feel fairly fixed, and there are others which are more difficult to classify (which I will discuss in Chapter 5).[5] It will not be possible to cover

---

[4] In fact, generally, it is recognised by the insurance industry that women are more careful drivers than men, with younger men being seen as the most likely to have serious accidents. Several insurers offer women lower premiums than men as evidence of this difference, with one UK/Australian company, Sheila's Wheels, catering only for women, and offering lower premiums.

[5] I have discussed overt sexism in more detail in my book *Feminist Stylistics* (1995b) and for this reason I will not give full details of the types of sexism which seem to me to be still current within

here all of the instances of overt sexism which have been documented, since there is a vast critical literature on this subject (see Vetterling-Braggin (1981)). What I will do in this chapter is to cover those areas which still seem pertinent and active at the moment. I will deal with them under the following categories: 3.1. words and meaning (including naming, dictionaries, pronouns, semantic derogation and surnames and titles); 3.2. processes (including an examination of transitivity, reported speech and jokes). In section 4, I focus on the effects of sexism and possible strategies for responding to sexism.

3.1.   Words and meaning

Throughout this section, I will be distinguishing between institutionalised sexism and the more 'creative' forms of sexism which individuals use. Sexist language has often been institutionalised in dictionaries and grammar books, in policy documents and government reports, through the use of generic pronouns (see 3.1.3) and particular terms to refer to women. This type of authorised sexism is one where, as Butler (1997: 25) puts it, the institution speaks through the individual, and she comments:

the ritual dimension of convention implies that the moment of utterance is informed by the prior and indeed the future moments that are occluded by the moment itself. Who speaks when convention speaks? In what time does convention speak? In some sense it is an inherited set of voices, an echo of others who speak as the 'I'.

In this rather complex statement, Butler neatly sums up the difficulty of trying to analyse institutional sexism. It is necessary to ask who is speaking when you utter statements which you have not invented (conventional speech which originates and is affirmed by institutions). This conventional speech seems familiar and known because it is based on stereotypical and commonsense beliefs about women. Because of their conventional and authorised nature, because the individual who utters them has not invented these ideas, in a sense s/he also does not have to take responsibility for them as they emanate from elsewhere, from the society or at least a part of the society. What is missing from Butler's account of the way sexism and racism work is that these utterances are challenged by other discourses within society. Whilst stereotypical views of women exist and have been affirmed by large sections of society in the past, this is no longer the case. Feminist discourses and discourses of equal opportunity have been taken up by many women, men and institutions and have become enshrined in legislation. These oppositional discourses pose a significant challenge to the commonsensical nature of sexist statements, even

British usage. However, I will be drawing attention to the way in which sexism has changed in the period since the publication of that book.

when there seems to be widespread antagonism to feminism *per se*. It is because these stereotypical views clash with many people's sense of their reality and their values and because they feel anachronistic and conservative that they are not simply authorised by society as a whole.

However, institutional sexism is not all that sexism is; in some ways, people interact with these institutionalised forms and create new forms of sexist usage in a similar pattern or model of the institutionalised form. Sexism may be seen as a form of language which is institutionalised and which is available to people to use. However, if people do use it, because it has begun to develop negative connotations amongst large sections of the society, and because it seems to be anachronistic, they might be considered to be conservative as well as being discriminatory. Thus, rather than seeing sexism as something which is imposed on women by men, I prefer to see sexism as a site of struggle over access to resources and positions of power. Kress (cited in Morrish, 1997: 344) argues that:

as material and social processes alter, . . . ideologically-constructed common sense is always out of phase with . . . practices; there is always a constant tension between social reality and social practices and the way in which they are and can be written about in language.

Discursive change is fairly slow and often out of step with the practices of individuals and groups within society (Mills, 1995a). Thus, for many within society, sexism is anachronistic but it still continues to be used and sexist discourses are still available as a resource.

3.1.1. Naming Many of the feminist theorists who analysed sexism in language in the 1970s and 1980s focused on naming practices. It was argued that language was 'man-made' and that women were excluded from the process of naming and defining. Spender (1980: 84) comments:

Names are essential for the construction of reality for without a name it is difficult to accept the existence of an object, an event, a feeling. Naming is the means whereby we attempt to order and structure the chaos and flux of existence which would otherwise be an undifferentiated mass.

Whilst it is clear that naming is important, there are a number of elements with which we need to take issue with Spender. Firstly, the focus on naming and nouns is not inevitable, but one which is partly determined by the Anglo-American linguistic and philosophical tradition within semantics of focusing on nouns almost exclusively. It also does not seem to distinguish between giving a name to someone, the existence of words to denote something and the development of names for new elements. We might usefully deal with these separately, since the system whereby we give family names to women and men, the development of terms for new elements and the existence of names for particular experiences are very different processes, and I shall be attempting to separate these off in the discussion below.

Whilst early feminist linguists such as Spender (1980) proposed that sexist language was a result of and reflection of a patriarchal social system, in recent years it has become clear that individual men do not necessarily 'control' the language, although certain elements of the way that language functions may seem to benefit or give value to the experiences and beliefs of men more than those of women. The view that the language system is fixed and encoded solely in men's interests has been challenged by feminists such as Black and Coward (1981). However, it is now not clear how we can describe the fact that the language is a system, albeit one which is constantly changing, which has embedded within it a set of stereotypical beliefs about women. It also has embedded within it a set of beliefs about women which are progressive and these can be seen to be differently valued to sexist stereotypes. The position of these beliefs about women are not 'contained' in any sense by the language, but they do seem to be a driving force which underlies the language as a system, and as such they lead to certain usages changing and certain usages being seen as authorised. Within Spender's determinist view of the relationship between language and reality, if you alter the terms within a language which seem to represent women negatively, then you will change also the way that women are thought about, as I discussed in the Introduction. However, other theorists considered that if you changed the social position of women, then words would in some ways reflect that change and alter accordingly. Neither of these views is very accurate, as it is clear there is a complex two-way process, whereby language items affirm and reflect and possibly contest the current state of play of beliefs about women and men.

Cameron (1990: 14) suggests that rather than seeing language as a reflection of society or as a determining factor in social change 'it could be seen as a carrier of ideas and assumptions which become, through their constant re-enactment in discourse, so familiar and conventional we miss their significance'. Thus, some sexist terms may be seen as so much a part of the language that we do not even notice them as sexist (and Spender's (1980) work was extremely important in terms of foregrounding those naturalised usages, so that we could see them as sexist). However, there are still lexical items which seem to be clearly sexist and which we might want to change or whose usage we might wish to resist. For example, there are certain words which refer largely to women and which have negative connotations. The adjectives 'shrill' and 'feisty' are used almost exclusively to describe women, and seem to have connotations of excess, even when they are used positively. 'Shrill' generally presupposes that certain women's voices are unpleasantly high or loud, in relation to an assumed female norm of quietness and a male norm of low pitch. 'Feisty' is used to refer to women who are strong and independent, but there is an association of this word with contexts which are relatively negative, which leads to the term having connotations of excessiveness. Although 'feisty' can be used in positive ways, it is generally used to refer to someone who is seen as exceptionally assertive, thus suggesting that women should not act in this way. Underlying these terms is a contrast with a male norm: males are 'independent' and 'strong' by right but not 'feisty'; male voices are at the 'normal' pitch, and even when they are high, they would generally not be described as 'shrill'. Thus, although Spender's views on sexism have perhaps been superseded by more recent feminist work and by changes in usage, there still exist many examples of overt sexism in naming and representing women. As Talbot (1998: 217) puts it: 'classifying people is part of the naming and ordering of experience; it both reflects and sustains existing social relations and identities. The categorisation of people is a powerful normative force.'

3.1.2. *Dictionaries* Hellinger and Pauwels (2007: 667) argue that 'dictionaries like grammars, are sites of codification and normative language'. Because of this they play an important role in the way that the language changes and they can act as 'gate-keepers' of authoritative usage. In the 1980s and 1990s, many feminists criticised dictionaries for featuring sexist terms without labelling them as offensive. Hellinger and Pauwels (2007: 667) argue that dictionaries 'have institutionalised sexist language in their choice of definitions and examples (use of androcentric generics, asymmetrical gender-marking, the communication of stereotypical gender roles)'. Kramarae and Treichler (1985: 119) comment on the process whereby dictionaries define terms and cite literary examples of their usage; they argue that:

A dictionary is a word-book which collects somebody's words into somebody's book. Whose words are collected, how they are collected, and who collects them all influence what kind of book a given dictionary turns out to be and in turn whose purpose it can best serve.

Drawing attention in this way to the specificity of the perspective of the sources which are drawn upon and the purposes the definitions serve challenges the portrayal of dictionaries as simply descriptive tools, objective collections of current usage. In response to this institutionalisation of sexist terms, several feminists constructed dictionaries themselves which did not function in the same way as other dictionaries, that is to standardise usage; instead they acted as a form of critique of conventional dictionaries and as a source-book of feminist knowledge and neologisms (Mills, 1989; Kramarae and Treichler, 1985). In this way they foregrounded the way in which all definitions are to an extent subjective. For example, in Kramarae and Treichler's *Feminist Dictionary*, the sources which they quote from as exemplary usages are often feminist writings rather than mainstream literature. Thus 'cosmetics' is defined as 'a mask used primarily by women which can be an aid for performances of various kinds, even for appearing a conventional woman' and 'man-made chemicals that clog your pores and make your eyelashes fall out'. The definition continues: 'the persistent need I have to make myself "attractive", to fix my hair and put on lipstick – is it the false need of a chauvinized woman, encouraged since infancy to identify her values as a person with her attractiveness in the eyes of men?' (Kramarae and Treichler, 1985: 108). 'Illegitimate child' is defined in the following way: 'it has traditionally meant that the person was born incorrectly because the father is not known or the parents are not married. This word is maliciously used even though the mother is known and knows that the child is hers' (Kramarae and Treichler, 1985: 206). This dictionary aims to foreground feminist theory and work on meaning and challenge the notion that conventional dictionaries are objective accounts of word-meaning. Kramarae and Treichler argue that dictionaries often make women's contribution to language invisible and/or downgrade them, for example when they label feminist terms such as 'herstory' a mere coinage ('all words are coinages', Kramarae and Treichler argue (1985: 4)). This feminist lexicographical project actively calls attention to the partiality of compilers of dictionaries and asks explicit questions such as:

What is the source of our knowledge of [language] norms (e.g. introspections, experi-ence, empirical research)? How do dictionary entries relate to each other and to objects in the world? What is the status of cultural knowledge in our understanding of the meaning of a word? What is the relation of word usage to conditions for speaking? (Kramarae and Treichler, 1985: 7)

Graham (1975/2006: 137) comments on her work in revising the citations in the *American Heritage School Dictionary* during the 1970s. She made a decision to change the examples given in the dictionary, because they seemed to present a sexist view of women and men; she argues:

if this new dictionary were to serve elementary students without showing favouritism to one sex or the other, an effort would have to be made to restore the gender balance. We would need more examples featuring females, and the examples would have to ascribe to girls and women the active, inventive and adventurous human traits traditionally reserved for men and boys.

She describes a moment of insight when she realised that she must change entries in the dictionary across the board: 'a computer citation asserted "he has *brains* and courage". In what seemed at the time an act of audacity, I changed the pronoun. "She has *brains* and courage"' (Graham, 1975/2006: 137). In the 2000s we are used to more gender-equal examples in dictionaries, but it is because of the work of feminist lexicographers that entries in dictionaries have changed.

These questions which feminist work on dictionaries has posed have shaped the way that dictionaries are now compiled. The new dictionaries of contemporary English usage such as the *Cobuild* dictionary have arguably been influenced by such feminist enquiry about the partiality of dictionary definitions, and, instead of using literary examples, they have chosen to examine usage within a large corpus of written and spoken examples (Sinclair, 1987).[6]

3.1.3. Generic pronouns and nouns Pronouns and nouns are important elements to consider when analysing sexism, as Hellinger and Bussmann (2001: 2–3) argue:

Personal nouns and pronouns…have emerged as a central issue in debates about language and gender. In any language personal nouns constitute a basic and culturally significant lexical field. They are needed to communicate about the self and others, they are used to identify people as individuals or as members of various groups, and they may transmit positive or negative attitudes. In addition, they contain schemata of, e.g. occupational activities and (proto- or stereotypical) performers of such activities. On a psychological level, an appropriate use of personal nouns may contribute towards the maintenance of an individual's identity, while inappropriate use, for example, identifying someone repeatedly (either by mistake or by intention) by a false name, by using derogatory or discriminatory language, or by not addressing someone at all, may cause irritation, anger or feelings of inferiority.

The 'generic pronoun' is when 'he'/'him'/'his'/'himself' is used to refer to both men and women. When the so-called generic pronoun is used to refer to groups of people (e.g. *when the student has finished **his** exam **he** should hand in **his** paper to the invigilator*), this usage in certain contexts may be confusing, since it is unclear whether it refers only to males or is in fact being used to refer to students in general (Spender, 1980). Sentences using the generic pronoun have the additional effect of affirming the markedness of female reference (i.e. male is the norm and female is the marked form) and contribute to the general invisibility of females within the language and within society as a whole.[7] This is something which is affirmed by Graham's (1975/2006) survey of the use of 'he', 'his' and 'him' in contrast to 'she' and 'her' in the *American Heritage School Dictionary*. She wanted to discover just how many of the uses of the 'he' pronoun were in fact generic and how many had singular masculine reference. Out of a sample of 100,000 words, there were 940 uses of 'he', of which 744 referred to males, 128 to male animals, 36 to professions which it was assumed were male (such as 'farmer') and only 32 referred to the singular subject used generically. Thus, for Graham, it is clear that generic reference is fairly low, but what troubled her in this study was that, relatively speaking, there were many

---

[6] However, even when large corpora of data are drawn upon, if sexist usages are institutionalised within the language and occur at significant frequencies, they will appear in dictionaries, sometimes unmarked as offensive or archaic.

[7] In other languages than English this so-called generic usage using the masculine pronoun is still grammatically the norm, as Hachimi shows of Moroccan Arabic (Hachimi, 2001).

more references to males than to females in the dictionary, as I will discuss later in this section.

Feminist campaigns to use pronouns which are truly generic have led to a radical change in the usage of generic pronouns, so that it is rare now to encounter 'he' used generically, since publishers advise authors not to use them and generally edit out such usage. Institutions such as trades unions and universities have produced guidelines for usage.[8] Cooper (1984) documented a decline of the use of generic 'he' and 'man' in a study of US newspapers. Pronoun use in English has perhaps changed more than any other area of language usage and it is the area where feminists have been most inventive, for example using 'she/he', 's/he' and 'they' instead of 'he'. The difficulty in using these forms is when one wishes to use a singular generic reference, for example 'the reader needs to pay attention to [. . .] language use', or 'when the baby asserts [. . .] will'. In these examples, 'his or her' can seem rather clumsy, especially when used extensively over a paragraph rather than just in one sentence, and 'their' seems, to some, to be ungrammatical. However, Eckert and McConnell-Ginet argue that 'they' used for a singular referent is perfectly acceptable, as for example in 'Someone called but they didn't leave their name' (Eckert and McConnell-Ginet, 2003: 256). They stress that this only works, however, if the original referent is indefinite (i.e. someone, a friend of mine), for example 'Someone said that they would pick that up for me'; whereas when the referent is definite, 'they' does seem odd, for example 'My teacher promised they would write a letter of recommendation.'

Romaine (2001: 161) reports that in American television interviews and talk shows, 'speakers used plural forms *they* and *them* 60% of the time to refer to singular antecedents of indeterminate gender like *person, everyone, anyone*, etc.'. However, there are a range of different strategies for dealing with pronoun reference. Writers such as Coates (1996) use 'she' and 'her' throughout their work for generic reference, and Sperber and Wilson (1986), in their work on Relevance theory, use 'she' to refer to the speaker and 'he' to refer to the hearer, a practice which most Relevance theorists have continued (Christie, 2000). Eckert and McConnell-Ginet (2003) have even coined a new reflexive pronoun 'themself' so that they can use a singular term for generic reference, for example 'it is unnerving to walk in on someone talking to themself'.[9] Holmes (2001: 124) notes that use of generics is not consistent; often there is a certain

---

[8] However, that is not to say that generic pronouns are not still in use. In a small-scale survey of generic pronoun use on UK BBC Radio 4 during the month of July 2007, I was surprised to find that 'he' was still used 'generically' fairly frequently, mostly when referring to workers in male-dominated professions. The use of 'he or she' was extremely rare. However, pluralisation, i.e. 'they', was used much more frequently than singular reference.

[9] It is interesting that my computer will not allow me to write 'themself' but insists on automatically correcting it to 'themselves'. It is a measure of the difficulty of feminist intervening in the conventions of usage, particularly when they are institutionalised through computer spell-checks.

'slippage' 'where an utterance starts as a generic but slips into masculinity before it ends'. However, Romaine (2001) suggests that we need to look not only at pronouns but at the number of times that males and females are referred to. In her analysis of the Brown corpus of American English, she found that in 1 million words, there were over 9,000 occurrences of 'he' and only over 2,000 occurrences of 'she'. She suggests that generics would not account for that discrepancy, and that we need to be aware of the relative lack of reference to women. This finding confirms Graham's earlier work where she reported that 'in books read by schoolchildren there are over seven times as many men as women and over twice as many boys as girls' (1975/2006: 136).

Despite this continuing difficulty with pronoun use, there are some theorists who think that feminists should not concentrate on the use of generic pronouns in the analysis of sexism. Most surprising amongst these was Robin Lakoff, whose early work on gender and language was so important for feminist research on sexism. She stated: 'My feeling is that this area of pronominal neutralisation is both less in need of changing and less open to change than many of the other disparities' (Lakoff, 1975/2006: 98). However, it is clear that the generic pronoun has changed, and even if its usage has not changed as much as some feminists, including myself, would have liked, we cannot avoid recognising that feminist campaigns have brought about this change in usage.

So-called 'generic' nouns such as 'man' are used to refer to both men and women but, in effect, often refer only to men. Spender (1980) commented on the fact that the use of 'man' generically is often interpreted as referring only to men. She reports on early research in this area:

Aileen Pace Nilsen (1973) found that young children thought 'man' meant male people in sentences such as 'man needs food' . . . Linda Harrison found that science students – at least – thought male when discussing the evolution of man, they had little appreciation of the female contribution even when explicitly taught it. (Spender, 1980: 152)

However, one of the effects of feminists campaigning about generic nouns and pronouns is that it is more difficult to use them easily. There have even been attempts to change the use of 'man' in church liturgy, for example Romaine shows that the 1995 Oxford University edition of the *New Testament* replaced 'the Son of Man' with 'the Human One' (Romaine, 2001: 162). There is a certain diffidence about using 'man' generically these days, and, when challenged, people will often rephrase their utterances. There does seem to be an attempt to use inclusive generics more, when referring to women and men, for example using 'postmen and women' rather than just 'postmen'.[10] However,

---

[10] There was an attempt in the 1990s by the UK Royal Mail to use the generic term 'postie' for both men and women post office workers, but this was met by opposition from the workforce and is not in use, mainly because it is an informal use and therefore would have been seen to trivialise the job.

there are words where the generic form already has another restricted meaning and therefore cannot be used for general reference, for example 'worker' is not a simple substitution for 'workman'. 'Workman' denotes a person who repairs something or builds something for you in your home, whereas 'worker' has a history within socialist and Marxist thinking which, whilst being generic, nevertheless does not make it the generic counterpart of 'workman'. Similarly, 'angler' has a slightly different feel to it than 'fisherman'; and 'fisher', although available, seems archaic. Other terms where there seems to be no generic equivalent are 'seaman', 'ombudsman' and 'craftsman', although 'craftsperson' and 'ombudsperson' are occasionally used. In some cases, there is dispute about the generic term and this intersects with other disputes over the term, for example 'dustman' is still used, partly because no generic has been developed apart from 'cleansing operative'.[11] However, certain occupational generic terms do seem to have been adopted, such as 'police officer' and 'firefighter'. This may be because certain police forces have taken the issue of language extremely seriously (Greater Manchester Police, 2000; 2001a). In the case of 'firefighter', it is noticeable that the change from 'fireman' to 'firefighter' was largely due to media reporting of the firefighters' strike in 2004 when 'fireman' was rarely used.[12]

Generic nouns are often still used for singular masculine reference. Eckert and McConnell-Ginet remark upon the use of generic nouns in an American anthropological text, where the authors stated: 'When we woke in the morning we found that the villagers had all left by canoe in the night, leaving us alone with the women and children' (2003: 243). This use of the generic noun 'villager' to refer to only the male villagers seems to assume that male villagers are the only 'real' people in the village. Eckert and McConnell-Ginet (2003: 244) comment on a similar example, in a statement made on a news broadcast: 'Over a hundred Muslim civilians were killed, and many women and children,' as if the women and children could not be considered to be referred to as civilians in their own right.[13] Eckert and McConnell-Ginet also note that generic terms can sometimes be used to refer only to females; they give the example of an air steward who stated that she had served on the first

[11] In the UK 'cleansing operative' seems to be resisted because it seems to be so euphemistic and overly technical and is often one of the terms mocked when 'political correctness' is discussed. However, this term seems to have developed less from debates about 'PC' than from a wish to find a more adequate term than the rather negative terms 'dustman' or 'bin-man'. Sometimes, to avoid these terms, workers say that 'they work in the cleansing department' rather than giving their job-title.

[12] This may be due to positive measures by firefighters' unions and employers to recruit more women into the fire service. Inclusive language is one aspect of those measures.

[13] They argue that although this 'and' could be taken to mean 'including' rather than 'in addition to' (and perhaps we do pragmatically infer this), the reporter did nevertheless use 'and' rather than 'in addition to'.

transcontinental flight and that 'back then people stopped working when they got married' (2003: 244). In this example, when she refers to 'people', she, in fact, means that only women stopped working on marriage.

Eckert and McConnell-Ginet comment on the way that terms which identify categories like 'men', 'heterosexual' and 'white' have been interpreted as the default term (i.e. they presuppose that a person mentioned is male unless it is mentioned that the person is female). They argue that when they are used as a default term, this often leads to the default term seeming to be erased and 'this sustains the distinctiveness of the marked category' (2003: 248).[14] They argue that this erasure of the default term and the marking of other terms ties into political and socio-economic disadvantage:

Where there is subordination of a social group, there is at least some default organisation of the field against which that group is defined. Belonging to the marked category is generally far more consequential for a person's life opportunities and sense of self than belonging to the often erased default category. (2003: 250)

Generally speaking, the male term is seen as the norm or the general term and the female the marked. For example, in a recent circular from my sons' school, I noticed that the heading 'football' referred to male football teams whilst 'girl's football' was discussed under a separate sub-heading, suggesting that football played by girls is exceptional or not conventional football.

Pauwels (1998) discusses the complex process whereby jobs for females have conventionally, in many European languages, used the masculine term. It is only recently that it has become possible to state that you are a lawyer or engineer in these languages using a feminine affix. However, in German, Pauwels comments on a rather strange occurrence: 'die Hebamme' used to be the word for midwife. When men began to work as midwives, this was changed to 'Entbindungspfleger'. For women to refer to themselves as midwives, they then had to add a feminine affix to the word, making for the much more unwieldy and masculine-derived 'Entbindungspflegerin' (see also Hellinger and Bussmann, 2001). However, this is not the case in Britain, where in the few fields where women are in the majority, for example in nursing or midwifery, males are referred to as the marked term, for example 'male nurse' and 'male midwife'.

This so-called generic use of pronouns and nouns is not necessarily built into the grammatical structure of a language. It is generally introduced into a language and subsequently regulated by grammarians, and, as I have shown, it can be changed, even though it feels deeply embedded in the structure of the language. Sunderland (2006), drawing on Spender (1980), examined the

[14] Romaine (2001) argues that the only terms which she could find where the male was the marked term were 'bride' and 'bridegroom' and 'widow' and 'widower'. Talbot (1998) noted that 'male prostitute' is also a marked term, as is 'male nurse'.

introduction of sexist structures into the language and the role of grammarians in regulating the introduction and maintenance of usages. She has shown how, in the sixteenth and eighteenth centuries, grammarians issued prescriptive statements affecting how gender should be handled in language. Wilson in 1533 argued that the male should precede the female, for example in 'man and woman', and in 1646 Poole justified this usage by stating that this was because males were worthier than females: 'the relative agrees with the antecedent in gender, number and person . . . the relative shall agree with the antecedent of the more worthy gender' (cited in Bodine, 1998: 129). In 1746 Kirkby argued that the precedence of males was because the male was more 'comprehensive' than the female (Sunderland, 2006: 12). Bodine (1998) also comments on the fact that an Act of Parliament in 1850 'legally replaced "he or she" with "he"'. She goes on to describe the measures which were taken in America and the UK to dissuade people from using 'they' for singular indefinite reference, for example an American grammarian, White (1880, cited in Bodine, 1998: 131) writes:

their is very commonly misused with reference to a singular noun. Even John Ruskin has written such sentences as this: 'But if a customer wishes you to injure *their* foot or to disfigure it, you are to refuse *their* pleasure.' How Mr Ruskin could have written such a sentence as that (for plainly there is no slip of the pen or result of imperfect interlinear correction of it) or how, it having been written, it could be passed by an intelligent proof reader, I cannot surmise. It is, perhaps, an exemplification of the straits to which we are driven by the lack of a pronoun of common gender meaning both he and she, his and hers. But admitting this lack, the fact remains that *his* is the representative pronoun, as *mankind* includes both men and women. [Original emphasis]

Thus, it is important to examine the history of the introduction and regulation of this particular type of pronoun and generic noun use, so that we recognise that we can bring about change in usages which seem embedded in the structure of the language.

3.1.4. Insult terms for women Many feminist theorists (Braun, 1999; Braun and Kitzinger, 1999) have noted that the insult terms used for women are sexualised, and, as a case study, I would like to examine the use of 'bitch', 'ho', 'pimp' and 'faggot' in gangsta rap music, since many argue that the use of these terms is highly problematic. US and British rappers such as So Solid Crew, Jay Z, Snoop Dog and Eminem have been attacked by journalists and politicians for their use of language which is seen to objectify women and glorify violence and gang culture. The rappers are accused of inciting violence towards and abuse of women, particularly because of the use of words such as 'bitch', 'pimp' and 'ho' in their lyrics, which assumes that the relation between men and women is in fact like that between prostitutes and their pimps. Gangsta rap or hip-hop is attacked primarily because of its association with gun culture and the glorification of violence. For example, in 2003 after an attack in Birmingham, where two black women were shot dead and two others injured in what seems to have been a 'turf war' between rival gangs, the then UK Home Secretary David Blunkett announced that he was appalled by the lyrics in rap and hip-hop music and demanded that the music industry put an end to glamorising violence (Zylinska, 2006).[15] The consistent recent UK media coverage of the shooting of young black men by gangs has prepared the ground for a moral panic around race which here interestingly also focuses on a concern with sexism. Very often these attacks on the sexism and violence of the lyrics are more like a channelling of racism. We have to be careful, as Chang (2006: 7) argues, that we do not project 'sexual excess and moral lack onto blackness' and inscribe 'black gender and family as dysfunctional' thereby enabling a 'displacement of misogyny and sexism onto blackness'.

Hip-hop is a 'masculinist' or 'hypermasculine' genre of music where the protagonists bolster their own sense of authenticity and 'realness' (Stephens, 2005: 23). The artists are very concerned to set themselves apart from teen pop music and mainstream music in general, which many of them consider to have 'sold out'.[16] Stephens (2005: 33) argues that 'hypermasculinity, signified by machismo and compulsory heterosexuality, are usually central markers distinguishing hip-hop from pop and other "softer" genres'. One of the key elements in this construction of 'realness' is the disdain for elements which are considered weak or soft and an emphasis on elements which demonstrate the masculinity of the singer, as McLeod (1999, cited in Stephens, 2005: 26) argues: 'within hip-hop, being a real man doesn't merely entail having a proper sex organ; it means acting in a masculine manner'. Particularly for white rappers, it is essential to present themselves as hard, tough and full of rage. This hypermasculinity is epitomised in the figure of the 'pimp' or 'mack' who features in much hip-hop.

Furthermore, 'realness' is derived from public perceptions that the stories told by rappers are in fact narratives about the real lives of the singers. However, as Stephens has pointed out, there is often a wide gap between the claims of rappers about their involvement in crime and gun culture and their real lives. And Ogbar (2005: 1073) has noted that there is a contrast to be made between the 'misogynistic lyrics of rappers with their real-life expressions of affection

---

[15] In terms of incitement to violence, Smitherman has argued that often verbal dexterity and play, even when exemplified in violent and offensive language, can in fact deflect action: 'while the speakers may or may not act out the implications of their words, the point is that the listeners do not necessarily expect any action to follow. As a matter of fact, skilful rappers can often avoid having to prove themselves through deeds if their rap is strong enough' (Smitherman, cited in Quinn, 2000: 128).

[16] This concern with authenticity is interesting considering that a survey in the *Los Angeles Times* in 1992 stated that 74 per cent of gangsta rap music is bought by white people (Quinn, 2000: 133).

and respect for female family members or women business partners. In a larger music industry of virtually no black women executives, many gangsta rappers proudly noted their preference for black women business managers, agents and professional handlers.'

Quinn (2000: 117) argues that we must take 'the stark misogyny in the lyrical content of [gangsta rap] tracks as a fairly well documented "given"'. However, we need also to:

demonstrate that gangsta rap, far from being a straightforwardly co-opted and debased form, comments in complex ways on the terms and conditions of its own popular and commercial-cultural mediation. There needs to be a greater engagement with the formal complexities of, and immense aesthetic pleasures derived from, these lumpen black repertoires, as they have transmuted into mass-mediated figures like the enigmatic mack [pimp figure] of gangsta rap. (2000: 117).

Thus, Quinn argues that we should not take the use of these misogynistic terms too literally, and must be aware of their complexity and self-reflexiveness.

Quinn documents the history of the pimp figure, deriving as it does from the trickster figure of African folklore, and the derivation of rapping from the black oral practice of narrative 'toasts' and 'playing the dozens' or verbal duelling. Because of its offensive lyrics, Quinn argues that not enough attention has been paid to the formal complexities of rap, because commentators are intent on reading rap polemically. Through verbal play, the 'pimp' establishes his sexual credentials. Rap artists represent themselves as pimps in their songs through their conspicuous consumption of expensive goods and food and drink and the commodification of women; however, Ice T argues that pimping is 'also used as a definition of a fly, cool lifestyle, which has nothing to do with prostitution' (Ice T cited in Quinn 2000: 124).

We should not assume that these insult terms are used only by male rappers. Some female rappers also affirm hypermasculinity and use these insult terms to refer to themselves. Quinn (2000) describes the black female group Boss who have released songs such as 'Diary of a Mad Bitch' and 'Recipe of a Hoe'. Quinn (2000: 116) comments: 'for these female artists in a male driven form, the central features of their hoe personae are materialism, their commodification of sex, and their rejection of romance-based courting rituals'.

Thus, when we discuss rap music we can see that there are two positions. One argues that rap music has a rich African-American cultural history and is complex and playful; as Quinn (2000: 129) puts it: 'pimp poetics share affinities with post-structural notions not only of signification but also of sub-jectivity, whereby the mack serves as an emblem of ontological indeterminacy'. Alternatively, we might be more convinced by those who argue that represent-ing black men as pimps entails representing women as 'hos' and objectify-ing them. There is a third position which recognises the complexity of these representations in rap music, but is still not comfortable with referring to women as 'bitches' and 'hos'. Perhaps this sense of ambivalence is summed up in Joan Morgan's review of Ice Cube's music, where she admits to feeling perverse pleasure in the lyrics at the same time as wishing to resist them (Morgan, cited in Quinn, 2000: 132–3). In an essay, she writes:

Is it foul to say that imagining a world where you could paint your big brown lips in the most decadent shades, pile your phat ass into your fave micromini, slip your freshly manicured toes into four-inch fuck-me sandals and have not one single solitary man objectify – I mean roam his eyes longingly over all the intended places – is like a total drag for you? Am I no longer down for the cause if I admit that while total gender equality is an interesting intellectual concept, it doesn't do a damn thing for me erotically? That, truth be told, men with too many 'feminist' sensibilities have never made my panties wet, at least not like that reformed thug nigga who can make even the most chauvinistic of 'wassup, baby' feel like a sweet wet tongue darting in and out of your ear. And how come no one ever admits that part of the reason women love hip-hop as sexist as it is – is 'cuz all that in-yo-face testosterone makes our nipples hard? (Morgan, cited in Chang, 2006: 547)

In the case of the white rapper Eminem, 'it is unclear if he is a sophisticated satirist and/or a shameless exploiter revelling in misogyny and homophobia for commercial gain' (Stephens, 2005: 21). There has been a great deal of criticism of Eminem because of his use of words such as 'faggot' and 'lez' in his songs and because of his representation of murder fantasy in relation to his girlfriend and hatred of his mother. Stephens argues that we should not see Eminem simply as a homophobe, but as what he terms a 'genderphobe', that is, someone who is not antagonistic to gay and lesbian people or to sexual acts which are not heterosexual, but who is antagonistic to certain types of behaviour which seem to him to connote weakness and femininity: 'Eminem, along with other hip-hop musicians, often espouses homophobic rhetoric but his most inflammatory attacks are usually directed at male rivals who deviate from gender roles' (Stephens, 2005: 23). Thus he is critical of what he sees as gendered behaviour or roles but does not see this as indicating a hatred of sexual choice or sexuality.

When Eminem's first album was released he was criticised by a gay and lesbian group in America (GLAAD), who argued that: 'Eminem's lyrics are soaked with violence and full of negative comments about many groups, including lesbians and gay men' and 'such defamatory material . . . encourages violence and hatred' and 'such disregard for others can lead to discrimination, physical abuse and even death' (Dansby, 2000, cited in Stephens, 2005: 25). Eminem responded in an interview: 'The term "faggot" doesn't necessarily mean a gay person. To me, it don't' (DeCurtis, 2000, cited in Stephens, 2005: 25). In another interview, he went further: 'Faggot is like taking away your manhood – you're a sissy, you're a coward . . . it doesn't necessarily mean you're being a gay person' (Douglas-Brown, 2002, cited in Stephens, 2005: 26). To further emphasise the semantic difference which Eminem feels he is making between faggot (weak) and gay (homosexual), in the 2002 semi-autobiographical film *8 Mile*, his character says, about a co-worker: 'Paul's gay/but you're a faggot.' It is important, particularly in the case of Eminem, to recognise that often Eminem is using irony and that he is speaking as a character – we must see that 'Eminem' is a persona developed by Marshall Mathers and that the 'Slim Shady' referred to in the songs is again another character. We cannot know the intentions and beliefs of the real singer and we must assume a distance between the singer and the persona. However, it is also not possible to simply decide to make something 'mean' something, unless this meaning is one which is affirmed by other discourses and groups within the society as a whole.

Thus, these insult terms used in the context of gangsta rap can be seen to have a multiplicity of meanings. It is clear that they are indeed sexist and homophobic, but they are not reducible to those meanings alone, since they have a history of usage which makes their meaning multi-layered. They are also part of a very theatrical form of music where the authenticity of the singer's persona depends on performing a particular type of hypermasculinity. The users of these insult terms intend them to be interpreted quite differently to the way in which they are often interpreted by the media. I am not trying to condone the use of these insult terms, but this analysis of a particular context forces us to be wary of making snap judgements about the inherent sexism or homophobia of particular words.

3.1.5. Semantic derogation Terms which have been associated with women or with femininity have historically become pejorative, according to Schultz, who argues that there is a 'semantic derogation of women' – a systematic process whereby words and phrases associated with women become negatively inflected (Schultz, 1990). Schultz traces the patterns in pejoration; for example, she shows that there is a 'democratic levelling' in terms referring to women in positions of authority. These are more likely to be used for women at lower levels – she cites the examples of 'lady', 'governess', 'mistress', 'madam' and 'dame', which were initially used only for powerful women but then degenerated to have wider reference, whereas the male equivalents of these terms retained their associations with high status. She notes that 'in their downhill slide, they slip past respectable women and settle upon prostitutes and mistresses' (Schultz, 1990: 136). She charts the process whereby 'huswif' (meaning the female head of a household in Old English) declined to mean, first: 'a rustic, rude woman' and then 'a lewd brazen woman or prostitute' (Schultz, 1990: 137).[17] Schultz (1990: 135) offers proof that these terms have negative associations:

[17] The current meaning of 'housewife' to refer to a woman who stays at home to look after the house and/or children is a very difficult term to use now, because of its negative associations. This is due partly to feminist campaigns about women being expected to stay at home and partly

if terms designating men are used to denote a woman, there is usually no affront. On the other hand, use a term generally applied to women to designate a man and you have probably delivered an insult.

As I mentioned earlier in this chapter (3.1.4), theorists in gender and language have documented the ways in which there are more insult terms for women than there are for men.[18] However, as Schultz suggests, it is even possible to insult a man simply by using the words 'woman' and 'girl', whereas it is not necessarily an insult to use the term 'man' or 'boy' to a woman. For example, if someone calls you an 'old woman' or 'old maid' you know that you are being accused of being weak or fussy (the actual sense of this term is not always clear, but it is clear that it is an insult, since it is often used in phrases like 'Don't be such an old woman'). 'Girl' is also used in this way to goad boys who are not considered to be sufficiently stereotypically masculine (as in 'Don't be such a girl') (see Sunderland, 2005).

Terms which refer to professions or contexts where women workers are in the majority tend to be trivialised and can have negative connotations; for example 'lollipop lady'[19] can have positive or negative connotations depending on the context, but the childish connotations of the use of the word 'lollipop' suggest that the job is not considered serious or worthwhile.[20] Similarly, when the Labour government decided to introduce untrained classroom assistants in the UK in the 1990s, they were termed by many tabloid newspapers 'Mum's army'. Instead of referring to the women who took up these posts in professional terms, this reference to the fact that many of the women were likely to be mothers was enough to trivialise the posts. 'Mummy track' is a term which has been used even in the left-leaning UK *Guardian* newspaper to refer to the lower profile career path which women who have children are encouraged to follow. In recent (2006) discussions in the UK about the government employing psychologists to advise the parents of offending teenagers on parentcraft, these psychologists were referred to as 'super-nannies', again using a term associated with a badly paid, largely female profession, rather than the professional term 'psychologist'. Both the *Guardian* and the news reports on 'super-nannies', whilst critical

---

to the increased involvement of women in the workforce, which has meant that there are fewer women who stay at home full-time. There has been a move on the part of those who care for children full-time (both male and female) to call themselves 'home-makers' instead, so that the labour involved in their work is recognised. However, this term has not been adopted very widely.

[18] In Britain, generally women are insulted in relation to their sexuality ('slag', 'slapper', 'tart'), their appearance ('dog', 'trout'), talking too much and too loudly ('gossip', 'bitch', 'nag', 'strident') and their non-compliance ('battleaxe', 'old bat', 'old boot', 'slut', 'cow', 'stroppy'). Male insult terms tend to focus on stupidity rather than sexuality (see Schultz, 1990).

[19] In Britain, this term is used to refer to a crossing attendant.

[20] The fact that these jobs are often part-time and are generally very badly paid plays a major role in the devaluing and trivialising of work associated with women.

of this development, nevertheless used the trivialising term throughout the report.

Hellinger and Bussmann (2001) comment on the way in which certain words used to refer to professions associated with females are of lesser status than those associated with professions where there are more males. For example, in French, 'couturier' (masc.) refers to fashion designers, and both males and females can refer to themselves using this masculine term. 'Couturière' (fem.) refers to seamstresses or tailoresses. The word 'tailoress' in English is rarely used, because of this association with low-status work.

Some of the examples of overt sexism which were given by feminist theorists in the 1970s and 1980s have a vaguely archaic feel today; for example, many theorists stressed the lack of equivalence between the terms 'host' and 'hostess' and 'spinster' and 'bachelor' (Lakoff, 1975; Spender, 1980; Mills, 1995b; Schultz, 1990). It has been argued that in pairs of words for women and men, the word to denote the female tends to pick up a sexual overtone which is not present in the word used for the male; thus 'hostess' can mean (a) a barworker who is sometimes a sex worker, (b) an air steward and (c) someone who hosts a party; whereas only the latter meaning is available for the male 'host'.[21]

Page (2005) analyses the way that the media represent and name Cherie Booth/Blair, the wife of the former UK Labour Prime Minister Tony Blair. As Cherie Booth, she is a successful barrister and head of a law firm. They represent Cherie Blair in terms of her appearance, her use of alternative therapies, her problematic friends, and as a mother, wife and consort, who is often criticised, whilst Cherie Booth is often represented as a powerful woman with a career. This image of Cherie Booth is in conflict with the traditional passive stereotype of the Prime Minister's consort. In both roles, however, she is criticised. From the analysis of the way that Cherie Booth/Blair is represented we can make generalisations about the way working women are represented and Page analyses the way that terms such as 'working mother' and 'juggle' are used. 'Working mother' is generally associated with problems and conflict; and 'juggle' is often used in relation to women at work, where women are seen to be trying to be both professionals and mothers at the same time. Page (2005: 576) comments:

[21] Other examples from British English are 'usher' and 'usherette', where the female term has become restricted to reference to women who work in cinemas (however, it could be argued that 'usher' has become restricted to the person who guides people to their places at weddings). 'Adventuress' used to refer to female adventurers, but also had picked up the meaning of someone who tried to gain advance through sexual relations with males. It is now rarely used with either of these meanings. 'Pro' and 'tramp' have different meanings for males and females, with the female reference having a sexual connotation, although the latter is largely an American usage.

I am not trying to claim here that altering naming practices in the media, introducing the term 'working father' or changing stereotypically negative representations of the working mother would result in a more equal situation for all women and men within and outside the workplace. However, exposing the ideological nature of these representational practices is still an important first step as a means of recognising that they can (and some might argue should) be reconstructed.

Feminists have argued that terms used to refer to women often seem to be diminutive. However, these terms are becoming more and more obsolete; for example, those words which end in -ette or -trix. 'Aviator' is itself obsolete and the female form 'aviatrix' is hardly ever used.[22] Hellinger (2001: 109) argues that these terms which refer to women using an affix were in fact always problematic: 'they never only denoted the female counterpart of a male referent, but generally carried additional negative connotations'. Because of the diminutive nature of these terms, it has been suggested that they should not be used to refer to women. Many people now use the term 'actor' to refer to women, rather than 'actress', just as 'authoress' and 'Jewess' are now rarely used. Indeed, Romaine comments that she realised that 'authoress' was used in a negative way, when she found a 'negative review of one of my books in which a male reviewer referred to me as an authoress' (2001: 158). Although this is not enough to prove that diminutive terms have negative connotations, perhaps we can see that negative environments of use have an effect on the meaning of these terms.

Schultz (1990: 137) suggests that this overall pattern of pejoration of terms referring to women could only have been initiated by men:

It is clearly not the women themselves who have coined and used these terms as epithets for each other. One sees today that it is men who describe and discuss women in sexual terms and insult them with sexual slurs, and the wealth of derogatory terms for women reveals something of their hostility.

However, whilst Schultz's work is important in seeing patterns of sexism, it is clearly not the hostility of individual men alone which is responsible for these patterns of usage.[23] As Deutscher (2005) has demonstrated, language change

---

[22] 'Suffragette' and 'majorette' are examples of words in fairly common usage referring to females using -ette. (It should be noted that the male term from which 'majorette' derives is 'major'; there is a significant difference in this binary pair.) However, there are few other words using -ette. The only situation where a recently coined word has used the -ette formation has been 'ladette', a suitably ironic use of this problematic form. Words like 'governess' (a derivative of 'governor') are no longer used because of changes in working practices.

[23] Although obviously the hostility of individual men will help to support this type of sexism. This hostility is only possible, however, because there are institutional supports for men to see this type of viewpoint as permissible or indicative of their membership of a group of men with similar beliefs.

is a complex process whereby a wide range of variants is available within the language at any one time; only some of these elements are adopted by large sections of the population, and this adoption occurs when there is a pattern of usage already in force, and that pattern is associated with institutional usage. When we analyse the way that words have historically changed, we may well find examples of semantic derogation, since dictionaries will try to list all of the variants, but we cannot assume that all speakers of the language use or even know these variants. Individual hostility is not enough to occasion the development and adoption of a negative term or to initiate patterns of changes in language meaning or connotation. However, once a pattern of derogation is established, particularly if its usage is associated with contexts of institutional power, it is available as a resource and may be drawn on by individual speakers and writers.

Very often terms which are associated more with women than men not only tend to take on negative connotations over time but also begin to be associated only with very restricted and specific reference. For example, in British English, 'landlady', from being a term which was equivalent to 'landlord', has now become restricted largely to the owner of a Bed and Breakfast or someone who rents out rooms in her house to lodgers. 'Landlord' has become the generic term.[24] Thus, when I wanted to refer to the female owner of a rented flat recently, I found myself calling her a 'landlord', as 'landlady' seemed to have a different reference and connotations. 'Manageress' has also become more narrow in reference; although it used to refer to female managers, 'manageress' is largely only used now to refer to women who manage shops. In other contexts, for example where a women is a business manager, the generic 'manager' would be used. 'Priestess' is restricted to reference to women priests in what are seen as pagan religious groups, and the generic terms 'priests' or the more specific 'women priests' are used instead. Thus, the process of change in women's employment has meant that the gendered terms are now being used in restricted ways, although the generic terms have become available to women as well.[25]

---

[24] In the UK, a Bed and Breakfast is a private house where the owner offers rooms for rent on a nightly or weekly basis, with breakfast included in the rent.

[25] As well as this problem of restriction in reference, there is also a distinct lack of words to refer to specifically women's experience. For example, as I noted in *Feminist Stylistics* (1995b), there does seem to be a distinct lack of words to name female genitalia informally, so that one is forced to invent words oneself or use a medical term or an offensive term (see Braun and Kitzinger, 1999). There is also a problem of vagueness about the words used to refer to female genitalia; whilst male genitalia can be fairly carefully described, female genitalia tend to be less distinct in terms of the way we talk about them. For example, 'vulva' is a word used to refer to both the entire genital area and particular elements within the area, and, as Braun argues, 'I don't think most of us are clear what the vulva includes' (Braun, 1999: 515).

Schultz (1990) suggested that there are three origins of pejoration: association with a contaminating concept, euphemism and prejudice. Contamination, she argued, may be a factor in this process, since she argues men always think about women sexually, and therefore any term used to refer to women will acquire sexual connotations; she gives the example of 'woman' and 'female', both of which have been avoided at different stages of their histories because of seeming to refer to 'prostitutes' or 'mistresses'. (Schultz found over a thousand words referring to women in sexually derogatory ways, but very few for men.) Euphemism plays a role, since despite this great variety of terms for prostitutes and sexually active women, there is a tendency to avoid naming prostitutes explicitly, which leads either to using words referring to other women, or to dysphemisms. Finally, Schultz argued that prejudice is the primary motivator for pejoration and is occasioned by the need for men to constitute women as an 'out-group' by focusing largely on their sexuality when referring to them.

3.1.6. First names, surnames and titles The first names which are given to women tend to have diminutive forms (for example, Debbie, Nikki, Maggie, Mandy), whereas male names tend not to be seen as diminutive.[26] However, there are a number of names which are shortened, more informal forms of male names which are now used by females, for example 'Charlie' and 'Jamie'. Whilst originally male names, these forms use the diminutive ending 'ie'. In Arabic, Hachimi (2001) has shown that whilst male first names often begin with '?abd' denoting a relation to Allah, for example 'Abdu-latif' – slave or server of the gentle, and 'Abdu-lmun?im' – slave/server of the benefactor, women's names cannot display a similar relation to Allah. The equivalent names for women are instead 'Latifa' and 'Naima', where the female is seen to be derived from the male form – Latif (gentle) + feminine form 'a'. However, Hachimi also notes that there are changes in the way that women and men are named in Morocco; for example, there are male names such as 'Aziz', which are shortened forms of 'Abdelaziz' but which are now used as full names, which do not indicate a relation with Allah. In a fairly recent development, certain names, such as 'Amal', can be used for both males and females.

In Britain, surnames have displayed a form of possession of the woman by her husband on marriage, largely because, until the 1930s, taking the husband's surname coincided with the appropriation by the husband of the wife's

---

[26] Shortened forms of British men's names tend to end with 'o' rather than 'ie' such as 'Robbo' or even 'er' such as 'Hezzer' for politician Michael Heseltine, 'Prezzer' for John Prescott. Whilst expressing certain negative emotions, these forms do not act as diminutives in the same way as 'Maggie' did when used of former UK Prime Minister Margaret Thatcher.

possessions and property (couverture).[27] The traditional loss of name on marriage has been fiercely debated by feminists.[28] Hellinger and Pauwels argue that the use of the male's surname on marriage, together with the use of titles 'which identify women in terms of their relationship to men (married or not married) . . . highlight their dependency on the male' (2007: 653). Since the 1970s, in Britain, there has been a change in terms of women's relation to men, partly because of the liberalisation of the divorce laws, which has meant that it is much easier for women (and men) to obtain a divorce. At the same time, the growth of couples choosing not to marry and to have children without marrying has increased greatly. This obviously has made a major impact on the choice of surnames. For many women, adding their partner's surname to their own on marriage is a partial solution to the problem; however, many women do not do this because of the class connotations of double-barrelled names in Britain.[29] Since 1855 when Lucy Stone began her campaign to retain her own surname rather than change it to that of her husband, there has been a sporadic pressure for women to be allowed to retain one's own surname on marriage (Kramarae and Treichler, 1985: 237).

In many other cultures, this problem does not arise as women retain their original name on marriage (Arabic-speaking countries), or add their name to those of their partners on marriage (e.g. in South American Spanish-speaking countries), or take their mother's name if they are female (Iceland). In Spain, when a child is born they are given two surnames, that is, they take their mother's first surname and their father's first surname (their mother's and father's second surnames are thus lost). Until recently there was no choice about the order of these surnames: the father's first surname came first, and the mother's first surname came second. This traditional practice of putting the

---

[27] This section is a thoroughly revised version of part of an article published in 2003 (Mills, 2003a).

[28] The fact that a woman's original surname is still referred to as her *maiden* name seems to many to be anachronistic, since the concern with virginity is now largely irrelevant, but equally, many feminists and non-feminists see it as paradoxical that feminists have argued to retain the name which belongs to their father in preference to taking the name of their husband.

[29] There is also a tendency for the woman's surname to become marginalised as it is the name which takes on the status of a middle name with the husband's name coming at the end. However, it could also be argued that since the woman's name comes first, it may be the one which is listed in the telephone book and thus is of greater prominence and importance. Wright and Hay (2000) have shown that in fact there are phonological reasons why certain names are put first, rather than this order being solely due to a patriarchal conspiracy. Wright and Hay found that in first names, the one which comes last is generally the one which is likely to end with a vowel, or have a long last vowel, and the one which goes first is likely to have an initial consonant cluster and be one-syllable. Because male first names seem to have the characteristics for initial position, they argue that male names come first; however, male names may have the characteristics of initial position because that is seen to be the most prestigious. The same is probably true of surnames in double-barrelled names. A combination of phonological preference and patriarchal stereotypes and also the 'rules' within one's own community of practice all play a role in such decisions.

father's surname first meant that most matrilineal lineages were lost. However, in the 1990s, a new law was passed which allowed parents to choose the order of their children's surnames. This means that either the mother's or the father's first surname can be placed first. Generally when referring to others, the first surname will be used. At present, many feminists use both surnames. However, in very conservative sections of the population, a woman may be referred to as 'señora Martín García': the wife of García, where García is the husband's surname. In Portugal, there is the same tradition of using two surnames, but traditionally the mother's surname is placed first and the father's second. The surname which is conventionally used and which is given value is the second surname (O. Castro, pers. com., 2007).

To give a brief example of the variability of the taking of the husband's surname on marriage and the naming of children in Britain at the moment, I would like to analyse the names of parents in a local Woodcraft Folk group.[30] Of 24 parents in one Woodcraft group, only 2 women had taken their husbands' surname, 15 of the children had taken the surname of their father, 4 had taken their mother's surname and 4 had taken a double-barrelled combination of their father's and mother's surnames. This small sample cannot be seen as being indicative of trends in the wider population. Amongst the white middle class (who are represented in this group) this is quite common, but within the wider population it is far more common to take one's husband's surname on marriage, and indeed, it would be fairly controversial to maintain one's own surname.

However, in recent years, there has been a trend for female celebrities to take their husband's names (Hughes, 2001). Hughes takes as symptomatic the fact that several famous women, such as Madonna and Victoria Beckham, changed their surnames to their husband's:

Women it seems are increasingly taking their husband's surnames when they marry, and not just in that 'Oh, let's just both be called Smith on the gas bill because it's easier' kind of way. Rather, it is a self-conscious means of marking a profound change in sense of self and wanting other people to witness it. (2001: 2)

However, for many, this seems regressive, signalling a 'whole suburban lower middle class fantasy evoked by my simple request to be known by [my husband's name]' (Hughes, 2001: 2). Hughes argues that:

Madonna knows that anyone can get married – she had already done it once. She also knows that with luck, pretty much anyone can have a baby, because she's already done that twice. What had eluded her up until now, perhaps was that trickiest of things, an enduring love relationship. And having finally found it, in the middle rather than at

---

[30] Woodcraft Folk is a socialist-inspired group emanating from the Co-operative Movement, which aims to provide activities for children that encourage co-operation, as an alternative to the more militaristic Scouts and Guides. This brief example is not necessarily indicative of trends in the wider population, but certainly may be indicative of middle-class trends.

the beginning of her adult sexual life, she wants to mark the moment for what it is: transforming. (2001: 2)

Where naming practices may bring difficulties for women is if they have children and have to make a decision about whose name the children will take. It becomes even more difficult when women divorce their husbands or leave their partners, and change their own names; then they are faced with the difficult decision about what to do about the children's surnames if they have their father's surname. If they then remarry and take their new partner's name, they are again faced with the question of what to do with the children's names.

The use of titles for women is equally fraught with difficulties, because of the need to choose between 'Mrs' and 'Miss' (where there is no equivalent distinction between married and unmarried men). The term 'Ms' was intro-duced in the 1970s, in the UK and US, in order to give women the option of choosing to represent themselves as something other than married or unmar-ried. Whilst Ms is still very much used by feminists in Britain, and is widely available as an option on official forms, for many it is often treated with some suspicion, as a title used only by divorced women, feminists, lesbians, 'man-haters' and women who are living with men without being married to them.[31] When it is used in the media it is often used pointedly in order to ridicule women. Walsh shows that prominent female politicians, when criticised, are often referred to as Ms (Walsh, 2001). The term Ms is also slightly difficult to pronounce and distinguish clearly from Miss in casual conversation. For many academic women, there is a further possibility of choosing to use the title 'Dr' or 'Professor'; however, the use of these titles outside the university or hospital context may implicate an assessment of the particular context as one in which power dynamics are at work (Thornborrow, 2002). Thus, feminist women seem to be forced into labelling themselves in relation to men (married or unmarried) or choosing a term which has a very marked feel to it (Ms) or using a term which relates to their professional status in contexts where it is not salient.

In order to test out the way that women talked about using 'Ms', Schwarz ran focus groups of women of different ages. One of the women said: 'I think Ms gives the idea that you choose to be that . . . whereas Miss you don't choose because you just haven't been saved by a man' (Schwarz, 2003/2006: 145). Some of the focus group participants stated that they considered Ms to refer to those who were divorced, those who were cohabiting, women who did not want others to know that they were in a relationship with a man, those who felt too old not to be married, and women who thought they might be treated differently if married. Thus, rather than 'Ms' being used to replace the terms 'Mrs' and

---

[31] Sunderland (2006) claims that Ms is much more widely used in North America than in Britain.

'Miss', in order that women would no longer have to indicate their marital status in their title, in fact there is now a proliferation of terms, each with a wide range of contested meanings. It is clear that the introduction of Ms has not been as successful as many feminists had hoped; however, Sunderland argues that 'the interventions were . . . effective discursively to the extent . . . that people *talked* about them' (Sunderland, 2004: 200).

In languages where there is no alternative title to 'single woman' and 'married woman', such as in German and Spanish, titles can be used in a very discriminatory way. Hellinger (2006) has analysed the way that the German Chancellor Angela Merkel is named in very different terms to her male colleagues. In a study of a number of national newspapers, of different political persuasions, she has found that the title which is used most frequently with reference to Merkel is 'Frau Merkel', a social title relating to her marital status, rather than a professional title. In Spanish, where there is a choice between 'señora' (married woman) or 'señorita' (unmarried woman), most feminists have decided to use 'señora' since it seems to be the nearest equivalent to the masculine term 'señor'. However, just as in French with 'madame' (married woman) and 'mademoiselle' (unmarried woman), these titles are also used to refer to women whose age leads you to believe that they should be married, even if they are not in fact married. Therefore, women above a certain age in both countries, whether married or not, tend to be referred to as 'señora' or 'madame'. However, female teachers in Spain are referred to as 'señorita' whether they are married or not; just as in English, all female teachers are referred to as 'Miss' in the vocative (O. Castro, pers. com., 2007). Thus, these titles for women draw attention to the marital status of women in a way that the term for men does not.

In a recent study which I conducted of British feminist women's use of their husband's surname (Mills, 2003a), I found that women's choice of surname and title at present can be seen to be at a crisis point in discourse where there are pressures exerted by our own perceptions of what is acceptable within feminism and what is deemed appropriate within other communities of practice. I found that just over half of the women I surveyed had taken their husband's surname. Just under half of the women surveyed kept their own name or changed their name to a name other than their husband's on marriage. Many of the women questioned stated that their reasons for taking their husband's name or keeping their original name were 'quite a volatile mix of practical, emotional and aesthetic factors' and some remarked that their decisions were guided by 'aesthetic and romantic reasons'. Many acknowledged that there was a complex range of pressures at work which informed their decisions about their surname and title, some of them locating these pressures specifically at the level of the family or particular feminist positions, and others stating 'it's just expected'.

However, rather than simply assuming that women therefore adopt one simple solution to this problem, adopting either their husband's name or retaining their own/their father's, using a title such as 'Ms', 'Mrs' or 'Miss', what women do is negotiate these conflicting pressures. They choose amongst these resources depending on the context, sometimes choosing different names and titles for use within particular communities of practice.

For some of the women I questioned, it was a matter of signalling an affiliation with certain members of a family; one woman who, together with her husband, changed their surname by deed poll to the maiden name of her husband's mother, did so because, on divorce, the mother-in-law had reverted to this name: 'we liked the sound of it with our first names better. There was the added factor that we were living in Scotland at the time and [our child] had a lot of family living locally with that name so again it was a cultural issue in that we thought it would give him a sense of kinship and a sense of geographical belonging. So although me and [my child] have the same surname as [my husband] it wasn't, in that second act of naming, that we took his name, it's more that we all acquired a name together.' This person's sense of her family's affiliation to a particular community overrode any other factors in her choice of surname. However, her feminist position dictates that she signals her awareness of the problem of seeming simply to be taking her husband's name. A similar process of affiliation and distinction seems to be at work with another respondent who stated that she took her husband's name because: 'I do not feel any particular loyalty to my father's name (I have a very difficult relationship with my father) and liked the fact that my partner's sounds more Irish than my family name.' Here, taking her husband's name involves a more explicit affiliation to a particular community from which she is geographically distant, and sets herself apart from her father. Another respondent who married a Turkish man stated: 'If I had not taken my husband's name relatives in Turkey may not have seen the marriage as valid or would not have trusted my commitment as Turkish wives do not keep their surname.'[32] For some of the women surveyed who took their husband's surname, the fact that they simply liked the sound of their husband's surname more than their own was a strong factor. Thus, aesthetic considerations and the sense of building a new identity for oneself with the adoption of this new 'nice-sounding' surname also come into play.

For others, taking their husband's name was seen to be a product of the time at which they were married, when this was more common than now. For them, there was often a sense of regret that they had not kept their own name, thus judging their choice from a later feminist position. Many of them remarked that

---

[32] This respondent, when commenting on an earlier draft of this work, mentioned that this was not the only reason that she had chosen to change her name to that of her husband. It was simply one of many other factors.

they felt that they had compromised their feminism or were judged as having compromised. One woman drew attention to this feminist position openly: 'at work they were surprised I had changed my name and thought for "professional" reasons I would use my maiden name'. Another stated: 'I had to explain my decision to a lot of my friends who know me to be an active feminist – the norm amongst them was to retain their own family name . . . I was surprised by the strength of feeling among my friends that what I had done was a betrayal, whatever "creative" excuses I came up with.' Thus, many of the respondents felt that not only their choice of surname but their relationship to their husbands was being judged by other feminists.[33]

Those women who kept their own surname on marriage remarked that they did so because of the need to signal their independence and, for many, as a way of making a public statement about their feminist commitment. However, many of them remarked on the difficulty of convincing others that they were married, sometimes having to provide proof of marriage to officials, and having constantly to correct strangers who called them by their husband's surnames. Many of the women who kept their name on marriage also gave their own name to their children.

Several of the respondents remarked upon the fact that, whilst they did not experience any conflict over their choice of surname, the use of a title was more problematic. For some, the shift to Mrs was seen in positive terms; one woman stated that 'while at University I had always been adamant that I would keep my own name when I married. But once we were planning to get married the thought of being Mr and Mrs with the same surname felt good. I didn't feel I lost my name, but that taking the new name was part of the new and married me . . . I had always said that I wouldn't be a Mrs and would keep Ms but I actually like being a Mrs, it all feels part of growing up.' For this woman, there is a clear sense of a feminist community who would expect her to retain Ms and which might argue that she had 'lost her name', but she has chosen to use Mrs as a signal of her maturity and affiliation with her husband.

In general, the chief difficulty that the women surveyed here remarked upon was other people's understandings and evaluations of their decisions, in relation to adopting a married title. One respondent stated that she was glad to take her husband's name because she felt that it showed her commitment to him: what she did not like was when friends and families addressed letters to her using Mrs followed by her husband's initial and surname, rather than her initial, thus characterising her as a conventional wife. Thus, awareness of the judgement of

[33] Obviously the age of the person responding to this questionnaire is of some importance since those feminists who married twenty years ago, when it was simply accepted that on marriage the woman would take her husband's name, may well feel differently about their choice of surname given the changes in social structures and attitudes since then.

others makes this a charged decision and illustrates the way that feminist women negotiate with the pressures from both feminist positions and conservative, sexist positions. This respondent is willing to take her husband's name and the title Mrs but on her terms, not within conventional sexist terms. What seems to irk her is the difficulty in separating her decision from those sexist positions. For Chouliaraki and Fairclough, this type of 'hybridity' is inherent in all social uses of language 'but particular social circumstances create particular degrees of stability and durability for particular articulations' (1999: 13). Thus, the practice which her family and friends engage in is perceived by her to be sexist, but, for them, there are particular stabilising forces, ideologies of women's role in marriage, which are brought into play because she has taken her husband's name and adopted the title Mrs.

It may still be the case that the majority of women in Britain do take their husband's name on marriage, but for feminists it seems that negotiating with the demands of what they perceive as sexism (largely the conservative anti-feminist forces in society), and what they perceive as anti-sexism (largely feminist ideas), results in them inflecting their choice of surnames within their own interpretative frameworks, or using different naming strategies depending on the context. Thus, reform is not the only possible response to overt sexism; naming is one of the areas where women negotiate positions for themselves and are very aware of the implications of the choices that they make. Their perceptions of other communities of practice and their position within these communities make a striking impact on their decisions about names and titles. Perhaps this type of negotiating change through the interaction of individuals with their perceptions of conflicting communities of practice, strategically choosing particular options for particular contexts, and inflecting those choices positively is a more productive model than the utopian notion that sexism can be reformed out of existence. However, it must still be remembered that interpretation of these practices can still be sexist. Working on sexism is not a once-and-for-all process, but rather an ongoing process of attention to discrimination.

3.2.   Processes

Very often, in analysis of sexism, it is largely nouns, pronouns and adjectives which are focused on. Here, however, I would like to examine instances of overt sexism in verbs or processes. Freebody and Baker (1987) in their survey of Australian textbooks for children found that there were some verbs associated only with boys, for example in subject position: 'answer', 'hurt', 'shout', 'think', 'work'; and in object position, 'play with', 'talk to', 'walk with', and there was only a small subset of verbs which were used for girls in the object position and not boys, for example 'hold on to' and 'kiss' (Freebody and

Baker, cited in Pauwels, 1998: 21). Whilst there have clearly been advances in the types of roles that female characters play in school textbooks, perhaps there is still some residual sexism in the types of verbs which are chosen. This process of association of verbs with males or females can also be seen in English-language textbooks for non-native speakers of English, although there has been some change in overtly sexist usage in recent years.

3.2.1. Transitivity Transitivity analysis examines 'who does what to whom' in texts. Burton (1982) argued that in much literature there is a tendency for female characters to be represented as 'acted upon' by other characters. Instead of their being represented as active and acting upon others, they are very often represented as the recipient of others' actions, in the object position rather than the subject position (see Wareing, 1994 and Mills, 1995b). Wareing (1994) has argued that, even in women's literature, where initially the female characters seem to be fairly active and self-determining, there are still tendencies for the characters to be represented as passive and acted upon at certain crucial moments of the text, for example in sexual scenes. Burton (1982) argues that, rather than focusing on individual language items, we need to see tendencies and patterning over the text as a whole. Not only is this important in representation in literature, but Burton argues that these tendencies to cast women into object position can be identified in the way women represent themselves in interaction. She suggests that because of stereotypical views, some women write themselves 'into a concept of helpless victim', their texts abounding in 'disenabling metaphors, disenabling lexis, and disenabling syntactic structures' (Burton, 1982: 201). She draws attention to the way in which certain women sometimes tend to say: 'You'll never guess what happened to me,' rather than: 'You'll never guess what I've just done.' She suggests that certain types of verbal habit – representing oneself as the recipient of actions – are seen as stereotypical for women.

Susan Ehrlich (1999; 2001) has also focused on transitivity choices. In a disciplinary hearing at a Canadian university where allegations of sexual harassment and sexual assault were made by two female students against a fellow male student, she shows that the male accused of sexual assault framed his actions as ones which suggested mutual engagement. Thus, whilst the female defendant stated 'he grabbed my hair' (which clearly foregrounds that this was not an action that she wanted to happen and categorises it as assault), the male stated 'I was caressing her hair' (which draws on the language of consenting sexual relationships and love, implying that the woman wanted this to happen). The male in this case also frequently used agentless passives, such as 'it was decided that' and 'clothes were removed', which do not suggest that anyone in particular was responsible for the actions, or that both of them were responsible jointly. The male who was accused in this case presented sexual activities as events which 'simply happened', for example, 'it started to heat up' and 'it started to escalate'. By using these agentless processes, the male sexual drive is categorised as a force which, once provoked by a female, inevitably has to run its course. Here, the male's responsibility is minimised, and Ehrlich argues that, in some ways, the court process itself affirmed this lack of responsibility on the male's part. The females, in this case, were criticised for not doing enough to resist the male or for not showing him clearly enough that they did not want to have sex, even though the female defendants both stressed that they were afraid and that they had in fact been very clear that they did not want sex with him. Thus, in this case, certain types of transitivity choices, which favoured male perspectives, resulted in rape being characterised as consensual sex. These transitivity choices had been institutionalised within the legal context of the tribunal (see also Cameron and Kulick, 2003).

A similar disenabling form of grammatical choice can be seen in two sections of an article about male and female participants in the British tennis tournament at Wimbledon in the UK TV and radio listings magazine *Radio Times* (one by Bates on men and one by Smith on women, 2004). In his article, 'The men to watch', Bates describes the male tennis players who are most likely to succeed in that year's Wimbledon. He describes male competitors such as Andy Roddick, Tim Henman and Roger Federer in entirely positive terms; for example, he says of Andy Roddick: 'He made a great effort last year and won at Queen's last year too, and he won the US Open after that. This year he recorded the world's fastest serve at 152mph which is good on any surface.' Of Roger Federer, he says: 'He's the reigning men's champion and he's the clear number one in the world. He's had an outstanding year.' Even when reporting on Andre Agassi, about whose form Bates has doubts, he states: 'he's one of the game's great returners. He's skipped much of the clay court season this year trying to save himself for Wimbledon, so physically he should be pretty fresh.'

In the article, 'The women to watch', which appears opposite the previous article, Smith describes the women competitors in starkly different terms. When she describes Amelie Mauresmo, Venus Williams and Serena Williams, she focuses not on their successes but on their injuries and self-doubts. On Mauresmo, Smith states: 'We know she can win at Wimbledon, but does she believe it too? She has the ability and the athleticism to be a contender and she can beat anyone on her day, but nerves might destroy her challenge.' When describing Serena Williams, Smith claims: 'No-one can stop Serena except Serena,' suggesting that Williams also suffers from self-doubt. Venus Williams is described only in terms of the effect of her injuries on her play. When complimenting Jennifer Capriati on becoming a 'big-time player once again', Smith states: 'a few months ago I would have advised you to look elsewhere for this year's champion'. Thus, in these two separate articles, there seems to be a clear difference between the way that male and female tennis players are represented, with the male players being represented positively in terms of their fitness and successes on court, and the female players represented as suffering from self-doubt. This differential treatment of sportswomen and sportsmen has become institutionalised; many different sports reports use the same sexist structures and verbal choices.

3.2.2. Reported speech Caldas-Coulthard (1995) argues that there is a tendency for the speech of females to be represented in news reports in indirect speech rather than in direct speech. She suggests that, because of this lack of direct quotation from women, women's statements are mediated by newspapers, which often leads to evaluative statements being made through the use of reporting words such as 'claim' or 'argued'. This can clearly be seen in the analysis of the representation of the former UK Foreign Secretary Margaret Beckett, which I discuss in Chapter 5, where there is very little direct quotation of Beckett herself, rather quotation of comments about Beckett from politicians and journalists. Because of this tendency, Caldas-Coulthard views women's voices as being relatively 'unaccessed'; when they are represented, they tend to be not the professional voices which are accorded to men but rather those associated with and emanating from the private sphere, for example those of daughters, wives and mothers. She argues:

The private/public distinction is a very important feature of social organisation. If women are represented mostly speaking in their personal roles, they are marginalised in terms of public or ritual speech. (Caldas-Coulthard, 1995: 227)

This institutionalised usage is not one which many might argue constitutes overt sexism and should be considered indirect sexism.[34] However, it remains the case that there is a clear distinction in the way that women and men are reported in newspapers.

3.2.3. Jokes As I will discuss in more detail in Chapter 5, jokes are a complex way of constituting women as a 'minority group' without taking responsibility for that exclusion.[35] Sexist jokes allow generally unacceptable views of women to be expressed, because the person who tells the joke generally can claim that they themselves did not make up the joke. As Davies (2004)

---

[34] The distinction between overt and indirect sexism is not clear-cut. There is a great deal of overlap between the two types of sexism.

[35] Often women make negative comments or jokes about males and we might argue that they must therefore be considered to be sexist in the same as males' denigratory comments about women. However, I would argue that for a comment to count as sexist, the recipient must be a member of a political minority group which has, historically, suffered discrimination.

states, sexism works with reference to an institutional status other than the personal or individual. A student told me a sexist joke which can serve as an exemplar here of the way these types of joke work:

Q: What do Barnsley girls use as protection during sex?
A: A bus shelter.

There is an assumption that the hearer will infer that girls from Barnsley[36] are renowned for their promiscuity and roughness. The verbal play is centred on the dual meaning of the word 'protection' (to mean 'condom' or 'the protection from the rain of a bus shelter during sex'). For those who tell and laugh at sexist jokes, the wordplay is seen as being more important than the sexist beliefs which underpin the joke.

Bing and Heller (2003) note that the jokes made about lesbians by men are generally concerned with sex (primarily oral sex), and appearance seen in terms of deviance from a heterosexual norm. However, Bing and Heller also note that lesbian humour takes issue with those representations and often foregrounds the living arrangements of lesbians rather than their sexual choices: 'in that sense lesbian humour constitutes a mode of social critique that offers transformative possibilities' (Bing and Heller, 2003: 178). In the debate about lesbian jokes in the pages of the journal *Humor*, it was asserted by Davies (2004) that jokes do not have a major impact on the real world. Bing responded:

Certainly a few jokes by themselves cannot dehumanise a group of people, even an underprivileged group. However when any group, be it lesbians or women in general are repeatedly treated as sex objects rather than as human beings in jokes, in pornography, in advertisements, in the media, in films, in books, etc, it is quite possible that this dehumanisation makes it easier for others to restrict, rape, assault and even kill individuals from these groups. (Bing, 2004: 325)

It is sometimes difficult to know whether to interpret insults as jokes, since often insults are used to indicate a particularly close relation with someone. If someone you do not know well calls you a 'dyke', in the phrase 'you fucking dyke' in an angry tone of voice, you can assume that you have been insulted and you would be justified in classifying the utterance as homophobic. However, in certain circumstances, amongst close friends, it may not be clear whether insults are intended to be interpreted as jokes and indicators of a close relationship ('I know you so well that I can use this insult with you'; thus the act can be classified as positive politeness, or affiliation). The interpretation of sexism is often equivocal and is largely a matter of interpretation. For example, if a workman at work calls me 'dear', he may be being sexist or simply using the sort of address term which he considers appropriate to use to a woman whose

---

[36] Barnsley is a town near Sheffield, UK.

name he does not know. It is this conflict over interpretation which is at the heart of the analysis of sexism.

4.   Sexism, racism and homophobia

Overt sexism, where someone openly denigrates a woman, can affect not only her sense of her place in the world but can force her to interrogate her sense of self. A similar process seems at work with racist language. James Baldwin stated in 1988:

In order for me to live, I decided very early that some mistake had been made somewhere. I was not a 'nigger' even though you called me one. But if I was a 'nigger' in your eyes there was something about you – there was something *you* needed . . . so where we are now is that a whole country of people believe I'm a 'nigger' and I *don't* and the battle's on! Because if I am not what I've been told I am, then it means *you're* not what you thought *you* were *either*! And that is now the crisis. (Baldwin, cited in Miller, 1995: 42)

Racism and sexism have very different effects.[37] For example, there have been several recent cases in Britain where children have been brought to trial because of having insulted others using racist terms. In the case of sexist abuse, this would not have reached a court. This is partly because racist insults may create an atmosphere of fear where people feel frightened to leave their homes or to interact with others, and also because very often racist taunts are part of violent campaigns against non-white people.

Because sexism works to demarcate certain people as belonging to a group, it draws on stereotypes and prototypes to make clearly distinguishable that which risks becoming indistinguishable. In the past women and men had more clearly defined separate roles and spheres, and, for many men and women, this lack of distinction is troubling, hence the necessity to assert sex difference as binary and natural (Cameron, 2007). Sexism works to re-establish these distinctions and seems to hark back to an early period of order when people supposedly 'knew their place'. A similar process can be seen at work in relation to language used about disabled people. The TUC argues that:

whenever we use words like 'cripple' we reinforce the assumption that disabled people are less than able people. When we work for equal rights, but talk about disabled people as helpless victims, we make the very objectives we have set ourselves more difficult to achieve. (TUC, 1998: 2; see also Wright, 2007)

One of the most significant difficulties with the model of sexism which has been used by feminist theorists, since the 1960s, is that it does not address any

---

[37] Because of recent legislation, racism is more likely to be acted upon by the police and legislature than in the case of sexism.

other issues than those supposedly determined by discrimination on the basis of sex difference. However, this is problematic, since if discriminatory language which is determined by prejudice on the grounds of class, race, disability and sexual orientation are not addressed, then the type of discrimination which is analysed under the heading of sexism is only concerned with women who are white, heterosexual, middle class and able-bodied. As Sedgwick argues with regard to homophobic language: 'It is unrealistic to expect a close textured analysis of same-sex relations through an optic calibrated in the first place to the coarser stigmata of gender difference' (Sedgwick, cited in Livia and Hall, 1997a: 6).

Whilst we must try to analyse discrimination in language across the board, at the same time, conversely, we must recognise differences. Many policy statements which are concerned with discriminatory language at present list all forms of discrimination in one document. However, if we do not deal with the elements separately to some extent we will assume that all discriminatory language is the same, that is, that it takes the same forms and will need to be addressed and combated in a similar way. It is clear that racist and sexist language have different histories. Wetherell and Potter (1992: 32) argue that racist language:

plunders – political ideologies of conservatism, liberalism and social reformism, the lay psychological analyses through which identity is construed and narrated in 'post-modern' consumer cultures, popular biology and social theory, the moral principles and practical dilemmas of Western ethics, the categorisation systems of 'race', culture and nation.

It is clear that sexist language does not have the same ideological history or provenance as racism or indeed homophobia. Furthermore, sexist language has different effects to other forms of discrimination. Whilst it may be responsible for creating what is termed a 'chilly climate' in the workplace where women implicitly are given the sense that they are not welcome, it does not seem to be associated with threats of violence which racist language often is (Greater Manchester Police, 2001c). In a similar way, homophobic language springs from different histories of oppression and activism and the conflicts over equal rights for gay, lesbian, bisexual and transsexual people (Leap, 1995; 1997; Livia and Hall, 1997b). It should not therefore be simply confused with the equal rights struggles of women in general. But we need to be aware that homophobic language does have similar effects to sexist language. Armstrong argues:

The use of [homophobic] language creates an atmosphere of uncritical acceptance of intolerance towards homosexuality, whilst reinforcing stereotypical attitudes towards gays. (1997: 327)

It is this acceptance of intolerance which needs to be combated, and campaigns against this type of language use are crucial. Leap (1995: viii) comments that:

language, like politics, is a product of negotiation and contestation. Speakers do not just 'acquire' language in some abstract or mechanical sense; speakers, learn, share, modify, exchange and maintain rules of grammar and discourse, based on their own experiences of text-making and on their encounters with the text-making efforts of others.

In conclusion, it is important to see that sexism is not a homogeneous entity. It can be reified in dictionary definitions and in the way institutions affirm or contest it, but it can often be ambiguous whether a remark is sexist or not. That is not to say that all meanings and interpretations are now up for grabs, because sexist statements are still those which seem to make sense with reference to a body of seemingly authorised gendered discourses. In order to assume that someone has been sexist, it is necessary to analyse what you think their intentions were in uttering what you have classified as sexist, and whether they directly or indirectly draw on this body of stereotypical thought about women.

The question of femininity is important here, for women who have a strong investment in femininity for their own self-identity may not consider sexist those statements which are interpreted as sexist by feminists. If we consider what are termed 'street-compliments' or 'sexual harassment', those who affiliate with traditionally feminine values may consider street compliments to be flattering and a recognition of their attractiveness, whereas for Anglo-American feminists, these comments will only seem like unwanted sexual attention.

In order to try to assess the way that overt sexism works, I would now like to examine an advertisement which appeared in a men's magazine in 2004 advertising Vaseline deodorant for men.[38] The advertisement features a half-length picture of a woman in a bra with her hands behind her head stretching; she does not look at the camera but instead poses with a look of sexual arousal on her face. Above this picture is the headline: 'What a lovely pair of pits.' The text continues under the picture of the woman: 'Beauties, aren't they? But why should women be the only ones to have armpits nice enough to fall asleep in?' The advertisement presupposes that some men find it difficult to use deodorant, because it is viewed as feminine or, as the advertisement puts it, 'wussy'. The advertisers tread a very careful path, since deodorants are generally considered feminine, arguing in suitably 'manly' joking language that many men have hairy armpits and that this may be unattractive, when in fact a man could have armpits as beautiful as the woman's. However, it

---

[38] I would have liked to include a copy of this advertisement at this point to illustrate this analysis; however, as I mentioned earlier, advertisers are extremely wary of granting permission for reproduction of advertisements, particularly in books about sexism. After an extremely lengthy negotiation with the producers I decided not to reproduce the advertisement.

can only make this very convoluted argument – have armpits like a woman's which smell nice, without challenging your masculinity – by using 'laddish' vocabulary. Firstly, the woman represented here is argued to have a 'lovely pair of pits' but the expected collocation, especially since she is pictured wearing a bra, is 'lovely pair of tits'. Later in the advertisement, jokes are made about male armpits being like 'an armadillo's scalp' and body odour is described in terms of 'pong'. The female represented here is presumably 'flaunting' her 'pits' and the male is urged to do likewise. However, this advertisement demonstrates clearly the very complex position advertisers are placed in when, in order to sell deodorants to males, they use illustrations of women. Thus, in this advertisement based on a sexist representation of women, a jokey laddish style of address is used to male readers, in an attempt to convince men to buy deodorant.

Thus, to summarise, there are a number of conventionalised and institution-alised ways of representing women which can be classified as overt sexism: where women are sexualised or trivialised in conventional usage and where they are represented as a deviation from a male norm. However, as I have shown in this chapter, many sexist forms have changed in recent years and feminists have developed alternative forms, some of which have been adopted and some of which have not. It is essential that feminists continue to campaign about overt sexism as it has an impact on the way women construct their sense of their own identity and their positions within institutions and communities of practice.

3   Language reform

When campaigners discuss linguistic reform, it is often assumed that they are only concerned with suggesting alternatives to particular terms of address, or ways of naming. Very often critics assume that linguistic reform is based on a very simplistic view of the nature of language and language change. In this chapter, I show that suggesting alternatives to sexist terms is only *one* of the strategies adopted by anti-sexist campaigners; it is only one of many strategies. Since sexism now manifests itself in complex ways, the notion of reform or even commenting on sexism has become much more difficult. Guidelines which were issued on language use in institutions are now much less visible than they were in the 1980s and 1990s.[1] This is partly because feminist campaigns on language have made an enormous impact on language use, at least in the public sphere. But it is also because the view of language reform has changed quite markedly, so that any campaigns on language are now considered to be a concern with 'political correctness' – a seemingly excessive concern with the replacement of problematic words with the 'correct' term (see Chapter 4). However, Cameron (1995: 143) argues that:

there is nothing trivial about trying to institutionalise a public norm of respect rather than disrespect, and one of the important ways in which respect is made manifest publicly is through linguistic choices: in the context of addressing or referring to someone, words are deeds (compare 'hey bitch!' with 'excuse me, madam').

---

[1] As an example of the type of toned-down guidance which is given to authors submitting a manuscript to a publisher, one publishing house offers the following advice:

Sensitive language Try to be sensitive in your use of terms that may cause offence, e.g. use 'Native American' rather than 'Indian'; 'White' and 'Black' are preferable to 'Caucasian' and 'Negroid'; use 'Humanity', 'people', 'humans' rather than 'Man' to describe the human race; use 'him/her' or 'them' rather than 'him' (but we prefer that you rewrite to avoid excessive use of 'him/her').

Here the publisher is clearly signalling that they do not wish their publications to cause offence, but they do not give great detail of the type of terms that they do not wish to see authors using; instead this serves rather as a signal for the type of language use which is seen to be objectionable, assuming that all of the authors will be able to intuit what other items are not acceptable.

In this context, language reform, however theoretically problematic (because of its assumption that it is possible to simply change language through issuing directives), forces individuals and institutions to see that their language usage may signal to others that they see them as inferior to themselves, when that may or may not be their intention. Attempting to reform the language also forces people to think about how their language affects others. If this usage is intentional, language-reform movements ensure that those individuals can be informed that institutions often do not support them in this type of language use. Hellinger and Bussmann (2001: 19) state that reform is not just a matter of calling for certain items to be changed in favour of what they term gender-fair terminology, but rather should be seen as a representation of a change in relations between the sexes:

Gender-related language reform is a reaction to changes in the relationships between women and men, which have caused overt conflicts on the level of language compre-hension and production. Reformed usage symbolises the dissonance between traditional prescriptions such as the use of masculine/male generics and innovative alternatives. In most cases it explicitly articulates its political foundation by emphasising that equal treatment of women and men must also be realised on the level of communication.

Thus, attempts at reforming and changing language may, at first sight, seem overly ambitious and feminist campaigners may be accused of trying to force individuals to change their language use, thus challenging individual autonomy and freedom of speech. However, Pauwels (2003: 561) argues that:

although many people disagree with the claim that there is gender bias in language, or refuse to adopt non-sexist language changes, they have nevertheless been made aware of the problematic nature of language in this respect.

Reform therefore works on a range of different levels, consciousness-raising, as well as at this more symbolic level, attempting to foreground changes in the status of women and men.

1.   Institutional language change

Since sexism seems to be invoked most often when women are considered to be encroaching on masculine territory, many of the campaigns about language use have taken place within the sphere of the workplace. Pauwels (2003: 561) argues that:

to date non-sexist language policies are in place in most public sector and in many large private sector organisations in English-language countries. They are also increasingly found in European countries and in supranational organisations such as UNESCO.

Cameron (1995) suggests that issuing guidelines for language usage is based on a simplistic model of language and language change. Simply replacing an offensive word with a neutral word does not for her mean that you eliminate sexist language. She uses the term 'verbal hygiene' (with all of the derogatory connotations of an excessive fondness for cleaning with which that phrase is associated) to refer to those campaigns against discriminatory language. When she discusses these campaigns over language she refers to 'language mavens' (that is, those who simply have particular dislikes about language use, such as those who campaign against the use of split infinitives). For me, anti-discrimination reformers are significantly different to those who are arguing against, for example, the use or misuse of the word 'hopefully', and it is because I see differences between these approaches and the strategies adopted by campaigners that I will not be using the term 'verbal hygiene' here.

Cameron (1995) also discusses the language guidelines which I wrote and which the University of Strathclyde's Programme for Opportunities for Women committee introduced in 1990. The Programme was a committee which was established by the university itself and which it hoped would enable it to live up to its claims in its mission statement of 'aiming for equal opportunities'.

The University of Strathclyde, at that time, was very largely a male-dominated technological institution and many of the female academics working there found themselves the sole female in their departments. The Programme for Opportunities for Women committee (POW) had decided that, in order to be successful in our work of changing the way that women were treated in the institution (on a wide range of issues and not just in relation to language), we would have to address the members of the university in a language that they could understand. If we had proposed anything too radical it would simply have been rejected.

The POW committee had felt that the language used within the university in relation to women needed to be addressed, since this was an issue which many women colleagues had brought up as of concern, and we felt that this might prove to be a symbolic issue which would also highlight the presence of women in the university. The language which was used by some male academic staff and administrators often reflected a belief that women staff and students were relative newcomers to the university who had to learn to adopt the university norms, which were in fact masculine norms. Sometimes women were treated in a patronising way, as if they were special and very different from the rest of the academic community, or they were addressed in university documents in language which referred to them as men. For example, I was once in a committee meeting, to which I had been co-opted, since there were no women on the committee (this strategy of co-optation was another of the POW's campaigns), and the chair started the meeting by saying, 'Gentlemen, if we could begin the meeting.' I was a co-opted member and I was there simply as a token female. This was signalled quite clearly to me by the fact that the chair behaved throughout the meeting as if I, as a female, was not there and was not part of the decision-making process. At another committee meeting where I was a co-opted female member, I was constantly asked at the end of many items of discussion, 'And what is the women's perspective on this?' as if I could represent the views of all of the women students and staff in the university. Women in the university were sometimes referred to as 'ladies' which seemed to be according them a level of courtesy and chivalry which was not appropriate to them being considered the equals of male academics.

The POW committee felt that this treating of women as newcomers who had to either conform to the masculinist norms of the university or be treated as exceptional, had to be challenged in some ways in order to encourage women staff to stay at the university. We therefore decided quite strategically to produce language guidelines. We could have produced quite a stark document which outlined the problems with the language used to and about women staff and students, drawing on our feminist positions, but we decided to use a discourse with which we thought all the staff within the university could agree. We also decided as a committee that although sexism was endemic within the university, part of the problem was that many people did not realise that they were being offensive to women and did not intend to be sexist. We could do little to change the language use of those people who did in fact intend to be sexist, but the vast majority of the staff and students, we felt, were unintentionally sexist, using language which they assumed was appropriate to the particular context. Sexism had become institutionalised. When we decided to put together a leaflet offering guidance on what we decided to term 'gender-free language' usage, we focused therefore on the notion of civility and offence, since everyone within the university would agree that being civil to others was necessarily 'a good thing' and offending others would be seen as necessarily 'a bad thing'. We therefore suggested that if they referred to female academics as 'girls' or 'ladies' they risked offending them and suggesting that women were not their equals. If they used 'he' to refer to all students, then they may suggest unintentionally that they considered the 'normal' student to be male and that female students were only allowed into the university on sufferance.

We decided as a group that it was better to suggest that sexism was not institutionalised and part of a social system (as most of us, in fact, believed to be the case), but rather to focus on the matter of unintentional offence, because in that way, these guidelines would not alienate other staff, would appear reasonable and could suggest ways of countering sexist language. Cameron (1995), who joined the University of Strathclyde after these guidelines had been introduced, has criticised this decision in her work, because she argued that if you adopt this particular approach which stresses that it is important to be civil to others and show respect, then you characterise sexism as simply a matter of individual intention:

From a 'civility' perspective the point of using non-sexist language is not to challenge androcentric linguistic representations of the world at large, but merely to avoid
offending/alienating women in the immediate context. This makes sexism a matter of
individual men giving offence to individual women, rather than a systematic social
process. (Cameron, 1995: 134)

We as a committee recognised this, but what we wanted to provide was a way
for each individual staff member to think about their use of language. But our
guidelines were not based solely at the level of the individual, as the very act
of issuing the language guidelines meant that the institution was also involved
in reconsidering language usage and recognising its role in the treatment of
women in the university. Drawing on our contacts with the trades unions within
the university, and supported by the university administration and management,
we distributed these guidelines throughout the university. With the support of
the union, AUT, we then circulated the guidelines to all AUT members within
Scotland, and to a number of other UK universities, either through the union
or through the institution itself.

Cameron (1995) discusses at some length the correspondence which was
received by the Programme for Opportunities for Women committee by those
who objected to the guidelines. Many of these were concerned with perceptions
of curtailment of freedom of speech, and discrimination against men. Despite
the fact that the guidelines did create some negative reactions, nevertheless they
did have a radical impact on many women staff and students at Strathclyde. The
guidelines gave women an institutional support for making claims about sexism
and referring to the guidelines made it possible to object to usages where it might
have felt intimidating, for example in large committee meetings. At several
meetings, female colleagues, when hearing sexist usages, simply asked: 'Since
the university has adopted gender-free language policies, could we possibly use
X instead of Y?' Therefore, it was possible to make the request for anti-sexist
usage a matter of institutional policy and not simply a personal request. The
POW committee did not see ourselves as 'verbal hygienists', simply concerning
ourselves with cleaning up the language used about women and making it less
offensive. We saw our language guidelines as part of an overall strategy to
make the university a more welcoming place for women staff and students by
making management, administrators, students and staff think of the changes
which needed to happen in the institution to accommodate women. Our other
activities involved setting up Women's Studies courses, publishing Women's
Studies bibliographies, to make those resources visible to both feminist staff
and others. In addition, in English Studies, we hosted day schools with students
to produce parallel curricula foregrounding the work of women writers, we held
day schools for women students on feminist theory, and we campaigned for
better childcare provision and promotion opportunities. With each of these

projects we thought carefully about how we could best achieve our end result, which was an improvement in the way that women staff and students were treated. Our overall aim was to encourage people in the institution to think carefully about what changes needed to take place, because, up until that time, the view which was most dominant was that the women who joined the university had to do so on the university's terms; they had to fit in and adapt to the masculinist ways of behaving and interacting. The guidelines which were produced on gender-free usage have to be seen as part of this overall strategy.

It should also be noted that policies such as the one adopted by Strathclyde and other universities are often not still in force, so it does seem as if the moment of institutional language reform is passed. However, the fact that language guidelines are not issued to new staff any more may suggest that they are less needed, since the reforms of the 1990s have been effective. In Cameron's recent (2006: 180) *Language and Sexual Politics*, in a footnote, she states that at Oxford University where she now works, anyone in charge of a committee is called a 'chairman'; she states: 'the experience of working . . . in an institution which does not even gesture in the direction of non-sexist language has made me rather less lukewarm and grudging . . . about the virtues of institutional policies'. Thus, issuing guidelines can be an effective way of opening up a debate about the type of language which it is advisable to use in relation to groups of people who are seen to be a minority. Whilst there are many debates about the most effective way to suggest changes to language at an institutional level, these reforming language guidelines did have a major impact on the way people use language within institutions.

However, as Pauwels (2003) notes, in the 1980s and 1990s these types of institutional reform were only one amongst many strategies drawn on by feminists to bring about discussion and change in language use. Pauwels describes how a great deal of the linguistic reforms which have taken place in Germany were brought about by essays in the German feminist magazine *Emma*. The English feminist magazine *Spare Rib* and other, more academic, feminist journals were all instrumental in publishing articles discussing feminist campaigns around language. Many feminists also used spray-can campaigns defacing sexist advertisements which foregrounded the sexism on many bill-board advertisements (see Talbot, 1998; Sunderland, 2006 for examples). On the London Underground, in the 1990s, there were highly visible sticker campaigns, where feminists posted stickers stating 'This Advert Degrades Women' on sexist advertisements. These popular campaigns to change the nature of the way women were represented within the public sphere, together with the campaigns to change language used about women within institutions, had a major impact on the debates about sexist language in the 1990s.

2.   Strategies of reform

Despite the fact that very often sexism is discussed as if it were monologic, simply a question of using a word or phrase to describe or address someone, in fact it is polyphonic. Sexist usage engages in a dialogue with views which have been expressed in the past and with ones which are currently circulating; it is in dialogue with sexist views and with feminist views and other anti-discriminatory discourses. Sexist language denotes an assessment of what is appropriate within a particular community of practice. It is a language which, whether it likes it or not, will be responded to, whether to be affirmed or met with criticism or silence.

When faced with sexist language at an institutional or individual level, feminists have adopted a range of strategies, some of them bottom-up strategies, where the individual who uses sexist language is challenged, or top-down strategies, where feminists have tried to encourage institutions to legislate to change language usage. For example, in France, the *Commission de feminisation de noms de métiers* examines the development of words to refer to female jobs, since in French it is the male term which is considered to be the generic term which can be used for both males and females. 'Le médecin' is the term used to refer to a doctor, but it is grammatically masculine, whether it is used to refer to a male or female doctor. Thus, feminists in France have set out either to develop new terms which are gender-neutral, or, more appropriately in a grammatical-gender language such as French, to develop a term which refers to women doctors. However, simply replacing terms is not the only strategy available to feminists, nor is reform taking place at simply the individual level. In this section, I consider each of the strategies which has been adopted as part of this process of reforming language and afterwards I will analyse the problematic nature of reform.

2.1.   Critique

The first stage in any reform movement is to analyse and critique what is considered be problematic (Spender, 1980). Pauwels (2003) has noted that there have been feminist language campaigns, criticising ways of referring to women, in the following countries: Norway, the Netherlands, Germany, Spain, China, Iceland, Lithuania, Italy, Japan, Poland, Thailand. Hellinger and Bussmann (2001) have edited three volumes of essays on the progress of these campaigns in many more countries and languages. Whilst simple critique is important as a first stage, since it sparks off debate, it often runs the risk of not providing alternative usages and also of simplifying matters for the sake of clarity.

2.2.   *Alternative terms*

Pauwels (2003) argues that we should see the work of feminist linguistic campaigners as language planning; generally the campaigns are not viewed in this way, as they are seen as *ad hoc* and not organised by a government, as is usually the case with language planning. When attempting to replace terms which are deemed to be offensive to women or when women have to use words which categorise them as male, there are a number of different strategies to be adopted – using gender-neutral language or using non-sexist usage. Frank and Treichler argue that:

Gender-neutral is a linguistic description: a gender-neutral term is formally linguistically unmarked for gender: *police officer, domestic violence, flight attendant*, in place of gender-marked *policeman, wife battering, stewardess*. Non-sexist is a social, functional description; a non-sexist term works against sexism in society. While many gender-neutral terms are consistent with non-sexist usage, the two are not the same. (Frank and Treichler, 1989, cited in Pauwels, 1998: 15)

Thus, with gender neutralisation, the same neutral term is used to refer to women and men. If this is adopted as a general policy, this would mean that the gender-specific terms (where the female term might have been considered to be the stigmatised or marked term, for example 'adventuress') would fall from usage. Another example of this would be the use of 'waiter' and 'actor' to refer to both males and females, in order for women not to have to use the less prestigious terms 'waitress' and 'actress'. However, this leads to invisibility or less visibility for women, and some theorists argue that it is better to develop terms specifically for women, but which are not negatively inflected.[2] Pauwels (2003) states that those who have argued for the development of feminine affixes have stated that 'it is better to be named and to be visible in language, even if there are connotations of triviality'. It is perhaps also a consequence of this argument that when there are many feminine terms within the language, perhaps these negative connotations will disappear over time (Pauwels, 2003: 558).

In grammatical-gender languages (see Chapter 2), such as Italian, French, Spanish, Galician, German and Arabic, the problem is slightly different, as there exist gender-specific terms, where the male term is used for both males and females. For example, female lawyers are termed in French 'l'avocat', the term referring to a male lawyer. This generally happens where it is only relatively recently that women have started working within these professions and they continue to be male-dominated. Here rather than being gender-neutral, the male term erases the presence of women in the profession. In this case, Pauwels

---

[2] However, that does not really deal with the question of how these terms have become negatively inflected and what strategy would combat that process.

(2003) shows that feminists have campaigned for gender specification, so that males and females are referred to using separate terms. This indicates that these professions are accessible to both men and women. Generally, within these languages there is usually a mechanism for modifying the male term with an affix, like '-in' or '-a', or by prefixing it with a different article such as 'la'. For example, in German the term for readers is 'Leser'. In order to refer to women readers, feminists have argued that 'LeserInnen' should be used, with a capital for the affixed segment to foreground the 'linguistic disruption', as Pauwels (2003) terms it. 'Pilot' can be used to refer to female pilots in German by adding the affix '-in', as in 'Pilotin'. However, there is sometimes resistance to adopting affixes to refer to female workers, and it is argued that feminist campaigners here do not understand the workings of grammatical gender, confusing it with sex difference. But feminists can see very clearly that grammatical gender and sex difference are very often inextricably linked.

In some languages, feminists have argued for gender neutralisation; for example in Dutch, 'de advokaat' (the lawyer) is used for both males and females instead of the gender-specific terms (Pauwels, 2003: 557). This is a more equitable solution in Dutch than in other languages such as German, since the definite article is not marked for gender: 'de' is used for both males and females. Pauwels (2003) argues that this is a simpler solution, since, in Dutch, there are a number of different feminine suffixes and it is sometimes difficult to know if 'dokter', for example, takes the feminine suffix 'in' or 'es'.

Thus, even within languages which have grammatical gender, it is not clear that there is one strategy for dealing with this type of reference. In some languages such as Dutch, gender neutralisation is the best option since it seems to allow sex/gender reference to be taken out of contexts where it is not salient. However, in English, gender neutralisation does not seem to be effective, since often those nouns which seem neutral, for many seem to have in practice a male reference. The feminisation of terms in many languages is effective because it makes women visible in the language. However, the disadvantage of feminisation is that it seems to suggest that the masculine form is the norm ('doctor' and 'female doctor'). Nevertheless if such terms are consistently used alongside a similarly gendered term for males ('male doctor'), they may lead to generic terms being restricted to terms where the reference is in fact generic (Castro, 2007).

A further strategy of replacement is needed for terms that have developed to refer to professions which have been traditionally dominated by women and which are not prestigious, for example 'air hostess' and 'cleaning lady'. In the case of these jobs, it is necessary to replace them with terms which bring greater prestige. For example, 'flight attendant' or 'air steward' is now used to refer to 'air hostesses'; they seem to be more prestigious titles than the term 'hostess' with all of its associations with 'bar hostess' and general waitressing.[3] However, the introduction of the terms may be resisted, since nothing about the nature of the job itself has changed, but only the term itself. There is also some resistance to adopting these new terms on the part of the general public and they are occasionally used ironically.

2.3.   Feminist renaming/neologism

Linguistic determinism, that is, the belief that language shapes our view of the world, is not particularly fashionable at the moment. There has been a widespread critique of the notion that, for example, if there are three main colour names in the language, all of the users of that language will only be able to distinguish those three colours. However, it must be the case that when there is a named category for a particular experience, that experience itself begins to feel more acceptable, or at least is more commonplace if you do not have to explain the experience in phrases developed from scratch.

   Feminists have felt it necessary to invent new words (neologisms) to describe critical ways of seeing, in order to challenge conventional perspectives on those experiences (see Kramarae and Treichler, 1985). Feminist neologisms have been very useful for women to recognise that certain experiences are general rather than specific to themselves. These neologisms also serve the purpose of defining experience from a feminist perspective rather than from a stereotypical or conservative perspective. The term 'date rape', for example, provides women with vocabulary to describe coercive sex with a known person as rape (in stark contrast to the woman-blaming vocabulary often used in tabloid newspapers). The development of the term 'sexual harassment' enables women to complain about unwanted sexual behaviour from their work colleagues, recognising it as a general type of behaviour which needs to be dealt with systemically, rather than at the level of the individual alone. The term 'abortion' has been generally referred to as 'termination' by feminist campaigners who wish to lessen the negative emotive qualities associated with the operation, by using a more neutral and technical word. In a similar way, feminists who argue that abortion should be available to all women have termed themselves 'pro-choice' campaigners,

---

[3] As I mentioned in Chapter 2, this is part of a larger movement for linguistic change in relation to job descriptions, so that there has been a general move by institutions, employees and unions to rename jobs which have developed negative evaluations and connotations to make the terms less trivialising or negative, so that in the UK 'cleansing operative' is used instead of 'dustman'. This change of terms relating to professions is more prevalent in the US and is often mocked in the UK and seen to be part of American influence. Many of these proposed changes have met with the same resistance that the feminist suggestions for change have, for precisely the same reason – it is not possible to change the way that people evaluate a profession simply by changing the term used to refer to it. However, it must also be noted that changing the name of something does have an impact, no matter how much these changes are ridiculed.

'choice' being a positively inflected term. This enables them to focus on the restrictions on the choices of the woman in relation to reproduction, rather than on the rights of the foetus.[4] These terms, implicitly and explicitly, provide both a feminist critique of the way that these experiences have been described in the past, and a more progressive feminist way of analysing the experience.

However, whilst some feminist neologisms are adopted by the linguistic community as a whole or by groups of women, other neologisms are less successful, partly because the words chosen themselves seem very marked. For example, the word 'seminal' is used to refer to something which is of intellectual significance. Feminist linguists, aware that it originated from the word 'semen', assumed that it inferred that the male contribution to reproduction was greater than the female, and that knowledge was indexed as masculine. Because of the problems of such assumptions, several feminists (some of them ironically and some not) developed the terms 'ovular', 'germinal' or 'generative' as alternatives (Eckert and McConnell-Ginet, 2003: 217). These words seem to clearly indicate a political position, that is, women-centred or feminist, and at the same time they assert a critique of the word 'seminal'. And for this reason, they may be resisted by certain sections of the community who do not share those values. Eckert and McConnell-Ginet (2003: 217) argue:

some feminists want to use 'seminal' to label the work of women who have made groundbreaking contributions in some field in order to highlight those achievements for the wider community, where alternatives to the familiar laudatory *seminal* might weaken or obscure the message.

As I have already noted in Chapters 1 and 2, one of the usages which has been focused on most in English is the 'generic he' pronoun. Several alternatives to the 'generic he' have been suggested: for example, 'they' is now commonly used to refer to those whose gender is not known. Hellinger and Pauwels (2007: 669) have demonstrated that in most studies of North American- and Australasian-spoken English, generic 'they' is used in 60–70 per cent of cases, whilst in British English this is not as yet the case. Eckert and McConnell-Ginet (2003: 256) note that when referring to someone scaling a high rooftop it seems appropriate to say, 'What do they think they're doing?' even when it is clear that there is only one person. They go on to argue that:

referring to babies, no matter what their genital appearance, as *they*, might begin to move us nearer to a stage where there are real live options to presupposing gender attribution in English singular third person reference.

While some feminist neologisms have been taken up within the society as a whole, others have not been used by those outside feminist communities; the

---

[4] Anti-abortionists tend to use the term 'pro-life' to describe themselves, rather than using the negative 'anti' affix.

use of 'they' for indefinite personal pronoun seems to be growing but there are many feminist alternatives to this pronoun (for example, 'per') which have not (Elgin, 1988).

2.4.   Critique by using marked words

Pauwels (2003) has shown that some women have reacted to perceptions of male bias in grammatical-gender languages by becoming 'norm-breakers', openly flouting the fixed conventions of languages in order to draw attention to discrimination. In German, Pauwels (1998) has demonstrated that some feminists, such as Louise Pusch, have used 'Frau' as a generic pronoun rather than the use of 'Mann', which is the masculine term used 'generically'. Pusch argues that it is important to use feminine forms generically, so that men experience how the generic use of the masculine form feels. Feminists have also argued that in German, when referring to males and females, one should use the neutral form 'das', for example 'das student'. Feminists have also begun to use comic reversals, for example developing the term 'Herrlein' (little man) on the analogy of 'Fraulein' (referring to young women), foregrounding the diminutive form 'lein' within 'Fraulein' (Pauwels, 2008: 551). Pusch has suggested drawing on the neuter form for generic reference, for example using 'das Professor' for generic reference, 'die Professor' rather than 'die Professorin' for female professors and 'der Professor' for male professors. Pauwels (2003) also draws attention to the use of 'gender-splitting' in German where feminine forms are included in all generic usages. In this way, gender-pairs are developed such as 'der/die Lehrer/in' – the male/female teacher, instead of 'der Lehrer und die Lehrerin', or new forms are developed such as 'der/die LehrerIn', which is a new composite form containing the masculine and feminine.[5]

In English, some feminist writers use 'she' as a generic pronoun. Occasionally, this may feel awkward as readers are used to 'she' as a sex-specific term, but when it is used in this 'generic' way it forces us to recognise just how sex-specific the 'generic' 'he' is. Mary Daly in her book *Gyn/ecology* (1981) suggested other disruptions which have critique of the masculine embedded in them. Her most successful neologism was the term 'herstory' to be used instead of 'history'. This playful rewriting of the word history demonstrated that women had been largely excluded from mainstream historical accounts. 'Herstory', at least in my experience, has always been used in this playful way, rather than being suggested as an alternative form to 'history'. Therefore, those who criticise the use of 'herstory' because they assume that it is based on a lack of knowledge of 'history's' etymology are missing the humour and politics of

---

[5] In German the use of '-in' as an affix runs the risk of signifying 'the wife of someone employed in this profession', but this usage is dying out.

this neologism. Although this term, along with terms such as 'wimmin' (which was used for a while to replace 'women' with its troubling etymology), were taken seriously by many feminists and non-feminists, they were developed to be used strategically as critique.

2.5.   *Inflecting pejorative words positively*

This strategy involves using pejorative or insult terms which have been used about women, but inflecting them positively or using them assertively as a counter-discourse. This can alter the usage of the word, but it is only possible with words where sexist usage is embedded in particular words or firmly associated with those words. Butler (1997: 15) suggests this as a more productive strategy than simply trying to propose alternative terms. She argues:

Those who seek to fix with certainty the link between certain speech acts and their injurious effects will surely lament the open temporality of the speech act... Such a loosening of the link between act and injury, however, opens up the possibility for a counter-speech, a kind of talking back, that would be foreclosed by the tightening of that link. Thus the gap that separates the speech act from its future effects has its auspicious implications: it begins a theory of linguistic agency that provides an alternative to the relentless search for legal remedy.

For Butler, taking legal action to limit offensive or discriminatory language is not the most productive form of action. Instead, she argues that we need to prise apart words and their associated meanings, and, by intervening in the meaning of words, by producing new meanings or associations for certain words (counter-speech), we can begin to disrupt the very mechanisms whereby discriminatory language makes sense. However, this type of intervention in language is only possible with certain types of discriminatory language and Butler here seems to be dealing with name-calling, as if this were the only type of offensive language. With indirect sexism, where there is a crucial distinction and distancing between the speaker and the utterance, this type of strategy cannot be effective. Similarly, there are only certain speech acts which can be reappropriated and used in an act of critique in this way. 'Nigger' is a case in point, as are 'dyke' and 'queer', where these words have been reinflected positively by the African-American and gay communities. However, this reinflection only works with a very limited number of terms which were originally insults and the use of these terms by opponents still unfortunately carries injurious linguistic effects. Butler (1997: 14) states that:

The revaluation of terms such as 'queer' suggests that speech can be 'returned' to its speaker in a different form, that it can be cited against its originary purposes and perform a reversal of effects. More generally then this suggests that the changeable power of such terms marks a kind of discursive performativity that is not a discrete series of speech acts, but a ritual chain of resignifications whose origin and end remain unfixed and unfixable. In this sense an 'act' is not a momentary happening, but a certain nexus of temporal horizons, the condensation of an iterability that exceeds the moment it occasions.

This 'returning' to the speaker for Butler confers power on the recipient. Thus, rather than seeing discriminatory language as a single 'momentary happening', we can see those who are attacked engaging in a response, refusing the terms which are used to define them and reframing those terms. In so doing, those who are discriminated against make the previous set of assumptions active but they also call them into question. However, these insult terms cannot be wholly reclaimed. Livia and Hall (1997a: 12) argue that:

no movement for the reclamation of pejorative epithets such as dyke, faggot and queer ever succeeds in eradicating their pejorative force entirely; indeed, it is in part due to their emotive charge that we are moved to reclaim them in the first place.

These appropriated terms can only be used effectively within certain contexts where you can be sure that your interlocutors will know and understand the way that the term is being inflected.

2.6.   Answering back/wit

As I mentioned in Chapter 1, there are a number of strategies which involve wit in responding to sexism. William Leap (1997) describes various strategies which have been used to deface homophobic graffiti; this strategy of answering back with humour and wit is something which Leap sees as an important political tool for gay, lesbian and bisexual people to carve out a space for themselves within a potentially homophobic and hostile world. When a message 'Death to faggots' was written on a lavatory wall, Leap documents the response 'That's "Mr Faggot" to you, punk' which was written next to the graffiti. He suggests that this response is highly effective as a response to insults since 'using an appeal to appropriate verbal etiquette to respond to a death threat is an especially delicious moment of queer phrase-making' (Leap, 1997: 318). Leap also points out that in gay and lesbian events many of the terms which have been used to denigrate gay and lesbians are used as a rallying call. For example, he shows that some posters for such events state: 'bring the whole pretended family'. This refers to the restrictive Clause 28 which was enacted by the British government in the 1990s to ensure that gay and lesbian family arrangements were not portrayed as 'real' families.[6]

---

[6] As I mentioned in Chapter 2, I am not suggesting, by including examples of discrimination against gays or lesbians, that homophobia is somehow subsumed within the study of sexism; these forms of discrimination are specific to their context, and must be analysed within that

This notion of joking at the expense of those who are insulting you is an important one and Bing and Heller (2003) have noted that the way that jokes developed within the lesbian community often explicitly responded to the types of jokes made about lesbians by heterosexuals. As I mentioned in Chapter 2, most jokes about lesbians seem to be about sex, and jokes by lesbians often challenge those assumptions by focusing on excessive romanticism and domesticity rather than on sex alone. For example, the joke which Bing and Heller analyse is:

Q: What does a lesbian bring on a 2nd date?
A: U-Haul.[7]

This joke, they argue, critiques the notion that lesbian relationships are about sex alone; the question presumes that the punchline will include some sexual reference, whereas it in fact suggests that lesbians are more likely to rush into long-term living arrangements than being concerned with sex. Jokes which overturn stereotypical views about women and witty responses can be powerful strategies in combating and challenging sexism.

Overall, it is important to realise that linguistic reform does not simply consist of replacing problematic or offensive words with alternative words, but also involves strategies such as mounting a critique through coining new words, using insult terms positively and developing witty responses to sexism.

3.   Effectiveness of reform

Many feminists enthusiastically adopted the cause of language reform during the 1980s and 1990s and lobbied within their workplaces for changes to be made to the way language was used in official documents. Many institutions, in turn, recognised the progressive message that reforming language usage gave to their employees and to the outside world (Pauwels, 1998; 2001; 2003). Hellinger and Bussmann (2001) chart the changes which have been brought about in a large number of European languages because of the campaigns of feminists to change language use – changes which are sometimes simply a matter of vocabulary choice and sometimes questions of grammatical features such as pronouns and word endings. Hellinger and Pauwels (2007) describe the major changes which have been brought about in legal and administrative documentation in Germany and Switzerland. They also comment on the changes which have been introduced by UNESCO since 1987 to eliminate sexist language from all

context. Different strategies may well be needed. But it is important in discussions of sexism that anti-sexist strategies are not simply focused on examples of heterosexual sexism, as if sexism *is* discrimination against heterosexuals alone.

[7] U-Haul is an American company from which you can hire removal vans or trailers to move house.

documentation in all six of UNESCO's working languages (English, French, Spanish, Russian, Arabic and Chinese) (Hellinger and Pauwels, 2007: 666),[8] and note that such linguistic reforms have been implemented in the Council of Europe (1990) and in the European Parliament (2003). These changes to the language have made a vital difference to many women who felt underrepresented in the language. Pauwels (2003) argues that these proposed changes have been surprisingly effective; her survey of the research on the effectiveness of feminist campaigning concludes that there has been a dramatic decline in the use of masculine generic nouns and some decline in the use of generic 'he'; the use of non-sexist alternatives to generic masculine nouns and pronouns has greatly increased. She notes that the use of sex-exclusive terms (such as '-man', as in 'barman') in job advertisements has been largely replaced by the use of the affix '-person'.[9]

Some of these changes which feminists have proposed to linguistic usage have been remarkably effective and are now used by the linguistic community as a whole. Other changes have been ridiculed and are generally not used even in feminist circles any more. Hellinger and Pauwels (2007: 665) argue that certain key factors contribute to the effectiveness of anti-sexist language reform: 'such factors include the question of whether the feminist critique of language is part of the country's political agenda [and] whether there are influential key agents who promote the change'. Thus, without this wider support of feminist principles in the society as a whole, and if the activists demanding change are not respected within the society, the proposed reforms will be ineffective. Pauwels (1998: 140) also argues that:

Language changes imposed upon a community by a government or official agency . . . may not be adopted despite far-reaching implementation strategies, because of the negative attitudes of the community towards the changes.

It might also be the case that the community is antagonistic towards the agency or government and therefore the reform fails because of this antagonism. Or the alternative terms may be used in negatively inflected ways. Hellinger and Bussmann (2001: 19) state: 'reformed usage has sometimes been appropriated by speakers who will use alternatives in ways that were not intended, thereby redefining and depoliticising feminist meanings'. As Holmes (2001) argues, in Australasia, 'Ms' is now used to mean 'feminist', 'divorced' or someone

---

[8] However, Hellinger and Pauwels also comment on the variability of effectiveness of UNESCO's language reforms, mainly because each of these languages represents gender differently, and therefore requires different mechanisms for reform. Generally, UNESCO advises those writing documents to use gender-inclusive generics, which may lead to the invisibility of females.

[9] This seems to be more true of job advertisements in the Australasian context than it is in the UK, where the use of '-person' (as in 'waitperson' or 'craftsperson') still tends to be seen as a marked form.

who is living with someone without being married (see discussion of Schwarz (2003/2006) in Chapter 2). The intention behind the development of the term 'Ms' was to create an equivalence between the way men were referred to and the way that women were referred to so that both men and women were referred to with one title. In other European languages, generally the change has been to abandon one of the titles used to refer to women. For example, in Germany feminists have argued for 'Frau' to be used to refer to all women, just as in Spain they have advocated the use of 'Señora' for all women. However, within the English-speaking community, males now have one available title and women have three, the alternative 'Ms' often being a stigmatised or specialised term whose connotations vary from community to community. Pauwels (2001) shows that in fact only 11 per cent of the women she surveyed in Australia stated that they had chosen to use Ms because of their feminist principles. Most of them used it because their friends used it. She also shows, however, that whilst 'Ms is being adopted [largely] by those who fall outside the traditional categories of "married" and "single/unmarried" ... there is some evidence that Ms use is also increasingly found among those who are married' (2001: 149). It is important to ask whether, when we assess the effectiveness of language campaigns, not only 'is there evidence of the adoption of non-sexist alternatives but also evidence that these alternatives are being used in a manner promoting linguistic equality of the sexes' (Pauwels, 2003: 566). For, as Hellinger and Pauwels demonstrate, the use of non-sexist language may not indicate 'a pro-feminist attitude, as linguistic choices may be informed by opportunism' (2007: 665).

However, it is not simply antagonism towards the government or towards feminism which contributes to linguistic changes not being adopted. Cameron (1995: 119) argues that language campaigns are never solely about language nor are they solely about the status of a minority group. She asks:

Why do so many people so deeply resent campaigns against sexist, racist, ageist and ablest languages? Is it because they are dyed in the wool bigots who want language to 'reflect society' by faithfully expressing widespread social prejudices? I think the evidence points in a different direction ... objections to linguistic reform tend to focus much more on *language* than on the social questions at issue, such as whether women are men's equals ... what many people dislike is the politicising of their words against their will.

She goes on to argue that:

opposition to politically motivated language change is not fuelled only by hostility to feminism or multiculturalism or whatever, but in many cases reflects a second and deeper level of disturbance to people's common-sense notions of language. (Cameron, 1995: 121)

It may well be that people find it possible to object to being 'forced' to change their language usage, whereas it is less possible now to openly object to being asked to consider women as the equals of males. What many people find difficult about this type of reform is that it is no longer possible to use a neutral term and to take up a seemingly neutral position when referring to women. Cameron (1995: 119) states:

> We also have to recognise that unless linguistic change holds some benefit for men and for more conservative women it will not be effective. By calling traditional usage into question, reformers have in effect forced everyone who uses English to declare a position in respect of gender, race or whatever. There is a choice of possible positions: you can say 'Ms A is the chair(person)' and convey approval of feminism or you can say 'Miss A is the chairman' and convey a more conservative attitude. What you cannot do any more is select either alternative and convey by it nothing more than 'a certain woman holds a particular office'. Choice has altered the value of the terms and removed the option of political neutrality.

Cameron (1995) has argued that feminist reforms of language seem, in some ways, very like other, conservative and perhaps reactionary reforming movements which had very problematic views about the nature of language. Furthermore, Cameron notes that the 'gender-free language' policies which institutions adopted seemed to her like 'the symbolic concession you can make to feminism without ruining your dominant status' (Cameron, 1998a: 155). Attempts to change language usage can be seen as simply papering over the sexist beliefs which fuel this type of usage. Holmes (2001: 118) comments that some view this change in language as a type of 'linguistic eugenics' where such forms pay 'lipservice to an ideal that belies the underlying reality of continuing sexism in the wider society'.

Thus, for Holmes and Cameron, although it is necessary to draw attention to the way that certain language items might be considered to entail negative attitudes to women, proposing alternative terms which might be used is not seen as challenging the sexist attitudes of speakers, but merely enables them to mask their sexist attitudes behind more 'politically correct' terminology (see Dunant, 1994 for a fuller discussion).[10]

Although clear-cut evidence does not yet exist that any particular alternative has completely displaced and replaced existing 'traditional' forms or practices, there is nevertheless sufficient evidence that most proposed alternatives are being used outside the group of originators and that their use is spreading through the speech community as a whole (Pauwels, 1998: 194). Crystal (1984) argues that the feminist campaigns on language are one of the most successful instances of prescriptivism[11] (Crystal, cited in Cameron, 1995: 118).

---

[10] See Chapter 5 for a fuller discussion of the notion of 'political correctness'.

[11] Prescriptivism is the view that it is possible for linguists or other groups to set out the language items and usages that language users within a particular community *should*

In cases where reform does not seem to have been effective, it is necessary to ask what other strategies can be used. For example, if 'police officer', the gender-fair alternative to 'policeman' being used generically, is itself construed as male (that is, because the majority of police officers are male, most people still see the term 'police officer' as having a male referent), then we need to ask what is an alternative strategy to foreground the number of women police officers. It is not possible to change this seeming generic to make it appear to refer to women; perhaps the only alternative here is to foreground the gender-specific term 'policewoman' and use it in a gender-pair ('policewoman and policeman') until gender-parity is achieved. This transitional strategic use of a range of different options is something which Eckert and McConnell-Ginet (2003: 261) focus on; they argue that:

there is no correct answer and no guarantee that any particular discourse choice will actually work as intended. This does not mean that processes like gender-neutralisation of job titles are not useful in helping change the gendered division of labour. They sometimes are. It does mean, however, that change does not always proceed smoothly. And it also means that there are no linguistic quick fixes.

However, there are individuals who vehemently and openly do not use gender-fair alternatives, who feel that they are being forced to change their language against their will. Romaine discusses the example of Lass who argues against the use of 's/he' as a gender-fair option. Lass states:

In my variety of English (and my wife's as well!) 'he' is the only pronoun usable for unselfconscious generic reference. Using 's/he' (which of course can't be pronounced: does anyone say 'ess-stroke-he'?) or 'he and she' or 'they' or whatever would count as an act (a deliberate flouting of grammatical convention in this case); but use of generic 'he' is not, since it's simply historically given and I can't not use it (without a conscious decision of a type not at all characteristic of 'normal' change) and still be speaking 'my own language'. Like all normal speakers, I am bound by the historically given. (Lass, 1997, cited in Romaine, 2001: 164)

As Romaine (2001: 164) goes on to note:

such a long comment is ironically testimony to the efficacy of feminist consciousness-raising which makes it increasingly difficult for authors such as Lass to hide behind a false illusion of neutrality and to claim that one has no choice because he is bound by the 'historically given'.

Although language planning is undertaken by governments in relation to which variety of language will be the standard language, and in some countries, such as French- and Arabic-speaking countries, official language institutes develop 'acceptable' words to refer to particular items, the notion of feminists reforming

employ. Prescriptivism has often been criticised since the role of the linguist is to describe the language accurately and not to suggest how to use the language.

the language is more complex, for a number of reasons. Firstly, feminists are not necessarily in positions of power and influence; secondly, the people who are in positions of power and influence in relation to language (dictionary makers, educators, writers) are not necessarily committed to feminist ideals; and thirdly, language is not so easily changed. It is surprising therefore that reform has been so successful within institutions and that feminist alternatives have been adopted.

As I mentioned in Chapter 2, hate speech and sexism should be analysed as different forms of discrimination. However, it is useful to analyse some of the proposed strategies in relation to hate speech, to evaluate whether they would be effective in relation to sexism. For some theorists of hate speech, the very notion of reform is problematic, however strategic and flexible it is, because as Whillock and Slayden (1995) suggest, if we try to eliminate hate speech, we may find that we consequently do not understand the very causes of this type of speech. Banning certain words will simply entail that other words or strategies are used. They suggest instead that we should accept hate speech as part of our culture as a whole: 'admitting hate as part of our culture rather than extraneous to it brings us more clearly in touch with its uses' (Whillock and Slayden, 1995: xiii). They argue that we should not try to reform language as such, but rather we should try to focus on what hate speech illustrates about our society. They claim that 'attempting to silence hate speech proceeds from a denial. If we don't talk about it . . . then it doesn't exist or it might go away' (Whillock and Slayden, 1995: xv). Whilst I agree that simply ignoring the issue of sexism is not productive, it could be argued that feminist strategies of reform are not an instance of trying to silence those views of women but rather of trying to foreground and critique those views of women in order to change them. Changing the language used about you may not change people's views about you as a member of a group, because change of that nature takes place over a much longer stretch of time, and as a consequence of changes within a wide range of other communities of practice and within the society as a whole. However, changing the way that you are addressed and referred to may enable some of the barriers between interactants to be lessened and stereotypical views of people to be challenged.

One of the problems which linguistic reform of sexism has brought about at an individual level is that overt response to sexism, for example naming something as a sexist statement, can lead to interactional crisis. Because anti-sexism implies a higher moral position, it can evoke a negative response. There are a number of terms which can be used to label verbal acts which are considered sexist. In the 1980s the term 'male chauvinist pig' was coined, and, although it sounds dated now, at least it enabled women to respond to sexism with reference to a body of feminist ideas about sexism, and hence accusations of sexism could be seen as not emanating simply from an individual.

The difference between the way that many feminists analyse sexism now and the way it was analysed in the 1970s and 1980s stems from the fact that it is clear that feminists have already made a major impact on the way that language is used. However, feminist ideas are not necessarily viewed positively. There is more institutionalised support available than there was before and many women generally feel that it is possible to respond to sexism either with humour or with recourse to a set of practices which have some formal institutional status.

We also need to recognise that not all women or even all feminists view sexism in the same way. Pauwels (1998: xii) argues that:

those who believe that language is the main force in shaping people's view of reality are greatly affected by the finding that language may be androcentric. They often see a direct, even causal, link between women's subordinate status in society and the androcentrism in language. For them language reform is a key to changing women's subordination in society. Other views among feminists do not assign such a central role to language. Consequently their desire for language change is less urgent. Some believe it important to eliminate this form of sexism, whereas others think it unnecessary to expend energy on a relatively trivial matter of sexual inequality.

A further difficulty with the notion of reform is that most of this work has been undertaken on examples of overt explicit sexism, those forms which seem relatively stable, where sexism is seen to 'reside' within individual words, for example in the 'generic' he pronoun or words like 'air hostess' or 'poetess'. However, this type of reform cannot be used on indirect sexism, which is a direct response to feminist campaigns on language. Furthermore, particularly in relation to indirect sexism, formulating a response is much more fraught since the meaning of indirect sexism, as I show in Chapter 5, is a matter of interpretation. If a sexist statement is framed using irony or humour, it is extremely difficult to challenge it without thereby appearing unable to understand the humour or play.

4.   Responses to anti-sexist campaigns

As I have argued above, whilst many of these campaigns have been very effective, some have been criticised and mocked. Those who oppose these proposed changes have drawn on different tactics when framing their language, either disguising their sexism more effectively, or openly arguing against gender-fair proposals. Van Dijk (1995: 9) argues that one of the responses to accusations of racism and sexism is that now speakers and writers work harder to hide their discriminatory beliefs, but they use words which can still, whilst coded, signify to others their beliefs: 'The discourse of ethnic affairs has become heavily coded in such a way that apparently neutral words are being used to avoid the racist implications of true intentions and meanings.'

Hellinger and Pauwels (2007) describe the way that opponents of language change have framed their responses. Firstly, many argue that they cannot change their language use because this type of reform constitutes an infringement of freedom of speech. Secondly, these opponents of anti-sexism argue that it goes against the traditions of the language. Rather than the language evolving 'naturally', such changes are seen to be interfering in the way that the language has been used over centuries. Thirdly, for opponents, these reforms are seen to be trivial, because they do not materially or economically improve the lives of women directly. Fourthly, opponents argue that reform is too difficult, expensive and impractical (for example, large numbers of documents would have to be revised). Finally, opponents generally argue that such reform is cumbersome (for example, proposed items like 'Ms' are difficult to pronounce) and unaesthetic (Hellinger and Pauwels, 2007: 654, 665). None of these objections is valid. Languages do not evolve naturally but are the constant site of struggle over whose meanings will be adopted (Deutscher, 2005). The reforms may seem trivial because they are 'only' language, but they do make an impact on the way women feel about their role within institutions, for example. It is costly to alter documents, but documents are altered all of the time in relation to changed circumstances. And finally, it is no more difficult to pronounce 'Ms' than it is to pronounce 'Miss' or 'Mrs' and, whilst relatively cumbersome, 'male and female doctors' need only be used initially once, before it is replaced by 'they'. Thus, I would argue that most of these objections can be easily countered and are simply indicative of a reluctance to take on board feminist demands. The first objection that anti-sexist campaigns constitute a curtailment of freedom of speech needs to be considered in more detail.

Some have argued that these attempts to reform language are tantamount to censorship and thus constitute an infringement of freedom of speech. Smith (1995: 230) states, in relation to hate speech, that: 'The government is without power to censor hate speech [and] such speech not only demands constitutional protection, but . . . its . . . protection is both politically beneficial and worth the cost.' I would argue that, although freedom of speech needs to be protected, particularly in cases where individuals wish to criticise the government or institutional policies, or simply wish to express an opinion, this protection of freedom of speech is significantly different to the freedom to discriminate against others through the use of sexist or racist speech. The effects of discriminatory language are such that sexism and hate speech create unwelcoming environments for certain groups and should not be tolerated. In America, the notion that linguistic reform is an infringement of civil liberties is much more prevalent. A US judge, Judge Douglas, argues that: 'A function of free speech . . . is to invite dispute. It may indeed best serve its high purpose when it induces a condition of unrest, creates dissatisfaction with conditions as they are, or even stirs people to action' (Douglas, cited in Smith, 1995: 236).

Thus, these upholders of free speech argue that sexist and racist speech should be allowed to be spoken and be responded to. Here Jensen argues: 'our responsibility is not to silence hateful speech, but to answer it' (Jensen, cited in Kellett, 1995: 143). However, although it is necessary to 'answer' individual acts of hate speech, it is important to move beyond this individual response to a wider, more global response which deals with racism and sexism as a systematic and institutional problem. What is needed is an individualistic response framed within a higher level solution.

In essence, we need to understand the appeal of hate speech and other forms of discriminatory language. Instead of seeing hate speech and sexism as an individual expression of emotion we should, I argue, see offensive language against a minority group as a means for a dominant group to coalesce as a group, by characterising themselves as threatened by a minority group, whom they characterise as attacking their values (D. Whillock, 1995; R. Whillock, 1995) (see also Wetherell and Potter, 1992). We 'forget that people often believe they hate for good moral reasons' (Muir, 1995: 163), but these beliefs are a misconstrual of the reasons for their antagonism towards certain groups of people.

There have been a range of responses to feminist interventions which might be termed 'backlash'. Those who believe that women are inferior or not fit for professions and tasks generally associated with males will continue to use sexist statements overtly. Others will use humour, which has been much in evidence in the media. Another strategy is the ironic use of sexist terms; in theory this should demonstrate a distance between the speaker and the sexist statement, but because of the curious interpretative position of irony, it often has the result of allowing sexist beliefs to be articulated at the same time as seemingly being criticised (see Chapter 5 on indirect sexism).

Thus, linguistic reform consists of a number of different strategies, some of them effective, but some of which have been responded to in negative ways, with opposition and humour. One of those responses to feminist interventions is the notion of 'political correctness', which I deal with in the next chapter.

4   'Political correctness'

In this chapter, I analyse the way that the highly contested terms 'politically correct', 'political correctness' ('PC') and 'political incorrectness' have developed, and I situate the usage of these terms within a broader strategy of responding to feminist, disability rights and race-awareness campaigns around language reform through ridicule and humour.[1] To clarify, in its general usage, 'political correctness' is characterised as an excessive attention to the sensibilities of those who are seen as different from the norm (women, lesbians, gays, disabled people, black people). This attitude is crystallised in a set of media-invented apocryphal terms (such as 'vertically challenged' instead of 'short'; 'follically challenged' instead of 'bald'; 'personhole cover' instead of 'manhole/inspection cover'; 'coffee with milk' rather than 'black coffee') which no anti-sexist or anti-racist campaigners have argued should be adopted. These invented terms are often listed alongside some of the terms which feminist campaigners have argued should be adopted (such as 'Ms' instead of 'Miss or Mrs' and 'chairperson' instead of 'chairman'). This mixing of 'real' and invented examples of proposed reforms, together with the use of the term 'PC' in contexts where it is uniformly negatively evaluated, has led to a genuine confusion amongst the general population about what 'PC' actually is.

The term 'political correctness' seems to have changed its meaning, as I show later in this chapter, from a knowingly ironic usage in leftist political circles to its current usage as a term of abuse largely by those on the right. Talbot (2007) argues that there are three themes central to 'political correctness': negativity, restriction and exaggeration. By this she means that the term is associated with negative evaluation and will occur in the context of problems and difficult topics; it will be associated with a desire to restrict the use of language of behaviour; and it will be associated with excessiveness. Talbot states that: 'the term ['PC'] is heavily implicated in the discrediting of a particular form of cultural politics by the political right' and she characterises 'PC' as a 'snarl

---

[1] Throughout this chapter I will be using inverted commas around the terms 'politically correct', 'politically incorrect' and 'PC' to indicate that I am using these terms whilst contesting their use.

word', which neatly encapsulates the sense that 'PC' is always used in contexts where it is negatively evaluated (Talbot, 2007: 759). Fairclough, in a similar vein, argues that the dismissive labelling of people's actions as 'PC' should be seen as part of a wider cultural politics; he states: 'this [labelling] in itself is … a form of cultural politics, an intervention to change representations, values and identities as a way of achieving social change' (Fairclough, 2003: 21). Thus, we should see the actions of those who characterise anti-discriminatory reforms as 'PC' as a form of political intervention.

A concern with 'PC' has been blamed for everything from the supposed decline of values in society to an excessive concentration on modern authors in university literature courses. Talbot (2007: 756) notes that 'PC has been held responsible for every imaginable form of restriction, well beyond concerns about racism and sexism.' Suhr and Johnson (2003: 5) remark that, in a BBC Radio 4 discussion programme on yobbishness:

'political correctness' was blamed for all of the ills perceived in British society: for some it was the hegemony of politically correct thinking which had rung in a new era of 'mock' politeness and led to a generation paralysed by a fear of denting the all too fragile egos of anyone who might belong to a so-called minority group. For others 'PC' was to blame for stifling the 'real' debates and conflicts which must be allowed to surface if we are to have any hope of progressing towards a more truly egalitarian society.

Thus, for some on both the right and the left, 'PC' is considered excessive concentration on the effect of language on the sensitivities of minority groups, rather than on the 'real' important issues which need to be addressed.

In the UK, as Johnson et al. (2003) have shown, the term 'PC' seems to have been used, especially in the British press, as a way of attacking a range of different political targets, but most notably the Labour Party of Tony Blair. Thus, it is part of a conservative political strategy, rather than a concern with a type of language use. The term 'political correctness' has been used to characterise the distinction between a veneer of superficial window-dressing (rhetoric) and a more reactionary political agenda (reality). But outside the sphere of newspapers, 'PC' is often used to describe those who are seen to be over-politicising issues which are outside the sphere of conventional politics (Cameron, 1994).

In the US the 'PC' debate has developed in quite a different way. As Talbot notes (2007), the affirmative action programmes in universities resulted in many universities adopting language reforms which were then criticised as 'political correctness'; this concern with language and with proposed reforms of the content of university curricula to reflect the new university population became known as the 'culture wars'. These reforms were much debated and seemed to engender a great deal of resentment. Lakoff (2001, cited in Talbot, 2007: 754) states:

they are forms of language devised by and for, and to represent the worldview and experience of, groups formerly without the power to create language, make interpretations,
or control meaning. Therein lies their terror and hatefulness to those who formerly pos-
sessed these rights unilaterally, who gave PC its current meaning and made it endemic
in our conversation.

Talbot (2007: 754) comments that this pejorative usage of the term 'PC'
'became a way of insinuating criticism, of delegitimising this new-found clas-
sificatory power'.

In France and Germany, the term 'political correctness' has functioned differently again. As Toolan (2003) has demonstrated, in his analyses of the use
of the term in newspapers in France, 'PC' has not been used in an ironic way
but rather has been used from the start pejoratively. In the French context,
'PC' seems to be used with disapproval but not with the antagonism that is
found in the US or UK. In Germany, the term 'PC' is used as a weapon to
brandish against the efforts of those who wish to re-examine National Social-
ism (Johnson and Suhr, 2003). However, despite these differences, we can see
that 'political correctness' is used as a way of attacking political activists by
simplifying and trivialising their concerns. Thus, an accusation of 'political
correctness' can be seen as an effective political intervention which has the
effect of wrong-footing political activists (Suhr and Johnson, 2003).

In order to gauge the way that 'political correctness' and 'politically correct'
are used in the UK, I kept a log of references to 'PC' on a range of programmes
on television and radio over a week in July 2007, and found that the references
were overwhelmingly negative. On BBC Radio 4 there was reference in a
political debate to 'bowing to political correctness'; on BBC Radio 2, there was
reference in a phone-in to 'political correctness gone mad' and many of the
instances of the use of the term 'political correctness' were prefaced by 'just',
indicating contempt and disparagement. Talbot (1998) notes that 'political
correctness' is used almost always in derogatory terms and in contexts where it
is characterised as a problem. The example she gives is of a political report in
1997 where 'the Health Secretary announced on the radio that he was "taking
steps to remove political correctness from the adoption process"' (Talbot, 1998:
229). In this context, a gloss for the phrase 'politically correct' might be: 'any
action which is engaged in solely to please minority groups and which, because
it is a superficial gesture towards those groups, is not actually beneficial to those
involved in the process of adoption'. Talbot gives another example of the use of
the term 'political correctness' where it is used in this negative way: in 2004 on
a Radio 4 programme, William Hague, the former Conservative Party leader,
stated: 'we must never put political correctness before the safety of the British
people'. Talbot notes that this statement was made in the context of Muslim
community leaders complaining about the disproportionate number of young
Muslim men being stopped by the police (Talbot, 2007: 755). To characterise
such political interventions as 'political correctness' and contrast them with

'the safety of the British people' effectively questions the legitimacy of such protests. She also draws attention to the fact that the phrase 'politically correct' occurs in a 2005 election leaflet from the neo-fascist British National Party. The leaflet states: 'The BNP would take the Politically Correct handcuffs off the police and put them on the criminals' (cited in Talbot, 2007: 755).

I have also found several examples of the phrase 'political correctness' used in similar ways. In the British National Corpus, there were few examples of the phrase but, where it was used, it tended to refer implicitly to an external body which was compelling certain actions, for example: 'I suspect after the PM's speech last night, it's no longer politically correct to talk about single parents.' Thus, here, 'politically correct' hints at a group of people whose aim is to ban certain beliefs. In another example, from the *Guardian On-Line*: '*Extras* [a British TV programme] represents blows against the monstrous and perhaps largely imagined regiment of politically correct thinkers, who impinge upon our basic freedoms on a daily basis' (*Guardian Unlimited* 2006). Here the group, although unspecified, is characterised as impinging 'on our basic freedoms', something which inevitably can only be viewed in negative terms. In all of these cases, we can see the term 'PC' being used to criticise anti-racist and anti-discrimination activists and to brand their activities as excessive. However, whilst it is politically inexpedient to criticise anti-racism, it is seen to be relatively acceptable to criticise 'PC'. The phrase 'politically correct' is thus being called upon to perform very complex semantic work.

Descriptions of 'political correctness' within the media tend to homogenise those active in campaigning for language change, whereas they are in fact a diverse group of individuals and pressure groups. This overlap and confusion have led to an undermining, perhaps deliberate, of any attempt to reform language. Fairclough suggests that the left have been 'divided' and 'disoriented' by the critiques of 'PC'. He asks: 'why is it that the critique of "PC" has been so successful? . . . Was it perhaps because the critiques of "PC" have a real target to shoot at, that there is something really problematic about the forms of cultural politics which were the primary target?' (Fairclough, 2003: 24). He answers these questions himself by suggesting that:

some (but only some) of the forms of cultural and discursive intervention labelled as 'PC' smacked of the arrogance, self-righteousness and puritanism of an ultra-left politics, and have caused widespread resentment even among people basically committed to anti-racism, anti-sexism, etc. (Fairclough, 2003: 25)

He argues:

the critiques are certainly reactionary, they certainly depend on a spurious construct called 'PC', they isolate one form of cultural and discoursal intervention from other forms, but like most successful ideologies they contain a partial truth. (Fairclough, 2003: 25)

Thus, perhaps for Fairclough, it is important to analyse the critiques of 'PC' in order to develop a more politically effective and less divisive form of action in relation to discriminatory language and discrimination in general.

The example that Fairclough gives of what he terms 'holier-than-thou' interventions is of a political meeting where there was a call for 'chairperson' to be used instead of 'chairman'. He suggests that the intervention which called for 'chairperson' to be used was 'irrelevant to the point at issue' and 'fetishized a rather minor matter of wording' (Fairclough 2003: 25). He characterises this intervention by feminists as an 'interruption' and as 'hectoring' (2003: 25). Feminist activists might disagree with this view of anti-sexist interventions and might not see it as such a minor issue or as 'damaging' as Fairclough represents it. As I have argued throughout this book, terminology which seems to suggest male-as-norm and female-as-exception does have a cumulative effect on how both women and men see their roles in the society as a whole. Perhaps Fairclough himself is characterising feminist interventions in this particular instance as trivial and as getting in the way of more important political discussions, a strategy consistently used by those attacking anti-discriminatory reforms.

Fairclough draws attention to the way that accusations of 'PC' have been a remarkably effective weapon in challenging the actions of those on the left. For example, he shows that, in the debates about asylum seekers in recent years, the UK political party the Liberal Democrats, amongst others, have complained to the Commission for Racial Equality about the way the leaders of the other political parties had used the term 'bogus' in relation to asylum seekers. As Fairclough (2003) shows, the *Sun* newspaper commented: 'What a sad commentary on this PC-obsessed country that instead of confronting the problem head on, we are talking about the "right" language to use . . . There IS a flood of illegal immigrants . . . the majority ARE bogus' (Fairclough, 2003: 26). The Liberal Democrats were clearly not simply complaining about the use of this particular phrase, but drawing attention to a range of discriminatory practices which could be seen to be crystallised in this consistent use of 'bogus'. The *Sun*'s response was to trivialise this political intervention by claiming that the Liberal Democrats were exclusively focusing on language rather than on serious issues such as immigration. Fairclough argues that we need to analyse examples of debates about 'political correctness' such as this, in order to develop a more effective form of political action. He states that we need 'a balanced view of the importance of language in social change and politics which avoids a linguistic vanguardism as well as dismissing questions about language as trivial, and an incorporation of a politics of language within political strategies and tactics' (Fairclough, 2003: 27).

This strategy of juxtaposing the concern with language with a very serious life-threatening issue is a common ploy, used to discredit anti-discrimination activists who argue that language and other ways of relating to certain groups of people need to be changed. For example, in an article arguing that we should move 'beyond political correctness', Bramson (2006: 1) juxtaposes a proposal to rename something in a more inclusive way with the issue of terrorism, in order to highlight what seems to him to be the ridiculous nature of some of the proposed reforms. He states: 'As recently as 1998 Congress felt compelled to rename its Christmas tree a "holiday tree" to appease non-Christians. In the post 9/11 world of constant political turmoil the luxury of spending time on such discussions seems to have evaporated.' What is interesting in this quotation is not only the juxtaposition of the seemingly trivial and the serious to discredit the proposed reform, but also the way that agency is handled here: note that Congress 'felt compelled' to rename Christmas trees (by using the passive voice with no adjunct giving the agency, it is possible to insinuate agency without naming explicitly who it is that is 'compelling'). This action taken by Congress is seen to be aimed at 'appeasing' non-Christians; the use of 'appease' here is significant, since it is a word which is rarely used outside the context of unsuccessful negotiations with and attempts to placate aggressive enemies. This action of trying to develop more inclusive terms for the Christmas celebrations, so that other religious groups may feel able to participate, is characterised as a 'luxury', that is, something which is not essential and which we need to do without in the face of more pressing issues such as terrorism. Although 'non-Christians' are only characterised in general terms here, rather than being referred to specifically, we can assume that they, in fact, are the same people who are seen to be responsible for the 'political turmoil' which Bramson feels we need to deal with, since he specifically mentions the 'post 9/11 world' (a phrase which is often used in this type of rhetoric as a euphemism for 'Islamic extremism'). Bramson characterises this type of call for reform as 'mostly a matter of semantics', rather than the serious business of political action (Bramson, 2006: 1).

What is interesting in many of the examples where the term 'politically correct' is used is that those who are seen to be trying to bring about linguistic reform are characterised as extremely powerful ('compelling' Congress to rename Christmas trees for example). Talbot (1998: 229) draws attention to this:

Inquisitive Martian scholars of Earth culture would get the impression that 'political correctness' was a powerful political movement based in universities and other cultural institutions. It would appear to have two specific objectives in education: one being to replace the traditional, established core of the culture with marginal elements (teaching Alice Walker instead of Shakespeare for example) and the other being to privilege some groups (women, ethnic minorities and the disabled) over others. In education and beyond, another apparent objective would be to control and police all language used to talk about those same groups.

Given this extremely complex situation, where notions of anti-sexism and 'political correctness' are confused, and where accusations of 'PC' are used to discredit campaigns, notions of simple reform of sexism have, in recent years, been cast aside, so that some feminists seem to be arguing that any intervention is impossible or politically inexpedient (Cameron, 1995). However, what is necessary is to develop a thorough analysis and critique of 'political correctness', in order to be aware of how it functions and what needs it is fulfilling politically and culturally. Furthermore, Fairclough (2003) claims, we also need a better theoretical understanding of the 'PC' controversy, so that new forms of anti-sexist campaign can be developed.

1.   Development of the term 'political correctness'

As a term, 'political correctness' or 'PC' has been problematic ever since it was developed. Cameron (1995) notes that, even when it was first used in the 1960s amongst those on the left, to denote someone whose political leanings were considered too doctrinaire, it was an ironising term, mocking the Maoist focus on 'correct thinking'. Berman suggests that it was 'an ironic phrase among wised-up lefties to denote someone whose line-toeing fervour was too much to bear' (Berman, cited in Suhr and Johnson, 2003: 9). Johnson *et al.* (2003) demonstrate that the number of newspaper articles on the subject of 'political correctness' was at its peak between 1985 and 1994 and they use Cameron's (1995) term 'discursive drift' to describe the process whereby 'the ironic in-group connotations of the term "PC" as used on the left were rapidly transformed into a derogatory catch-all with which to denigrate a plethora of left-liberal concerns' (Johnson *et al.*, 2003: 29–30). It is paradoxical that it is this ironising usage itself which seems to have come to stand for the type of attitudes which critics argue that anti-discriminatory language campaigners actually hold (Cameron, 1994; 1995). Indeed, for many feminists the term 'politically correct' now seems to be simply a term of abuse; for example, Morrish argues that '"political correctness" has no meaning in itself and ultimately no reference, because it is never contrasted with anything' (Morrish, 1997: 340).[2] It is this difficulty of defining what 'PC' actually refers to which leads to methodological difficulties, as Johnson *et al.* (2003: 30) point out when they argue that the confusion about what 'PC' is:

renders problematic any attempt to describe the empirical effects of 'PC' on actual language usage ... it also places the analyst in the methodologically awkward position of having to stipulate a priori both what does and does not 'count' as linguistically 'PC'.

[2] The definition of 'political correctness' is made even more complicated by the fact that 'politically incorrect' is so often used as a positively evaluated phrase rather than as a criticism (see Johnson *et al.*, 2003 for a discussion of the frequencies of the usage of 'politically incorrect' and later on in this chapter where I discuss the uses of 'politically incorrect').

The term 'political correctness' began to be used outside leftist circles and in the process picked up such negative connotations 'that the mere invocation of the phrase can move those so labelled to elaborate disclaimers, or reduce them to silence' (Cameron, 1995: 123).[3] Suhr and Johnson (2003) suggest that 'PC' is used to refer to those who are seen to over-politicise issues which are considered to be outside the realm of conventional politics; thus, one way of denying the claims of feminists and anti-racist campaigners is to accuse them of bringing politics into contexts where it is not appropriate, for example within educational establishments or local government. The arguments about 'political correctness' have therefore not simply been arguments about language. Fairclough (2003: 17) states:

we might see the controversy around 'political correctness' as a political controversy in which both those who are labelled 'PC' and those who label them 'PC' are engaged in a politics which is focused upon representations, values and identities – in short, a 'cultural politics'.

Thus, in the UK, the struggles between Margaret Thatcher, the then Prime Minister, and Ken Livingstone, the leader of the Greater London Council, and other members of what was characterised in the tabloid press as the 'loony left', and the struggles between progressive staff members and the educational establishment in the US, around issues of so-called 'political correctness', can be seen to be an ideological battle over whose political and moral vision should prevail (see Lakoff, 2000). As Fairclough notes, politics has changed from party politics (centred on political parties and social classes) towards 'single issues and to a politics of recognition, identity and difference as much as to a politics of re-distributive social justice' (Fairclough, 2003: 20). One can sense the disappointment in Fairclough's statement as much as in the statements of those on the right who are uncomfortable with this new more cultural model of political activity. But, for him, there is a sense in which these debates about what type of language is appropriate when referring to women is 'small beer in comparison with the systematic diffusion and imposition of neo-liberal discourse through international organisations such as the World Bank and the OECD' (Fairclough, 2003: 20).[4]

The focus on 'political correctness' is, in a sense, a way of doing politics by other means, and of the opponents of anti-discrimination campaigns simplifying and polarising complex political struggles. Suhr and Johnson (2003:15) argue:

---

[3] It should be noted that this is the case in the UK, but the development of 'PC' in France and Germany is different (see Johnson and Suhr, 2003; Toolan, 2003). For a description of the development of 'PC' in the United States see Lakoff (2000).

[4] This wider focus on discursive change and the influence of neo-liberal discourse is of course of vital importance; however, it is possible to engage in both of these campaigns.

a media driven umbrella term such as 'political correctness' can be drawn upon as a means of discursively suppressing (sub)-cultural contradictions and dilemmas... In many cases 'PC' not only simplifies and trivialises – but ultimately collapses – complex social political and economic phenomena in the manner of what Bourdieu (1991) refers to as 'symbolic violence'.

The development of the term 'political correctness' with its negative connotations has undoubtedly made the process of linguistic reform advocated by many feminists much more complicated and problematic.

2.   'Political incorrectness'

The phrase 'politically incorrect' is used in a range of diverse ways. Rather than simply signifying the opposite of 'politically correct', it has accrued to itself a range of connotations and associations, because of its use in particular contexts, which have inflected its meaning. In order to investigate the meanings of the terms 'politically incorrect' and 'political incorrectness', drawing on the methods used by Johnson *et al.* (2003) and Johnson and Suhr (2003), I undertook a small survey of the way the phrases were used in the on-line version of the left-leaning British *Guardian* newspaper, *Guardian Unlimited* (GU), the right-wing *Times* on-line newspaper, *Times On-Line* (TO), and the *British National Corpus* (BNC). By analysing the occurrences and contexts of these phrases, 'politically incorrect' and 'political incorrectness', it is possible to map a range of meanings of these terms.[5]

The first group of meanings (A) can be characterised as broadly positively evaluated: a positive association with risky humour and fun, as a term of praise for those who are doing something daring, and as an accurate, if unpalatable to some, assessment of affairs. The second group of meanings (B) can be characterised as when the phrase 'politically incorrect' is used to refer to a set of opinions which are considered trivial or concerned with the banning of offence. The third group of meanings (C) is when 'political incorrectness' is portrayed as ridiculous. Finally, there is a fourth group of meanings (D) where 'political incorrectness' is used as a synonym for sexism or racism. I will examine each of these groups of meaning in turn.

A.   *Positive evaluation of 'political incorrectness'*

A i. Fun and humour Generally, 'political incorrectness' is used in contexts which are associated with slightly risky fun and humour. Here it is

---

[5] This type of survey of course only indicates to us the range of meanings that 'politically incorrect' has in certain newspapers, at a particular time, and should not necessarily be seen as indicative of the range of meanings that the term might have for the population as a whole.

a positive evaluative term, reflecting the complex relation between 'political incorrectness' and 'political correctness' (if 'political correctness' is viewed as an over-zealous concern with the rights of political minorities, then 'political incorrectness' can be seen as a positive mocking or undermining of such concerns, with a stress on the fun which 'PC' is trying to eliminate).

In the sources which I examined, there were many examples where the phrase 'politically incorrect' was used in association with words signifying fun and humour, for example:

> 'a politically incorrect imp' (BNC)
> 'politically incorrect jokes' (GU 2007)
> 'politically incorrect wise-cracks' (GU 2007)
> 'small fast cheeky and politically incorrect' (GU 2007)
> 'a raucously funny, politically incorrect and satirical look at our celebrity obsessed culture' (GU 2006)
> 'this novel . . . in a delightful and deliciously politically incorrect manner' (GU 2006)
> 'they are so innocent that they say the most hilarious politically incorrect things' (GU 2006)
> 'the brothers are famous for their politically incorrect comedies Dumb and Dumber' (GU 2006)
> 'because of its graphic scenes and politically incorrect humour' (GU 2006)
> 'wincingly politically incorrect comedy' (GU 2006)

Here, the words which are in the lexical environment of 'politically incorrect' entail that the connotations of the phrase are positive. In the examples, 'small fast cheeky and politically incorrect' and 'the most hilarious politically incorrect things', the fact that the words 'small fast cheeky' and 'hilarious' all have positive connotations entails that they have an impact on the range of meanings that 'politically incorrect' can have. This ensures that, here at least, 'politically incorrect' is positively inflected.

Occasionally, the phrase is used in stark contrast to the phrase 'political correctness' which is negatively evaluated, for example: 'yet the vogue for politically incorrect television is sure to spread . . . tiring of a relentless diet of politically correct cop shows' (TO 2007). Here again, the lexical environment where 'politically correct' is associated with 'tiring' and 'relentless' is enough to ensure that 'politically incorrect' is inflected positively.

A ii. As a positive term for people who are seen as risk-taking and daring 'Politically incorrect' is often used as a term of approbation for individuals in the public eye who are considered to be daring in terms of the opinions they hold and who are respected because of their beliefs, despite the fact that these views may be seen by some to be contentious.

> 'isn't there something refreshing about a cantankerous old boy [the astronomer Sir Patrick Moore] who is shamelessly right wing and politically incorrect' (TO 2007)
>
> 'a man who managed to grow very rich, that most politically incorrect of things, by founding his own stockbroking firm' (GU 2007)
>
> 'he enjoys the good things in life: good food, good wine, holidays, politically incorrect cars' (TO 2007)
>
> 'It's just possible that this new Jeep Grand Cherokee SRT-8 is the most politically incorrect car you can buy. It is much more than just another overweight SUV. Its carbon dioxide emissions are so high' (TO 2006)
>
> 'we annul a vital part of our sons if we say that such competitive masculinity is only ever anti-social and politically incorrect' (TO 2006)
>
> 'humour of that Indulgences column would be considered too ripe and politically incorrect for a serious newspaper' (GU 2006)
>
> 'Murray feels no inhibition about tackling such a politically incorrect subject as high Jewish IQs' (TO 2007)
>
> 'Murray puts his trademark politically incorrect slant on Christmas' (GU 2006)

In the first example above, referring to the astronomer Patrick Moore, 'political incorrectness' occurs within the lexical environment of terms such as 'refreshing', 'shamelessly', 'old boy'. Particularly because of the positive connotations of 'refreshing', all of these terms together with 'political incorrectness' take on a positive connotation.

In some of the other examples, 'politically incorrect' is used as a term of praise. For example:

> 'a desire to pay tribute to Benny Hill, the politically incorrect comedian' (BNC)
>
> 'if a poll were taken tomorrow . . . to determine who was the most politically incorrect artist in town, Steve Giankos's name would surely zoom to the top of the list' (BNC)
>
> [Jeremy Clarkson, a British TV presenter] 'outspoken, politically incorrect' (GU 2007)
>
> [Bernard Manning, a racist, sexist British comedian] 'king of the politically incorrect one-liner' (GU 2007)
>
> [Boris Johnson, a Tory MP] 'has practically cornered the market in the politically incorrect soundbite' (GU 2007)

> 'She is jolly, bright and, with the exception of the occasional politically
> incorrect remark about black people making good runners because
> of lions, an all round good egg' (TO 2007)

This last example is an especially complex use of the term, because here
it allows the writer to indicate that they disapprove of the person's racism
(here simply described as 'politically incorrect' rather than racist), whilst
characterising the person in positive terms as 'an all round good egg', thus
implicitly suggesting that the racism is only an occasional and not very important lapse in her character. In practically all of these examples, 'politically
incorrect' occurs alongside very positively evaluated lexical items: in the
example of Boris Johnson, 'cornered the market' generally has positive connotations; and Bernard Manning is described as 'king of the ... one-liner'.
These positive terms in the lexical environment of 'political incorrectness' give
the term its positive connotations. There is, however, a hint in all of these
examples that 'political incorrectness' signifies a daring rudeness, which the
author would like to be associated with. Implicit in all of these usages is the
sense of a group of killjoys who would like to criticise these people, and
this meaning of 'politically incorrect' can only function against that implicit
background.

   *A iii. 'Political incorrectness' as an accurate, if unpalatable, assess-
ment* There are a number of usages of the phrase 'politically incorrect' which
seem to characterise its meaning as being an accurate, if unpalatable to some,
assessment of reality. For example:

> 'featuring wry observations about farming practices and some politi-
>   cally incorrect views on environmental issues' (GU 2006)
> 'a painfully truthful and politically incorrect picture of the country'
>   (TO 2007)
> 'The concept that children should somehow be cocooned is crackers.
>   Let me be even more blunt and politically incorrect. Stress is often
>   very good for you' (TO 2007)

In all of these examples, the phrase 'politically incorrect' could be substituted
by the phrase 'blunt but truthful', a truth that most people cannot face up to.

*B.   'Political incorrectness' as a term of disparagement for those who
would seek to ban something*

   B i. Accusing someone of a trivial concern 'Politically incorrect' is
also used to refer to something which is ridiculous, for example a ruling by the

government or local council which is seen to be concerning itself with trivial issues (not necessarily to do with language):

> 'another ruled that a grassy lawn was politically incorrect on the grounds that not all children have gardens' (BNC)

Very often, with this meaning of the phrase, it occurs alongside the phrase 'called' or 'accused' of being 'politically incorrect', as with this example:

> 'you could express an opinion without being called a racist, politically incorrect or being sued' (GU 2007)

In the examples below, 'politically incorrect' is something which others have attributed to what are represented as perfectly reasonable actions:

> 'at different times it has been politically incorrect to assume that homosexuality is environmental' (TO 2007)
> 'the first thing I discover is that the term "elf" is politically incorrect. "We call them helpers," says the grotto manager' (TO 2006)
> 'the word "empire" has become so politically incorrect these days' (GU 2006)
> 'human resources, or what used to be given the now politically incorrect label "personnel department"' (GU 2007)
> 'boxing has been deemed politically incorrect in recent years' (GU 2006)

In all of these phrases there is an implicit reference to groups of people who would disapprove of the actions/beliefs referred to, although the readers are invited to agree that the actions or beliefs are innocuous. This can be seen in the following example:

> 'So what makes it politically incorrect to teach children parenting?' (GU 2006)

It is assumed that the reader will agree with the author that whoever thinks that children should not be taught parenting is wrong, and the grounds for not wanting to teach them parenting are thus shown to be spurious.

B ii. External compulsion In many examples of the use of 'politically incorrect', there is a sense of an ill-defined group whose aim is to compel the majority of the population to believe certain things or to act in certain ways. For example:

> 'now clearly sentiments like that are rooted in the British Empire, which it has become rather politically incorrect to admire today' (TO 2007)

> 'it really is young men between 15 and 30 who are responsible for the vast majority of crimes, although it is politically incorrect to say this too loudly' (TO 2007)

In the first example, by using 'it has become', it is possible to leave vague who it is that is making it difficult for the empire to be admired. In the second example, such is the power of this external force that it is not possible to voice such sentiments aloud.

C. Ridiculing/irony

The phrase 'politically incorrect' also occurs in contexts where it is ridiculed, that is, where the lexical items with which it is associated are negative or are being mocked. For example:

> 'complaining that a recent photograph showed him with an unrecyclable styrofoam coffee cup, he denounced it as "politically incorrect"' (BNC)
> 'is a suntan just politically incorrect?' (BNC)
> 'politically incorrect carbonated drinks' (GU 2006)

Here, 'politically incorrect' is not associated with holding beliefs about the rights of minority groups, but about whether it is 'correct' to use styrofoam cups, to have suntans or to drink fizzy drinks. Because of this ridiculing, the term itself is devalued.

D. As a synonym for 'sexist' or 'racist'

There are few examples in these sources where 'politically incorrect' is used as a straightforward synonym for 'sexist' or 'racist'. In the following example, it seems as if the person referred to is not being accused of either sexism or racism. 'Not only is he self-parodyingly awkward, hostile, rude, politically incorrect, grumpy, morbid, selfish, tactless, rich and balding' (TO 2007). Here, the phrase occurs amongst many terms which have negative connotations, such as 'grumpy', 'morbid' and 'balding', and it seems to refer to beliefs. Occasionally, however, it is used almost as a euphemism for racism, for example, in a review of *The Mousetrap*, Agatha Christie's play: 'a chilling work . . . having migrated through politically incorrect titles referring to 10 little niggers and 10 little indians' (GU 2006). The word 'nigger' is not 'politically incorrect' but racist and the term 'Indian' for 'Native American' or 'First Peoples' is highly contentious and also considered by some to be racist.

Sometimes, the phrase 'politically incorrect' is used to refer loosely to issues which are contentious, for example: 'The CUF is run by Richard Berman, a lobbyist criticised for his work on politically incorrect causes. He represented the tobacco industry in a failed quest to prevent a ban on smoking in restaurants' (TO 2006). Here, it is unclear to me how this qualifies as 'politically incorrect' behaviour, except that perhaps it could be seen to be a cause which is generally negatively viewed by most of the population.

What is interesting is that the term 'politically incorrect' is used just as much in left-wing as in right-wing newspapers (I had expected that it would be used more by right-wing newspapers as a simple term of abuse). Both the *Guardian*'s and the *Times'* use of the terms seem to be equally complex.

Thus, overall, the phrase 'politically incorrect' has a range of meanings which are generally associated with risky humour and fun, external compulsion, uncomfortable truths, triviality and irony. I was therefore surprised, given the complexity of this usage, associated with both negative and positive connotations, to discover that there is now a series of books called *The Politically Incorrect Guides*. One assumes that the series editors have made the decision that in general 'political incorrectness' has positive connotations which can be seen as a positive selling point for the books. Thus, they have published guides such as the *Politically Incorrect Guide to Global Warming and Environmentalism*, the *Politically Incorrect Guide to Islam*, the *Politically Incorrect Guide to the Bible* and the *Politically Incorrect Guide to Darwin and Intelligent Design*, amongst many others. Here, the term 'politically incorrect' is assumed to have connotations of daring to voice unspeakable truths which the 'nanny' state would prefer to keep hidden, a positive connotation of the term which runs through many of the meanings that the term has accrued in its use in the press.

3.   Anti-sexist campaigns and 'political correctness'

Because of campaigns by various groups to change language usage, it is assumed that anti-sexist activists would like to 'ban' certain terms, and this imagined 'banning' of terms has led to resentment. D. Whillock (1995: 123) argues that:

in an era of political correctness, overt expressions of hatred are diminishing. This does not mean that people have fewer feelings of hatred, but that public forums for its expression are becoming less tolerant.

For Whillock, the antipathy towards women still remains but the forms of expression of that hatred are assumed to have been restricted. In this sense, ridiculing the supposed banning of words is one of the possible responses to these campaigns and this is largely how the very notion of 'political correctness' has developed.[6] This notion of banning and censorship is quite interesting as

---

[6] Another response is indirect sexism which I discuss in the next chapter.

feminists have rarely been in positions of power to implement these proposed changes and there have rarely been government edicts about this issue. However, there has been some institutional support for such changes, and it is this institutionalised support for what are often portrayed as minority group interests and representation which have occasioned such negative reactions within certain sectors of the population. Pauwels (1998: 67) argues that:

The allegations made by feminist language critics about the sexist nature of languages are challenging deeply-rooted views about language as a semiotic system, as a means of human communication and about the relationships between languages, their users and societies. It is not surprising then that a major reaction coming from both professional and lay sectors of speech communities was (and still is) one of denial.

There have been protests from some sections of the population that language reform is not necessary, because they do not recognise that there is discrimination within the language or within the wider society. Mockery of language reforms and minority groups' claims to equality are the origin of 'political correctness'. It is because of this parodying and mocking that many people confuse anti-sexist campaigns with 'political correctness'. In a similar way, anti-sexist campaigns have been criticised for focusing on something which is considered to be relatively trivial. As Lakoff (2000: 18) argues:

There are moralists and pundits who are incensed at the amount of attention paid to what they feel ought to be ephemera, especially since it's impossible to get anyone to care about what ought to matter: campaign spending, corruption, genocide in Yugoslavia, the collapse of the Asian economy, the stand-off in Iraq. Why doesn't anyone want to argue about those?

It is the assumption of such criticisms that concern with language use necessarily precludes an interest in wider, more conventional political issues. Furthermore, such criticism ignores the profound impact discriminatory language and hate speech can have on individuals and minority groups as a whole.

As I mentioned earlier in this chapter, many of the current problems which society is experiencing are laid at the door of 'political correctness', and 'political correctness' is often represented as a much wider movement than simply a language-reform issue. As Cameron (1995: 124) puts it, it is seen to be about:

Giving preferential treatment to members of certain social groups (e.g. women, ethnic minorities) in schools and universities; constructing educational curricula in which the traditional ideas of cultural heritage and artistic excellence are replaced with an emphasis on non-western, non-white and female cultural contributions.

Thus, these campaigns are seen to be demands for rights for those who are marginalised within society. Prescribing the type of language which can be used about those minorities is only one part of a much larger series of campaigns for equality (if you are an equal rights campaigner) or for preferential treatment (if you are a conservative).

This confusion about what anti-sexist campaigns are trying to do and what 'political correctness' is has led to a great deal of confusion. The complex relationship between the discourses of anti-sexism and 'political correctness' has had the effect of bringing into question notions of both a unified community and a unified language. It is also clear that this debate about the use of language has foregrounded questions about whose interpretation of a term holds, and very often in these debates there are some very problematic notions of meaning being used. Cameron (1995: 121) argues that:

Radicals charge that a certain word is, say, 'racist'; their critics indignantly deny this on the grounds that when they use the word they do not intend to be racist, and accuse the radicals of 'reading things in'. At other times, the critics stress that words *do* have meanings independent of speakers' intentions in using them, and that 'political correctness' precisely perverts those time-honoured meanings.

Thus, these arguments about anti-sexist campaigns and 'political correctness' are largely discussions about who has the power to have their interpretation of a term accepted in the society as a whole. But it is also clear that campaigners and critics alike have used very different models of interpretation of linguistic items at various times, sometimes arguing that the meaning of a word is authorised and in the word itself, whereas at other times they have asserted that the meaning of a word is simply a matter of interpretation.

Cameron (1995) draws attention to the fact that there is no agreement on what constitutes 'political correctness'. For feminists, 'political correctness' is a term of abuse and ridicule, a fictional issue which has been invented by the media, whereas for many others throughout society 'political correctness' refers to a set of real terms and beliefs. Paradoxically, although it is often a term which is associated with feminist campaigns, there are no feminists that I know of who use the term. It is only the opponents of such reform who use it to characterise feminist and anti-racist campaigns. This makes it difficult for feminist campaigners to describe their own work seriously, because, in effect, the term 'political correctness' has been used extensively to refer to their work within the society as a whole and necessarily presupposes certain values, views of language and views of society (for example, that one word can be substituted for another, that a word can be banned, that changing words automatically changes social relations, that there is a 'correct' way of referring to someone, and so on). This very simplistic notion of language reform implicit in the notion of 'political correctness' has meant that feminist campaigners have to start any discussion about language reform by unpicking some of these assumptions and explicitly stating, defensively, that they do not hold certain beliefs.

It is clear that there is a complex relation between the terms and discourses surrounding 'politically correct', anti-sexist and sexist, and in order to try and understand the nature of 'political correctness', it is necessary to analyse the relationship between these three discourses. In recent years, the debates about sexism, anti-sexism and 'political correctness' have become increasingly complex, so that very few feminists feel that it is now possible to make simple claims about the nature of sexism or about what effective anti-sexist measures are possible, particularly given the ridicule which 'political correctness' is generally accorded in the media, and the confusion or overlap that many people seem to feel that there is between anti-sexism and 'political correctness'.

This complex situation is largely a result of very effective feminist campaigns over language which have meant that, in the public sphere, sexist language is often viewed by employers and employees to be incompatible with equal opportunities in the workplace. However, as I mentioned earlier, many of the anti-sexist language policies which were introduced in institutions in the 1980s are no longer in force. This is partly because of the fear that these policies might be seen to be trying to be 'politically correct' (i.e. only superficially changing the language but not altering the status quo) and partly because it is assumed that the battle has largely been won and the explicit policies are no longer necessary.[7] These anti-sexist campaigns have effectively created a situation where, as I discussed in the last chapter, institutions, such as publishing houses, trades unions, public corporations, public service providers, universities and so on, have defined what they consider 'acceptable' and 'unacceptable' language (Pauwels, 1998). Because of the development of alternative terms by feminists, such as 'chair' instead of 'chairman', 'flight attendant' rather than 'air hostess', and so on: 'the radicals have effectively politicised all the terms, so that, in any interaction, the choice of certain words will announce your political stance in relation to women' (Cameron, 1994: 31).

Thus, what many people react against in these language reforms is not so much the idea of changing language, since we accept changes in language on a day-to-day basis, it is rather that they object to being openly judged on their political positions through their use of language items which for them have before been seen as neutral.

For many feminists, anti-sexist campaigns have been made problematic pre-cisely because of this ridiculing of any attempts to reform or call for change to sexist-language usage. Thus, any anti-sexist-language campaign now has to define itself in contradistinction to what has been defined as 'politically correct' by the media. It is the interaction between perceptions of, and arguments over, these three discourses: sexism, anti-sexism and 'political correctness', which

---

[7] A notable exception to this trend for the dropping of anti-sexist language policies is the very proactive Greater Manchester Police policy on discriminatory language (2001a).

has led to considerable debate and confusion over sexism, particularly where there is a backlash against feminism, and a questioning within post-modern feminism of the fundamental bases of Second Wave feminism, together with larger scale changes in society in relation to women's employment and representation in the public sphere (Whelehan, 2000; Brooks, 1997).[8]

One of the effects of the conflict between feminist campaigns for reform and the contestation and ridiculing of some of those reforms has been that it is not possible to say clearly what constitutes sexism, anti-sexism or 'political correctness'. Whilst, in the past, sexism seemed to many feminists to be a clearly defined set of practices which reflected a particular set of attitudes towards women, in fact now sexism, anti-sexism and 'PC' are all contested terms and have a range of meanings for different people. This has led many feminists to develop other forms of anti-sexist campaigning, since overt challenging and calls for reform cannot be effective in relation to these indirect practices.

For many feminists, 'PC', as I mentioned above, is simply a media invention used to denigrate feminist anti-sexist campaigns, and, thus, it is a term to be contested or at least used with great care. Feminists do not wish to have their political action denigrated by being associated with a set of practices which are characterised as ridiculous and the object of scorn, and with which they would not agree. Thus, whilst anti-sexist measures might involve discussing with a male colleague if he referred to secretaries as 'girls', if it seemed that this was demeaning and resented by the secretaries, feminists would nowadays seek to distance themselves from any action which called for the banning of the term 'girls' in all contexts. The particular context here and the judgement of the participants in that context determine whether the meaning of a particular phrase is offensive, rather than it being assumed that a phrase can be considered to be sexist in all contexts, for all people. For many feminists, therefore, there is a distinction to be made between anti-sexist practices, which are largely local and context-specific, and 'PC', which is an abstracted set of rules extrapolated from these practices by the media and generalised to absurdity.

However, for others in the wider community, 'PC' is perceived to be the same as anti-sexism, consisting of a real set of rules, developed by 'loony left' councils and radical feminists and imposed *inter alia* on schoolchildren, university students and council workers, which should be challenged in the name of free speech (Matsuda *et al.* 1993). To illustrate this confusion, to take just one example: an older female relative of mine, on meeting me one day, said: 'Oh, you look nice, though I expect I'm not supposed to say that, because

---

[8] The current situation in relation to feminism cannot be regarded as simply one of backlash, since it could be argued that many feminist claims which seemed radical in the 1970s have now been incorporated into conventional 'common sense'. Thus, young British women, whilst not necessarily calling themselves feminist, assume that they will self-evidently be economically independent and autonomous (Whelehan, 2000).

it's not very "PC".' For her, 'PC' had become a term which complicates all expressions of evaluation in relation to women and has become confused with sexism itself.[9]

4.   Model of 'political correctness' and anti-sexism

Because of these problems with reifying sexism, anti-sexism and 'PC' (that is, viewing them as a concrete set of rules or language items which we can all agree on), what is needed is a model of discourse which can reflect the complexity of the inter-relations of these discourses and the fact that there are diametrically opposed interpretations of each term. Sexism, anti-sexism and 'PC' should be seen as functionally different, as – respectively – a set of discursive practices interpreted by some as discriminatory, a set of metadiscursive practices aimed at combating discrimination, and a negative characterisation of that position of critique. However, whilst functionally different, these discourses operate in relation to one another.

The model of discourse used to examine this complex set of discursive practices must also be able to analyse these discourses less as concrete objects or sets of linguistic practices but rather as evaluative positions which are taken in relation to others' behaviour, as was clear in my earlier analysis of the use of the term 'politically incorrect'.[10] Vetterling-Braggin was one of the first to remark upon the fact that labelling someone's statements as sexist involves taking a moral position in relation to them and their beliefs, and may provoke a breakdown of relations with that person (Vetterling-Braggin, 1981). However, it is not quite as simple as this, since often sexism, anti-sexism and 'PC' are themselves hypothesised positions which we attribute to others and which then have an impact on our sense of what it is possible for us to do or say. Thus, in forming our own assessments of what is sexist, we try to map out the parameters of the beliefs of others which would allow our own beliefs to be acceptable (Volosinov, 1973; Toolan, 1996). For example, a postgraduate student told me, with a certain amount of trepidation, that she was getting married and was going to change her name to that of her husband, stating 'Of course I know that you won't approve.' She had made certain assumptions about my beliefs, based on her knowledge of feminist debates about sexism and surname change, and had assumed that I would disapprove. For this person to discuss her future

---

[9] It should be said, however, that this comment was followed by a fairly heated debate between members of the family as to what 'PC' can be used to refer to and what its effects on language use are. What was striking about this incident was our inability to agree on what 'PC' was, even within a fairly homogeneous group.

[10] I argue this more fully in *Gender and Politeness* (2003b), where I suggest that politeness itself is less a concrete phenomenon and more an assessment and evaluation of one's own and others' hypothesised intentions. Sexism and 'political correctness', in a similar way, are hypothesisations and evaluations of others' positions in relation to gender.

plans with me meant her making hypotheses about the set of beliefs that she felt I might hold which would determine my reaction to her new surname, and this dictated the way in which she presented this information to me.

Bourdieu's (1991) work is very instructive in the analysis of these complex discursive formations; rather than seeing sexism, anti-sexism and 'PC' as rules or as practices/sets of words, we should instead view them in the context of specific interactions between individuals and what those individuals perceive to be others' use of the terms, and the way those terms are used in what is perceived to be the society as a whole. We should also see the use of the terms sexism, anti-sexism and 'PC' as vehicles by which people establish or contest their positions within communities of practice. In this sense, one's choice of words can be seen as defining one's position within a group or community of practice: 'relations of communication – linguistic exchanges – are also relations of symbolic power in which the power relations between speakers or their respective groups are actualised' (Bourdieu, 1991: 37). Bourdieu defines the notion of 'habitus' as the set of dispositions which one draws upon and engages with in order to perform one's identity through discourse: 'the dispositions [which] generate practices, perceptions and attitudes which are "regular" without being consciously co-ordinated or governed by any "rule"' (Bourdieu, 1991: 12). This set of attitudes or practices which are seen as constituting a norm by individuals are then discursively negotiated by individuals in terms of their own perception of what is acceptable for their own behaviour: 'The habitus "orients" their actions and inclinations without strictly determining them. It gives them a "feel for the game"' (Bourdieu, 1991: 14). And this practical sense of the 'feel for the game', what other people think and what others consider acceptable, 'should be seen, not as the product of the habitus as such, but as the product of the relation between the habitus on the one hand and the specific social contexts or fields within which individuals act on the other' (Bourdieu, 1991: 14). Drawing on Bourdieu's work, Eelen (2001: 223) argues that we assume that there is a common world, that is, a set of beliefs which exist somewhere in the social world and are accepted by everyone, which we as individuals need to agree with or contest:

On the one hand, collective history creates a 'common' world in which each individual is embedded. On the other hand, each individual also has a unique individual history and experiences the 'common' world from this unique position. The common world is thus never identical for everyone. It is essentially fragmented, distributed over a constellation of unique positions and unique perspectives.

This is precisely the case with 'political correctness', where we often assume that our understanding of the term is the only 'real' definition.

Stone's (2004) work on 'genealogies', drawing on Foucault's use of the term, is instructive in relation to 'political correctness', as through analysing the relation between anti-sexist campaigns and 'political correctness' we can trace a genealogy of accrued meanings and political positions.[11] She argues that: 'the genealogist traces how some contemporary practice has arisen from an indefinitely extended process whereby earlier forms of the practice have become reinterpreted by later ones' (Stone, 2004: 91).

It is that notion of reinterpretation which is crucial here, as 'political correctness' is clearly an attempt to reinflect and appropriate feminist anti-sexist campaigns on language in order to discredit and ridicule them. She goes on to argue that:

genealogists treat any current phenomenon as arising as a reinterpretation of some pre-existing practice, which it harnesses for a new function, and to which it assigns a new direction. (Stone, 2004: 91)

Stone argues that through this history of reinterpretation, elements become yoked together 'within chains of reinterpretation that bring them into complex filiations with one another' (Stone, 2004: 93). For feminists, the challenge now is to respond to this most recent reinterpretation of their interventions in relation to language, which seems to be so diametrically opposed to their political intentions.

Sexism, anti-sexism and 'PC' are regarded by individuals as practices and knowledge which exist in the 'common world', but which each individual in fact creates for themselves within a particular context. These hypothesised discursive positions then exert pressure on their actions. Thus, a feminist might, in trying to work out whether an utterance made to her is sexist, draw on a hypothesised notion of a feminist community of practice with a clear anti-sexist position, where such an utterance might be assessed as sexist. A person's position on sexism and 'PC' is thus not a simple repetition of, or reaction to, a set of conventional beliefs, but rather a complex process of hypothesising that 'common world' of positions on sexism, anti-sexism and 'PC', and one's own stance in relation to those hypothesised positions, which is worked out through discourse, through an assessment of one's position in the particular communities of practice with which one is engaged. This working out of one's position in relation to hypothesised norms is not a neutral process, however, since institutional pressures inform our stances on sexism, 'PC' and anti-sexism differently. As Butler (1997) has shown in her work on racism, discriminatory language is sometimes 'authorised' by institutions who do not condemn or take measures against it. However, it should be remembered that anti-sexist measures are also 'authorised' to an extent, because of the way that they have been adopted as policies by a range of institutions. This 'authorisation' may

[11] Stone's work is based on tracing a genealogy of women, but her feminist appropriation of the notion of genealogy is instructive here.

be undercut by the way that 'PC' is presented and confused with anti-sexism, and indeed I would argue that the ridiculing of 'PC' has led to many anti-sexist policies being withdrawn from many institutions.

To illustrate some of these arguments, I would like now to examine the complex ways in which institutions, in particular, deal with what they see as 'political correctness' imperatives, where 'anti-sexism' is confused with 'political correctness'. Many institutions can see that they need to pay lip service to equal opportunities, even whilst their structures or working environment are profoundly discriminatory. Fairclough argues that 'there is a stage short of inculcation at which people may acquiesce to new discourses without accepting them – they may mouth them rhetorically, for strategic and instrumental purposes, as happens for instance with market discourse in public services such as education' (Fairclough, 2003: 26). I would like to analyse an advertisement aimed at recruiting female managers by the British supermarket chain Somerfield, in order to see the extent to which institutions often gesture towards equal opportunities and use a superficial discourse of 'political correctness' rather than inclusive positive-action policies.

The advertisement appeared in a women's magazine in 2005. It features a picture of a smiling woman store manager and next to this photograph is the statement: 'My team didn't want a female manager, just a good one.' On the face of it, this seems to be suggesting that Somerfield are only appointing people on merit, in line with discourses of equal opportunity, since the advert goes on to state: 'Being a Somerfield Store Manager is about ability. Nothing else'. However, there are a number of different forces at work in the text which complicate its message. In a sense, this text is formed out of a conflict of equal opportunities/feminist discourses with discourses of 'political correctness' which results in a contradictory text which is sexist indirectly rather than directly.

If we take the dominant reading first of all: this advertisement seems to be saying that Somerfield does not discriminate against anyone, and that they are not interested in gender. A resisting reading might focus on this opposition between a good manager and a female one, in which the female manager is in fact positioned as the opposite of a good manager. The advertisement as a whole articulates a belief that some workers do not want a female manager, which is a common complaint in many workplaces ('my team didn't want a female manager'). It also refers indirectly to firms which promote women not on ability but because of the imperatives of 'political correctness' or 'affirmative action' ('Being a Somerfield Store Manager is about ability. Nothing else'). So even though 'political correctness' is not referred to directly, it is referred to indirectly in these sentences. The 'nothing else' refers indirectly to equal opportunities legislation and pressure from feminists which might cause women to be appointed on the grounds of being from a group which has been excluded from positions of power. However, this suggests that such affirmative action or positive discrimination results in people being appointed when they do not merit such positions. Thus, even though the advertisement appears to have an overall positive message about equal employment opportunities at Somerfield, the advertisement contains mixed messages about female managers; it seems to have a veneer of 'politically correct' views grafted onto an indirectly sexist text.

In conclusion, 'political correctness' and 'political incorrectness' have a complex relationship with sexism and with anti-sexist campaigns by feminists and other anti-discriminatory campaigns (Wright, 2007). All of these anti-discriminatory campaigns have been characterised as irritating and as an obstacle to communication; when characterised as concerned with 'political correctness', they have been seen as excessively focused on changing language rather than on bringing about real political or economic change. However, perhaps the degree to which the term 'political correctness' is used is also an indicator of the degree to which feminist campaigns have made an impact. Johnson *et al*. (2003) have charted the decline of the use of the term 'political correctness' in British newspapers and suggest that perhaps the peak of its usage was in the 1990s. Therefore, perhaps it is time to consider what needs to be done in the wake of 'PC'. What is challenging now for feminists is to develop strategies which can deal with indirect sexism and also recast the representations of anti-discriminatory language campaigns in the media, so that they more closely reflect the work on language that is being done by feminists.

5   Indirect sexism

I have argued that overt, direct sexism can be and has been challenged through a variety of reforming measures. However, this challenging of sexism by feminists has led to two responses: one, the development of the notion of 'political correctness' and 'political incorrectness', both of which implicitly criticise feminist interventions, and the other, the development of what I shall be calling indirect sexism (see Lazar's (2005) subtle sexism). In order to describe indirect sexism, it is necessary to consider in more detail the proposition that I have referred to throughout this book so far, that sexism can be best described if we consider it as a *resource* available within the language. I will therefore describe the model of language I am using which enables us to describe sexism as a resource; then I go on to analyse the notion of stereotype more fully, since it is clear that stereotypes of women are not necessarily agreed upon, even within one particular society. I then examine the way that indirect sexism manifests itself.

1.   Language as a system

In analysing sexism, we need to be very aware that the language available to us is not a static system, although it sometimes feels as if it is (especially if we focus on the analysis of written texts). A language is a product of negotiations over meaning in the past as well as in the present, and even some words which we find archaic still remain in use amongst sections of the population. We, as individual users and interpreters of the language, do not necessarily know all words or meanings within the language, and each individual and community of practice of language users will interpret and inflect language items in different ways. Language should then be seen as a pool of available meanings, some of which are ratified and affirmed by their usage within institutions. However, that does not mean to say that those usages which are not ratified disappear; they linger on in texts and in individual usage and are still available as a resource. Thus, the history of sexism is embedded in the language which is available to be used; those words about which feminists have campaigned, such as 'chairman' and 'weathergirl', have not disappeared, but exist as an inflection or pressure on current usage of related or opposed words. Sometimes, the usage of a particular word is stigmatised and individuals then avoid the use of that word, but that stigmatisation then has an effect upon related language items. The past meanings and usages of a word exert themselves on current usages and interpretations.

Deutscher has argued that the mechanics whereby language changes constitute a complex process of decay and renewal; he argues that 'languages cannot remain static' and 'they manage to change so radically through the years ... without causing a total collapse in communication' (2005: 9). Deutscher analyses the general changes which have occurred in language in relation to case, pronunciation of vowels and pronouns; however, this model of language change can also be used when discussing what is judged appropriate within a society as a whole. In order to be able to make statements about what norms are in place at any given moment at the level of a culture, we need to be able to describe language as a dynamic entity. Deutscher argues that we have to acknowledge that within all language communities there is great variation in terms of norms and that changes will occur if certain usages within those particular communities come into prominence. Rather than assuming that cultures and language groups are homogeneous in their usage, we need to be aware of the heterogeneity within cultural groups. Deutscher (2005: 68) argues:

Language is not a monolithic rigid entity, but a flexible fuzzy system, with an enormous amount of synchronic variation ... there is variation between the speech of people from different areas, of different ages, of different sexes, different classes, different professions. The same person may even use different forms depending on the circumstances ... and it is through variation that changes in language proceed, for what really changes with time is the *frequencies* of the competing forms. [Emphasis added]

Rather than assuming that the fixed rules for usage represented in grammars and dictionaries are accurate descriptions of a language, we need to be able to see language as much more dynamic: the rules in grammars and dictionaries are attempts to stabilise something which is not stable. In a sense, what grammars and dictionaries do is to assure individuals that the language *can* be described. Thus, when feminists campaign against certain usages, they are not necessarily trying to ban them or erase them from the language, since this is not possible. Even when words which seem sexist are used less frequently, they are still available for use, for sexist or for humorous effect. This helps us to explain the way that sexism, as a stereotypical way of representing the relations between women and men, with an associated lexicon of words, is for some anachronistic and offensive and for others is an accurate or even humorous representation of women and men.

Individuals inherit this system of conflicting meanings and have to pick and choose amongst these conflicting discursive systems in order to position themselves as particular types of individual, belonging to or affiliated with certain groups. There are some meanings which individuals will wish to align themselves with and others which they will wish to contest and hold in contempt. In this way, sexism is a resource which is available to individuals to affirm or contest in the construction of their own identity. As Ochs states: 'Members of societies are agents of culture rather than merely bearers of a culture that has been handed down to them and encoded in grammatical form' (Ochs, cited in Holmes and Meyerhoff, 2003: 35). Thus, individuals create themselves as subjects through the very active role that they play in choosing their forms of expression.

2.   Stereotypes

When discussing sexism, the notion of stereotype is often evoked, but it is often assumed that we all have access to the same stereotypes. Instead of this general view of stereotype, Cameron (1998b: 452) argues that her approach:

treats the structural fact of gender hierarchy not as something that must *inevitably* show up in surface features of discourse, but as something that participants in any particular conversation may, or may not, treat as relevant to the interpretation of utterances. Furthermore, it insists that where assumptions about gender and power are relevant, they take a form that is context-specific and connected to local forms of social relations: however well founded they may be in structural political terms, global assumptions of male dominance and female subordination are too vague to generate specific inferences in particular contexts, and thus insufficient for the purposes of discourse analysis. [Original emphasis]

However, whilst it is important not to over-generalise about the stereotypes of men and women (since, as Cameron argues: 'they take a form that is context-specific'), we must nevertheless acknowledge structural inequalities and the stereotypes that are hypothesised on the basis of those inequalities. Drawing on Bourdieu's (1991) notion of habitus, we can define a stereotype less as a fixed set of characteristics than as a range of possible scripts or scenarios (sets of features, roles and possible narrative sequences) that we hypothesise. Thus, some extreme perceived or imagined aspect of some members of an out-group's behaviour is hypothesised and then that feature is generalised to the group as a whole. In this sense, the stereotype is based on a feature or set of behaviours which may have occurred within that community, but the stereotype is one noticeable form of behaviour which is afforded prototypical status, backgrounding all of the other more common, and in a sense more defining, forms of behaviour (Lakoff, 1987; see Mills, 1995b for a discussion of scripts and scenarios). This notion of the prototype is quite important, since hypothesisation of stereotypes often informs judgements made about males and females and sets often unconscious notions of what is appropriate. The notion of the prototype also allows us to acknowledge that stereotypes of femininity which circulate within British society now may have originally been descriptions of certain aspects of white middle-class women's behaviour within a certain era, but that even within that class, at that time, there were other forms of behaviour which conflicted with and challenged them.

The stereotype is not a fixed set of behaviours which exist somewhere, but the hypothesised version of the stereotype is something which is played with by those arenas where our 'common' experience is mediated, for example on television, in advertising, newspapers and magazines. The media develop new types of stereotype: as Gill (2007: 111) notes, 'new stereotypes have not necessarily displaced older ones but may co-exist alongside these or perhaps merely influence their style'. In a similar vein, Thornborrow describes the way that the relatively new stereotype of the working mother has been developed by the media, particularly in advertisements: she argues that the image of the stressed woman juggling work and childcare responsibilities is represented in order to demonstrate her need for products and services (Thornborrow, 1994). Gill draws attention to the fact that even stereotypes of feminism are drawn on by advertisers to present images of independent female consumers; she argues that advertisers 'render feminism as a visual style' (Gill, 2007: 95). It is clear that we as a nation do not share experience, but the media work on the assumption that we can consider certain types of information as 'common' to all readers/viewers. Members of audiences however take up a variety of positions in relation to this information, some affiliating with the values of the stereotype and others rejecting them.

The hypothesised forms of stereotypes are, I would argue, equally damaging to both males and females, since they consist of assumptions about us which often clash with our own perceptions of ourselves. These stereotypes are often authorised, in some sense, through being mediated by the media and thus they have an impact on us; they are not simply someone else's personal opinion of us but they appear to be affirmed at an institutional level. The stereotype that women should take the major role in childrearing and household management is one which is challenged by many oppositional discourses such as feminism; nevertheless, it is still a stereotype which can be activated by many men when considering and mapping out their own roles within the household, because it is still kept active by certain groups within the society and implicitly authorised (Sunderland, 2004).[1] These stereotypes of appropriate behaviour for males and

---

[1] Sunderland (2004) shows that the representations of, for example, men as carers for babies, generally resort to sexist stereotypes, even when they appear in seemingly progressive parenting journals which stress the importance of the father in childrearing. The father is often represented as inept and bumbling and as needing to refer to the mother for advice and guidance.

females have been challenged by feminism, so that the notion that women are weaker than men or that they should not compete with men in the workplace are notions which cannot be drawn on without also drawing upon discourses of feminism.[2]

To give an example of stereotypical assumptions, let us consider the analysis of an anecdote by Cameron (1998b). Cameron relates how a friend's father, when he sits down to eat his dinner, always asks his wife: 'Is there any ketchup, Vera?' and this indirect question is interpreted by all as a request by the man for his wife, Vera, to fetch the ketchup for him. Conservative stereotypes of the role of wives in relation to husbands, which here are shared by both the wife and the husband, lead to both of them interpreting this as a request for the ketchup to be brought to the husband, rather than as a request for information about the availability of ketchup. However, their feminist daughter is angered by the way in which the couple collude in this stereotypical behaviour and Cameron draws attention to the way in which this type of requesting behaviour can only be effective if we assume that women's primary role is to serve men. For me, this example would qualify as indirect sexism, as gender is not oriented to explicitly in the interaction; however, the presuppositions underlying this utterance are gendered and based on sexist beliefs.

There is clearly not just one stereotype of femininity. If we consider the stereotypes of the nagging woman and the gossip, these can be seen to coexist with other stereotypes which are not concerned with excessive linguistic pro-duction and excessive demands, for example the stereotype of the over-polite woman who is concerned only with surface appearances, or that of the self-effacing woman silenced by a dominating male partner. As Liladhar (2000) has shown, feminists have begun to change their views of traditional femininity; it is no longer seen solely as a set of negative behaviours which keep women in a subordinate position, but rather there is potential play within the behaviours which have been traditionally seen as denoting powerlessness, particularly when they are used ironically, as in the demeanour of the Soap Queen and the Drag Queen. Whilst in the past traditional femininity seemed to denote a con-cern with one's appearance to the detriment of one's intellect, femininity itself now seems to denote a range of stereotyped behaviours which can be ironised and played with (Bell et al., 1994). Both of these positive and negative aspects of stereotypical femininity are kept in play whenever femininity is referred to.

Skeggs (1997: 10) argues that 'femininity brings with it little social, political and economic worth'. In that feminine behaviour is not generally valued, we might be led to ask why women do in fact orient themselves to such behaviour,

---

[2] As Whelehan (2000) has shown, there are a range of positions, for example, on whether singers such as the Spice Girls and Madonna are positive role models for women or whether Girl Power constitutes a form of acquiescence with patriarchal norms.

as there are women who are more feminine-affiliated than others (Crawford and Chaffin, 1986; Gilbert and Gubar, 1988).[3] However, Skeggs has shown that, in relation to caring, which is an important aspect of femininity, it can be considered to be a means of achieving some sense of value when in a position of relative powerlessness: 'a caring identity is based not only on the fulfilment of the needs of others and selflessness but also on the fulfilment of [the woman's] own desire to feel valuable' (Skeggs, 1997: 62). Thus, even though the adoption of certain feminine positions does not bring great status within the society as a whole (caring jobs are not economically rewarding), they may however define women in ways which are of value, for example they may construct a woman as respectable and therefore aligned to what are seen as middle-class values. Through the alignment with middle-class femininity, many middle-class (and indeed working-class) women can gain some power and assert their difference from other groups of what are for them 'non-feminine' women. Thus, investment in femininity provides some status and a moral position, in relation to both working-class and other middle-class women (for example those who work outside the home). Furthermore, in previous eras, conventional femininity, whilst not exactly valued by the society as a whole, was at least expected as a behavioural norm. Now, however, it seems as if the representation of stereotypically feminine women is rarely presented on radio or TV without mockery or ridicule.

Stereotypes of femininity can be considered to be sexist when they are evaluated negatively. For example, if we assume that women are more considerate of other people's feelings, this might not necessarily be considered to be sexist, since some might argue that considerateness is a valuable type of behaviour. However, if consideration for others is seen as weak or as a waste of time, then it would amount to sexism.

These stereotypes of gender are important in the process whereby we assess others. Cameron (1998b: 445) asserts that:

Information about who someone is and what position she or he speaks from is relevant to the assessment of probable intentions. Since gender is a highly salient social category, it is reasonable to assume that participants in conversation both can and sometimes (perhaps often) do make assumptions in relation to it.

But as Cameron makes clear, whilst we may be making assumptions about gender in our interactions, stereotypes of gender, because they are hypothesised rather than actual, may not be shared. Where conflict in conversation often occurs is when assumptions about gender are not shared by participants, and

---

[3] The notion of feminine-affiliation allows us to describe the way that for some women, femininity is an important part of their identity-construction. By affiliating with the values of femininity, however contested they are, women derive value for themselves. However, there is a sense in which this is a question of degree rather than being an all-or-nothing choice.

this is not a conflict which is restricted to a struggle between women and men, but can be a conflict between women, where some hold a more traditional view of what women should do, whilst others aim to challenge those stereotypes.

Femininity has often been associated with the private sphere and the values associated with that sphere. Therefore, caring, concern for appearances, emotional excess, incompetence in relation to non-domestic tasks, have all in the past been markers of the feminine; however, with the changes which have taken place in relation to women's employment within the public sphere, these aspects of femininity are more difficult to maintain. Greater social mobility, greater choice in relation to marriage, divorce and conception, have made major impacts on women, and, whilst many women would still not openly identify as feminist, nevertheless many of the values of feminism have become common sense. That does not mean that the ideals of femininity have simply disappeared, because they are constantly invoked, sometimes ironically, but often in contradictory ways in relation to this commonsense feminist set of ideas about women's position. Halberstam's (1998) work on 'female masculinity' has been important in mapping out forms of behaviour and style available to women other than conventional feminine forms and Holland (2002) has shown that women can appropriate notions of femininity to describe their own forms of dress and behaviour which seem to directly challenge feminine values. Thus, one of the many important advances made by feminism is to open up, within the notion of what it means to be a woman, a distinction between femininity and femaleness, so that one can be a woman without necessarily considering oneself to be (or others considering one to be) feminine. Furthermore, one can play with notions of femininity, without assuming that these are necessarily negatively evaluated.

Masculinity has often been posited as the direct opposite of femininity. One of the defining features of masculinity is seen to be aggression, which is often considered to be a biological part of being male (caused by testosterone), rather than as a set of characteristics which are acquired in a complex negotiation between the individual and what they hypothesise to be the values of their communities of practice and the wider society. Masculinity is frequently described in terms of battle and warfare. Stereotypically masculine speech is seen to be direct and forceful, arguments between males are described as 'cut and thrust' or as verbal 'sparring' (Coates, 2003; Pilkington, 1998). Tannen's (1991) work also seems to characterise masculine speech as a speech style aimed at establishing a position in the hierarchy and getting the better of your opponent. De Klerk characterises '"high-intensity" masculine language as constituted by dominance, interruption, disputing and being direct' (De Klerk, 1997: 145). Swearing seems to have a stereotypical association with masculinity, and indeed most of the studies of swearing have concentrated on adolescent males. However, for many men, this characterisation of the 'hard man' is not necessarily one which they want to adopt wholesale, but neither do they want to adopt the persona of the 'new man' (Benwell, 2006). Edley and Wetherell have described the way that young men 'exploit the critical or rhetorical opportunities provided by the subject position of the "new man"', not necessarily to claim the position of the 'new man' for themselves, but rather to construct a way of being a man which does not involve wholesale adoption of 'macho' or 'new man' forms of masculinity (Edley and Wetherell, 1997: 208).

Because of changes in men's and women's employment patterns and involve-ment in the public sphere, together with the impact of feminism, there is a sense in which men, at least at a stereotypical level, are often represented as in crisis about their masculinity. Whelehan (2000: 61) argues that:

there is much evidence in recent years that men as a group are feeling more disen-franchised by increased unemployment and the figures for the incidences of violence and suicides among young men are frighteningly high. The popular press speak of the 'feminising' of the workplace as one cause of increasing male unemployment, clearly signalling that the more women make up a significant part of the workforce, the more men have to pay . . . men are undergoing a crisis in the way their identity is defined, and this crisis is alleged to be directly related to female emancipation. Feminism is roundly viewed to be at fault. While it is true that the new lads are assuredly the product of identity crises, it is not just generated by feminism, but also by gay liberation and anti-racist movements, which act as a reminder of what mainstream male culture, such as big budget competitive sport, regularly excludes.

Thus, macho masculinity is considered to be a set of (valued or problematic) behaviours which are under threat from changes in the behaviour considered appropriate for women and homosexual males. This challenge to masculinity has been embraced by some as a positive opportunity for men to explore different aspects of their identity, but others have seen it as intensely threatening. Thus, media stereotypes such as the 'new man' (the feminised and often mocked mythical figure) and the 'new lad' (the man who rejects this feminisation and embraces patriarchal values ironically) are available for men and women to react against and incorporate into their own sense of appropriate behaviours (Benwell, 2006).

Not all males feel comfortable with macho speech styles and attitudes, for example Stearns (cited in de Klerk, 1997: 145) comments:

Malely male gatherings confuse me a bit; they leave me feeling out of place. Gratuitous obscenities strike me as an unilluminating form of speech and I cannot hold my own in skirt-lifting stories. I have always, in sum, viewed manhood with a bit of perplexity.

Particularly given the changes that have taken place in terms of the social position of women, many men's attitudes to women have changed considerably. But these changes have also brought about the rise of 'laddish' behaviour, indirect sexism and backlash (Whelehan, 2000; Benwell, 2006). Nor should we assume that there are no differences within the types of stereotypes hypothesised for particular groups of males, as Jackson has demonstrated in his analysis of the sexualised representations of black males (Jackson, 1994). Furthermore, many men may feel 'forced' to engage in stereotypical masculine speech behaviour because of the fear of otherwise being labelled homosexual by others in their community of practice, as Cameron (1997) has shown.

We should therefore not assume that stereotypes are permanent, unchanging discursive structures, but we should see them rather as resources which can change fairly rapidly, with certain anachronistic aspects being available to be called upon by certain speakers and writers within particular communities of practice. In an article on discursive anachronism (Mills, 1995a), I argue that discursive structures, by their very nature, because they are constantly being challenged and used in new ways by speakers and texts, are in a process of continual change; however, certain of these structures seem as if they are more stable, simply because they have endured over a relatively long period of time. I would argue, however, that it is perhaps the community members' interactions with these seemingly more stable stereotypes and discursive structures in general which change and thus colour speakers' use of them as part of their linguistic resources or assumptions. Sexism is indeed, for many, anachronistic. Nevertheless, it remains within the language, for some speakers, as an active set of resources, and, for others, simply as a set of attitudes which need to be eradicated or challenged.

3.   Institutions and language

As I have argued throughout this book, sexism is not simply a question of individual language use, but is a complex negotiation between an individual's sense of what is appropriate within a particular context or community of practice, and the routines and resources available to them, which are affirmed or challenged by institutions such as the media, the government and educational institutions. The language which is deemed to be appropriate to particular contexts and institutions may be gendered. To give an example, Holmes and Stubbe (2003) have described the way that certain workplaces are themselves gendered as more masculine and feminine, the more 'feminine' workplaces being those where there is less formality and more of a crossover between social life, family life and the world of work. Freed (1996) has also described this feminisation of particular discursive environments, which she terms 'gendered domains', and McElhinny (1998) has analysed the masculinised environment within police forces. These gendered domains have an impact on the speech styles which individuals consider appropriate and what individuals think that they can say. Thus, Holmes and Meyerhoff argue that: 'To focus on gender in activities alone may be to focus on the gender of individuals, but to lose sight of the gender of institutions' (2003: 31). This plays a major role in the way that individuals judge whether their language is appropriate. They go on to state that:

because certain linguistic strategies are indirectly and indexically linked with certain groups, institutions need only be organised to define, demonstrate and enforce the legitimacy and authority of linguistic strategies associated with one gender while denying the power of others to exclude one group without needing to make that exclusion explicit. (Holmes and Meyerhoff, 2003: 32)

Thus the expression of sexism is dependent on the assumption that the context is a masculinised one where the utterance of such beliefs will be acceptable.[4]

4.   Indirect sexism

Because overt sexism is something that many institutions have tried to eradicate or discourage, at least within the work environment, there is less overt sexism in the public face of organisations, for example in mission statements and general documentation intended for consumption by the general public. That is not to say that overt sexism has been eliminated in informal interaction, but at least within public discourse it is stigmatised.[5]

However, it could be argued that within the context of the media (certain newspapers, television and radio programmes), sexism is very apparent, but it is a form of sexism which has been modified because of feminist pressure and because of male responses to feminism. For example, in British men's magazines such as *GQ, loaded* and *Viz,* there is a great deal of sexism, but it is accompanied by humour and irony; it is assumed that men and women are entirely different and the discriminatory statements which are made about women are seen to be simply reflecting that 'natural' difference: women are represented largely as sexual objects.[6] A similar ironising sexism can be seen to underpin many advertisements in the UK, where products are associated with a stereotypical masculinity – for example in TV advertisements for Burger King, the chorus for a song about the 'double meat whopper' is 'I am man.' Similarly,

---

[4] I recognise that it is not necessarily the case that sexist utterances depend on a masculinised environment, but, generally speaking, it would seem to be the case that utterances are made in the belief that they will not be seen as inappropriate or outlandish. Sexist remarks are sometimes made to shock or cause irritation, but they seem to make sense through their relation to an institutionalised context where they are viewed as normal and not aberrant. The aim of sexist remarks is to indicate that the addressee is considered the one who is aberrant.

[5] Nevertheless, in languages other than English, at least in languages which have grammatical gender, sexism is still overt and blatant, since the masculine form is used to refer to both males and females fairly consistently.

[6] Men are also represented in stereotypical ways. Benwell describes the content of men's magazines as drawing on working-class culture and values: they are not represented as concerned with the world of work but focus instead on drinking, partying, watching football and going on holiday, as well as addressing women only as sexual objects (Benwell, 2006: 13).

McCoy's crisps are advertised as 'man crisps'. We have to assume, because of a range of signals which indicate excessiveness, that we are not to take these advertisements seriously. The overstatedness of these advertisements and this type of ironised representation of men and women emanates from what Benwell (2006) has described as a crisis in masculinity, which seems akin to a regression to adolescence and 'schoolboy humour'. What is apparent in men's magazines is how much the representation of masculinity has changed in recent years, since the rise of Second Wave feminism. Benwell describes the development of the 'new lad' ideology which is largely a reaction to the representation of the 'new man' (where males were shown to be developing caring and more compassionate perspectives). The new lad, by contrast, is 'an attempt to reassert the power of masculinity deemed to have been lost by the concessions made to feminism by the "new man"' (Benwell, 2006: 13). For Benwell, the new lad: 'marked a return to traditional values of sexism, exclusive male friendship and homophobia' (Benwell, 2006: 13). However, 'new laddism' is not a simple return to traditional masculinity because of its 'unrelenting gloss of knowingness and irony, a reflexivity about its own condition [which]... arguably renders it immune from criticism' (Benwell, 2006: 13). Thus, there is a playfulness and self-reflexivity which distances new laddism from overt sexist attitudes, but which also protects it from feminist critique. Benwell cautions against seeing new laddism as a simple backlash response to feminism, but argues that it is a complex reaction to concerns about the perceived feminisation of men. However, she also notes that there are articles within men's magazines which are clearly hostile to feminism and even hostile to women in general. Thus, not all representations of women and instances of sexism are playful and ironic.

This ironising of sexism I am terming 'indirect sexism', since it both challenges overt sexism and keeps it in play. Benwell (2006) terms this type of indirect sexism 'new sexism' (see also Lazar's (2005) 'subtle sexism'). I prefer to retain the notion of indirect sexism, since it feels to me that this is very reminiscent of, if not identical to, past forms of sexism, but the only difference to overt sexism is the way it is used. Williamson refers to this type of sexism as 'retro-sexism' because it seems to be drawing on very outdated notions of sexual difference and male and female identity. She states: 'retro-sexism is sexism with an alibi: it appears at once past and present, "innocent" and knowing, a conscious reference to another era, rather than an unconsciously driven part of our own' (Williamson, 2003, cited in Gill, 2007: 111). The fact that humour and irony are used when being sexist does not change the nature of the sexism itself, but rather simply changes the way it can be responded to. Indeed, Benwell remarks upon this continuity when she states that masculinity in men's magazines is not so much evolving as 'cyclical, repetitious and parasitic upon its predecessors' (Benwell, 2006: 26).

On British radio programmes such as the Chris Moyles and Scott Mills shows on Radio 1, where the audience is largely young people, both overt and indirect sexism are common. In a similar way, television programmes like *Top Gear*, a programme ostensibly about cars, which features three 'laddish' male presenters, seems to address a young male audience, because of the amount of overt and indirect sexism of the presenters.[7] However, because the social status of women has changed and because of feminist campaigns about sexism, changes have been brought about in what is considered appropriate language in the public sphere. Women now feel that they have institutional support in terms of questioning the type of language which is used to describe them. Overt sexism is now largely seen as anachronistic and so it has been driven underground; indirect sexism is one which in some ways attempts to deny responsibility for an utterance, mediating the utterance through irony or disguising the force of the sexism of the utterance through humour, innuendo, embedding sexism at the level of presupposition, or prefacing sexist statements with disclaimers or hesitation (Mills, 1998). For example, someone wishing to make a statement which might be interpreted as sexist may begin an utterance with 'I don't want to be sexist or politically incorrect but . . .' in order to deflect criticism for the sexism of the statement and to position themselves as someone who is aware of the difficulties entailed in sexism. This allows the sexist statement to be made whilst permitting the speaker to avoid charges of intentional sexism. This indirect sexism is in a sense more pernicious because it is more difficult to deal with, since it is difficult to 'unpick' and respond to.

However, it must also be admitted that the use of seemingly sexist terms has become even more complex, since women themselves have started using some of these terms in ironic ways. To give an example, from the 1960s onwards, 'girl' has been used to refer not only to female children but also to adult females, for example in pairs such as 'weatherman'–'weathergirl'. This was seen to be discriminatory because 'boy' was not used in the same way. However, now 'girl' is used by women sometimes to refer to adult women, for example in the phrase 'girls' night out'. 'Girlpower', a term used by the Spice Girls, was also used to refer to adult women in a powerful way. Relatedly, the term 'girlie' was originally used to describe soft porn magazines ('girlie mags') or things which were seen to be rather trivial and associated with excessive femininity, for example in the phrase, 'that's a bit girlie' or 'girlie talk'. However, now this term has been adopted by some women to describe things relating to women in an ironic or humorous way, for example in the British comedy TV show *The Girlie Show*.

---

[7] The sexism is made more apparent because nearly all of the guests on the show are male, nearly all of the studio audience is male and the presenters engage in 'blokey' banter with one another. The subject matter is one which is stereotypically associated with masculinity.

It seems as if there is now a certain instability within sexism itself, so that whilst Second Wave feminism regarded sexism as a clearly defined set of practices which reflected a particular set of attitudes towards women, in fact now sexism has a range of meanings for different people. This makes sexism much more difficult to deal with and difficult even to confidently identify. If sexism is now considered simply a matter of opinion (it may be sexist to you, but it's not to me), then it is practically impossible to describe the linguistic constituents of sexism as Second Wave feminism did. Linguistic practices can only be interpreted as sexist in particular contexts but these local meanings depend on a notion of an outdated and highly problematic form of overt sexism against which these indirect sexist meanings are negotiated.

We must differentiate between different types of sexist practice, so that some sorts of linguistic routines can be seen to be more sedimented than others (such as the use of the generic 'he' pronoun to refer to men and women). These seemingly more sedimented forms of overt sexism are changing rapidly and do not form part of many people's repertoire (Pauwels, 1998; 2001). It is only through the use of a Second Wave feminist analysis which can describe global systematic uses of language that these uses of language can be combated and changed. In other contexts, where the sexism is a particularly local, context-specific type, where, for example, the sexism is indirect – ironic or difficult to generalise about – then a Third Wave feminist linguistic approach is more productive. However, there has to be a close relation between these different forms of analysis. Whilst one demands a general campaigning and reform, the other demands a more local and immediate response. Anti-sexist campaigns are necessarily complex and feminists differ on what they see as the most effective way of dealing with those elements which they consider to be discriminatory. It is not always possible to agree on what is sexist, in that sexism is an evaluation of an intent to be sexist rather than an inherent quality of the utterance or text alone. There will therefore be disagreement about what constitutes sexism and in a similar way there will be differences in the type of response that is considered appropriate.

However, it is not even as simple as this, since often sexism is a hypothesised position which we attribute to others and which then acts on our own sense of what it is possible for us to do or say. Thus, in forming our own assessments of what is sexist, we try to map out the parameters of the beliefs of others which would allow our own beliefs to be acceptable (Volosinov, 1973). Rather than seeing sexism solely in terms of abstracted general sets of words where the sexism is considered to reside in the words themselves, we must be able to see that there are local interpretations and strategic responses to what is evaluated by participants as sexist. Thus, rather than seeing Second and Third Wave feminist analysis as simply chronological – that is, one has displaced the other through being a more effective analysis of sexism – we might perhaps see them as each suited to particular types of sexism. Second Wave analysis can analyse those sedimented forms of overt sexism which seem to be embedded within the morphology of the language system itself, whereas Third Wave feminism is better able to analyse the ambivalences and uncertainties about and within indirect sexism, within particular contexts. In the rest of this chapter, I will be considering what constitutes indirect sexism and what are the most effective responses to it.

As an example of the way that sexism pervades institutional representational practices in an indirect way, I would like to analyse the way that British newspapers represent women in positions of power, because it is clear that, although there is nothing overtly sexist in these texts, nevertheless they are indirectly sexist in that they represent women in very different and ultimately trivialising ways, in contrast to males in power.

In a report in the British left-of-centre newspaper the *Guardian* (White, 2006) about Margaret Beckett when she was appointed as Foreign Secretary in the Labour government, there are a number of ways in which the text displays a sexist attitude towards women, but the sexism is indirect (see also Walsh, 2001).[8] In a sense, the text represents Beckett in a very positive way as 'Labour's great survivor' and stresses the importance of her becoming the first woman Foreign Secretary. However, despite that overall positive message about Beckett, there are a number of ways in which the newspaper undermines her as a minister and presents her instead in indirectly sexist ways. Because these strategies for representing women within the public sphere occur in many texts, I feel that they constitute institutional sexism, that is, a type of sexism which, because it is drawn upon repeatedly by various institutions, becomes routinised.[9] If we analyse the collocation in this article (that is, the words which 'keep company' with each other), we will see that words used to represent women in the public sphere are here associated with conflict or problems, for example the words which occur in references to Beckett are 'survivor', 'savaged', 'undermining' and 'menacing'.[10] This sends a message to the reader, particularly when this is not an isolated example of this type of strategy, that women do not belong in the public sphere in the way that men do. In this, as in many other texts about women in the public sphere, Beckett is described in terms which draw attention to the fact that she is exceptional – she is a 'survivor against the odds', she is the first female foreign secretary and she is compared to Margaret Thatcher. Thus, as well as stressing her success,

---

[8] Although I would have liked to reproduce the article from the *Guardian*, the difficulty of obtaining permission to reproduce the text in a book explicitly on the subject of sexism proved too great.

[9] I presented a version of this analysis in a paper on 'Institutionalised contempt' to the 'Feminisms' conference, held in Sheffield Hallam University, July 2006.

[10] See later in this chapter for further discussion of collocation and indirect sexism.

the article gives an implicit message about how difficult it is for women to succeed. There is also a trivialising message here about Beckett's enjoyment of caravan holidays, a fact which is consistently brought into news reports about her, for at the end of the article, we read: 'the Westminster wits were asking yesterday if the Beckett holiday caravan will now be fitted with all the high tech communications equipment the foreign office enjoys'. In this way, through associating Beckett with trivial concerns, the newspaper is able to characterise Beckett as unfitted to fully assume the role of Foreign Secretary. Also consistently drawn into reports is her supposed lack of fashion sense and her alleged physical likeness to Princess Anne. Furthermore, there are other trivialising comments such as, 'If she were a cat she would be the scratching kind,' which can hardly constitute a serious assessment of her capabilities and yet this sentence is followed by, 'But she has been a solidly competent minister since 1997.' The 'but' seems to suggest that there is some contrast between her 'cat-like' qualities and her ability to perform as a minister, and this 'cat' metaphor is picked up later in the article where reference is made to her 'claws'. At the same time as she is portrayed as a competent minister, she is also characterised as overly feminine in a way which is inappropriate to public life: she is described as 'cautious', 'a safe pair of hands', 'too dilatory in search of consensus', 'feminine', 'courteous', 'charming' and 'well turned out'. Although these words in isolation are not problematic, when used repeatedly throughout a text, they begin to signal an excessive femininity. It is also stated that 'she is cautious but never stupid'; the very fact that 'stupidity' is mentioned at all forges an association, even whilst denying it. Alongside this devalued femininity, she is accorded some masculine characteristics, some of them seen as inappropriate for a woman (her speech to the Tribune rally was 'menacing'; she 'undermined' her colleagues) and some of them are presented neutrally or positively (for example the fact that she can bat away tough questions, that she has 'inner steeliness').

A number of direct quotations about Beckett seem to elide the position of the newspaper and the critics: 'one Tory MEP stated "her tenure at DEFRA was frankly disastrous"'.[11] In this way the newspaper can give negative reports on her performance without being held responsible for them. She is not accorded direct speech or indirect speech herself, a common strategy in reporting on women in the newspapers (Caldas-Coulthard, 1995). Furthermore, again without referencing particular critics, the newspaper states that 'some judged' her speech to be menacing; the only response from Beckett which is cited is that she found these comments to be: 'exaggerated, she insists'. This is not a direct

[11] MEP: Member of the European Parliament; DEFRA: a government department concerned with agricultural regulation, which no longer exists.

quotation from Beckett and seems more like free indirect speech.[12] As in much indirect sexism there is a certain amount of humour used at Beckett's expense, but again this is done indirectly by referring to 'Westminster wits' who are asking questions about Beckett's caravan.

This text seems to be characteristic of a type of indirect institutionalised sexism, whereby women within politics are undermined through focusing on their appearance, and ridiculing them for being either/both too feminine or too masculine. There are linguistic elements which we can focus on as part of this analysis, but it seems to me that what we are analysing is the meaning of the accumulated force of a range of different language items. Thus, what we are analysing is sexist attitudes which have insinuated themselves into ways of representing women.

However, the following week a letter from a reader, Noreen Randle, was published by the newspaper. The letter states: 'Margaret Beckett is a politician not a model. We should be celebrating the appointment of the first woman as foreign secretary and an older woman at that. What a relief we can't rerun history: "Charlotte, Emily, you'll never get anything published until you show a bit of leg." Margaret Beckett always looks neat and presentable; what counts is how she does the job' (*Guardian*, May 2006). Such a letter makes it clear that women and men do not necessarily respond uncritically to institutionalised sexism and are quite able to unpick this discursive strategy; furthermore, in publishing this letter, the newspaper acknowledges that its representation of Beckett was problematic.

We can also identify the different discursive frameworks operating for women and men from an examination of two texts which were published in the same issue of the *Independent*, the first about a vice-chancellor of a university, Baroness Blackstone (Hodges, 2004), and the second about a trade union official, Paul Mackney (Midgley, 2004). As in the analysis of the newspaper report on Margaret Beckett, Blackstone is described in terms of her appearance: she is dressed 'as ever, in a beautiful suit' and she is described as an 'elegant grandmother' whose 'exquisite clothes belie a sharp and serious mind' as if good clothes and intellect are in conflict. The reader is left uncertain as to why the fact that Baroness Blackstone is a grandmother is considered relevant to a discussion of her role as vice-chancellor of a university. She is also described as 'formidable', a term which seems to be reserved for women. Whilst the rest of the article focuses on her plans as Vice-Chancellor of Greenwich University, the focus on her clothing potentially undermines her seriousness as a vice-chancellor. In the same issue of the *Independent*, the article on Paul Mackney,

---

[12] Although free indirect speech, as Simpson (2004) argues, is often an eliding of the narrator of the text and a character and can be read as endorsing the position of the character, in this case, the fact that the verb chosen is 'insist' suggests some distance between the position of the narrator/writer and Beckett. 'Insist' suggests excessiveness.

the then-general secretary of trade union NATFHE, discusses his qualities as a leader and as a person, his background and his experience, but there is no discussion whatsoever of his clothes or appearance, or whether he is a grandfather. Whilst the heading under the photograph of Baroness Blackstone reads: 'Well-suited: Baroness Blackstone, the new vice-chancellor of Greenwich is keen to attract American students', which plays on the meanings of 'wearing good clothes' and 'being a good choice for the position', the heading under Mackney's photograph simply refers to his professional qualities: 'Rabble-rousing: Paul Mackney has even been expelled from the International Socialists'. At a discourse level, texts representing men and women have a range of different discursive rules which have been internalised by journalists and writers, which constitute a form of indirect sexism.

My approach to analysis is essentially a pragmatic one, that is, one which attends to an analysis of the meaning of utterances and words in context (Christie, 2000). However, my approach allows for an analysis which is both *localised*, i.e. analysing how gender is addressed/oriented to/constructed within a particular interaction/text, and *generalised*, i.e. analysing the general and fairly regular patterns of production and interpretation of discourses. This type of analysis examines the relation between these two views of gender: gender as constructed within each particular context and gender as a variable (without assuming that this variable is fixed or static). Through focusing on context, we can see that each particular context is informed by and negotiates with notions of what is appropriate/acceptable within that community of practice. Indirect sexism therefore is a complex negotiation between participants' assessments of what is stereotypically appropriate, or what they assume is appropriate within a particular community of practice and their notion of their own gendered identity.

5.   Types of indirect sexism

5.1.   Humour

As I have shown in Chapter 2, humour often exaggerates certain features associated with a group or draws on and plays with stereotypical knowledge for comic effect. For example, humorous utterances will presuppose that men and women are different and exaggerate that supposed difference. This type of joke can help to create a sense of solidarity amongst men. As Lakoff (1990: 270) comments:

Saying serious things in jest both creates camaraderie and allows the speaker to avoid responsibility for anything controversial in the message. It's just a joke, after all – can't you take a joke? In a lite and camaraderie society worse than being racist or mean-spirited is not getting a joke or being unable to take one.

To give an example of sexism being used humorously, a male colleague of mine in a meeting with female colleagues, when seeing that the phone call on his mobile phone was from his wife, said to us all 'It's OK, it's the wife.' The use of the term 'the wife' is so excessively sexist (there is no equivalent term such as 'the husband') and all of the women in the room were feminist academics, so he presumably assumed that he would be seen to be being humorous in his use of this phrase. However, a great deal of discussion of this phrase ensued with many in the group unsure whether ironic use of a sexist phrase is sufficiently critical.

A great deal of research on humour has shown that women are often the butt of jokes by males (Crawford, 1995; Grey, 1994; Banks and Swift, 1987). Crawford (1995) has reported on research which shows that often humour is used in a way to reinforce unequal power relations: for example, male doctors tend to tell jokes and female nurses tend to laugh at them. She argues that street remarks made to women by construction site workers have the effect of reminding 'their targets that men control public spaces and that women's bodies are acceptable objects for public denigration' (Crawford, 1995: 146). We might disagree that public space is entirely under men's control. However, street remarks perhaps are illustrative of the difficulty of analysing sexism at present; for very often these remarks are 'positive' appraisals of women's appearance and could in certain contexts be interpreted as complimentary. Here, however, they also serve the function of demonstrating to women that they are 'fair game' and available to be commented on sexually by strangers, in a way that men are not.

Crawford also notes, in an analysis of Spradley and Mann's study of cocktail waitresses in America, that sexual joking and sexual comments about the women's bodies are often used by the male bartenders as a way of keeping the waitresses under control. One of the waitresses in the study commented:

The only way to get back at them is to get on their level and you can't do that. You can't counter with some comment about the size of his penis or something without making yourself look really cheap. (cited in Crawford, 1995: 133)

Crawford (1995: 146) argues that: 'Cocktail waitresses and investment bankers alike can be effectively silenced when those who denigrate them have institutionalised power over their employment.'

Irony is a common strategy for humorous remarks about women. Benwell (2006: 21) observes that:

the operation of irony in the expression of sexism rarely works to subvert or oppose the object of irony, as we might assume the traditional function of irony to be, and indeed this kind of irony rarely has a clear object at all. Rather it operates as a pre-emptive disclaimer which places the burden upon the receiver to share the joke, regardless of their usual politics.

Because I teach on language and gender courses, I am often sent examples of humour about men and women by colleagues, to use as examples or as research data. Here is one of the examples I received recently, which had been circulated by e-mail within a work environment:

Women's language translated

Yes = No
No = Yes
Maybe = No
I'm sorry = You'll be sorry
We need = I want
It's your decision = The correct decision should be obvious by now
Do what you want = You'll pay for this later
We need to talk = I need to complain
Sure, go ahead = I don't want you to
I'm not upset = Of course I'm upset you moron
You're so manly = You need a shave and you sweat a lot
You're certainly attentive tonight = Is sex all you ever think about?
Be romantic, turn out the lights = I have flabby thighs
This kitchen is so inconvenient = I want a new house
I heard a noise = I noticed you were almost asleep
Do you love me? = I'm going to ask for something expensive
How much do you love me? = I've done something today you're not
    going to like
I'll be ready in a minute = Kick off your shoes and find a good game
    on TV
Is my butt fat? = Tell me I'm beautiful
Are you listening to me? = Too late, you're dead
You have to learn to communicate = Just agree with me

Men's language translated

I'm hungry = I'm hungry
I'm sleepy = I'm sleepy
I'm tired = I'm tired
Do you want to go to a movie? = I'd eventually like to have sex with
    you
Can I call you some time? = I'd eventually like to have sex with you
May I have this dance? = I'd eventually like to have sex with you
Nice dress = Nice cleavage
What's wrong? = I don't see why you're making such a big deal out
    of this

What's wrong? = What meaningless self-inflicted psychological
    trauma are you going through now?
I'm bored = Do you want to have sex?
I love you = Let's have sex now
Yes, I like the way you cut your hair = I liked it better before
Let's talk = I'm trying to impress you by showing you that I am a
    deep person and maybe then you'll have sex with me

This type of e-mail message is often sent out to friends and colleagues at work. The humour resides in the fact that, even though males and females are presented as polar opposites, both of them are represented as ridiculous. Thus, generally this type of message is not considered sexist, because it is humorous about both men and women. As Connor states in an analysis of this type of sexism in advertising: 'the putdowns of women . . . are knowingly ridiculous, based on the assumption that it's silly to be sexist (and therefore funny in a silly way) and that men are usually just as rubbish as women' (Connor, 2002, cited in Gill, 2007: 40). Here, the men are represented as obsessed by sex and the women are represented as manipulative. However, I would argue that this type of humorous e-mail is indirectly sexist, since in fact the perspective from which this text is constructed is predominantly androcentric, that is, from a masculine perspective. Women are represented as saying exactly the opposite of what they mean; they are portrayed as manipulative, ambitious, self-centred, selfish, materialistic, and as resisting sex and undergoing 'meaningless self-inflicted psychological trauma'. Men, on the other hand, are represented in a more positive light as direct, plain-speaking and obsessed with sex. Thus although these e-mail jokes are generally seen to be humorous they still keep in play unchallenged and largely negative stereotypes about women.

Sunderland (2007) asserts that there are a range of positions that feminists can adopt in relation to this type of humour. She argues that the first is to critically reject the jokes, for example by sending a response to the person who sent the e-mails asking not to be sent further jokes. The second reading position is a resistant reading which analyses and contests the presuppositions of the jokes. Thirdly, and perhaps more problematically, Sunderland (2007) suggests that there is a third position, that of critical enjoyment of the joke; the feminist reader 'may co-construct the text's ironic potential . . . and take critical intellectual pleasure in that'. She then goes on to argue that there is a fourth position of feminist reclamation of the joke, where we 'refocalise (ironise?) the jokes for ourselves and take the woman's perspective, actively moving the 'object' of the joke (women) to subject position and mak[ing] the original focalisers, men, the object'. This feminist reclamation of the jokes might work if, in fact, women and men were treated equally in society, and we could assert that these jokes are simply 'silly' as Sunderland does. However, I regard them as a small part of a much wider discursive structure which discriminates against women. Ignoring jokes like this, actively enjoying them or characterising them as 'silly' will not alter those discursive structures and will perhaps reaffirm them and allow them to proliferate.

An example of sexist humour being used in a complex and indirect way is the British television programme *Men Behaving Badly*. In this programme, the two central male characters use sexist humour in order to affiliate with one another; they comment at great length on women's bodies and discuss their own lack of comprehension of women's behaviour, but they always do this in an ironic or exaggerated way. It is assumed that the producers of this programme intend that we are to laugh at the male characters rather than to find the sexist humour amusing, but it is not clearly evaluated apart from by their long-suffering female partners. The male characters are seen as slightly pathetic and not as competent on any level; but the viewer is also encouraged to find them slightly endearing, as if they were boys who had not quite grown up. However, their female partners are forced to deal with their incompetences and their excessive drinking and to modify their behaviour in relation to them. In one scene, for example, when the male characters are looking through a soft porn magazine together, they comment on one of the women that she is 'top totty'. 'Totty' is a childish, schoolboy term for an attractive woman, but this term, especially when used together with 'top' – again a childish humorous form of expression, rarely used by adults – is such an exaggerated form of sexism that within the terms of the programme it cannot be objected to as sexist as we are to assume that it is intended to be humorous and tongue-in-cheek. If we wish to categorise 'top totty' as ironic, we need to consider what it is that is being ironised; it seems very difficult to locate an object of irony – is it the male characters themselves, their adolescent and exaggerated attitudes, or is it the women whom they are looking at in the soft porn magazine? Are we to assume that the makers of this programme are distancing themselves from this type of statement because of, as Benwell puts it, the assumption that 'serious expressions of sexism [are] implausible in a contemporary context' (Benwell, 2006: 21)? Such an avowedly schoolboyish approach to women is difficult to respond to seriously. This is a problem for many feminist viewers, who do not wish to be seen as puritanical or lacking a sense of humour, but who have little possibility of contesting these ways of presenting sexist ideas, even though sexism is still kept in play by these means.

To give another example of indirect sexism, we might consider the television advertisements for Yorkie chocolate bars. The advertisements, following on from the association of Yorkie bars with truck-drivers, claim that Yorkies are 'Not for Girls'. In the TV advertisement a woman disguised as a male builder with a hard hat and false moustache goes into a sweet shop and tries to buy a

Yorkie bar. The shopkeeper tries to test whether she is a man or not by asking her to define the offside rule in football, and to decide whether stockings or tights are better. Finally, he manages to show that she is female because she responds to flattery. If this advert had been shown in the 1980s, the feminist response would have been clear – classifying the product as 'not for girls', suggesting that women are not 'man enough' to eat large chunks of chocolate would have been seen as sexist. But this advert is playing with stereotypes; the woman is not disguised convincingly as a man; the advertisement ridicules men as much as women, suggesting that men are obsessed with football and sex. So if we laugh at this advert because we think it is ironising sexism, we could be seen to be buying into sexism, that is, rejecting femininity and valuing masculinity; if we don't laugh at the advert and take it as sexist, we could be seen as humourless and unable to see the overt playfulness and critique in the advert.[13]

Thus, it is possible to make overtly sexist statements in a very knowing, 'post-modern' way, drawing attention to the ludicrous nature of such attitudes, but at the same time keeping those sexist attitudes in play. For example, on Radio 1, DJ Chris Moyles often uses overtly sexist terms such as 'tart', 'cow' and 'dippy' to his female colleagues, mocking and belittling them if he interprets them as having stereotypically feminine concerns, but he does so by framing these remarks within an ironic, playful mode. When challenged about the use of such terms, the BBC generally responds by suggesting that Moyles is adopting a persona and his use of these terms should be seen to be making fun of such sexist usage. Anyone who complains is thus seen as lacking in sophistication in that they are unable to distinguish between an assumed persona or character and a real person's beliefs. For many feminists, there is thus little possibility of contesting this type of usage without appearing puritanical, humourless and overly literal.

5.2.   Presupposition

Sexism at the level of presupposition is also much more difficult to challenge, as Christie has demonstrated, since it is necessary to make overt the assumptions upon which the sexism is based; the reason this indirectness is in fact often chosen is to mask the sexism and to give the speaker the potential for denying any intended sexism (Christie, 2001). For example, in the phrase 'So, have you women finished gossiping?' there are a number of presuppositions about

---

[13] Interestingly, Yorkie bars now carry the slogan 'Not for Girls' on their wrappers with a symbol of a girl crossed out. Thus, although the TV adverts seem ironic, the bars which are for sale deploy less clear ironising. Many other advertising campaigns have chosen to use this explicitly sexist form of address to viewers, for example advertisements for men's magazines, beefburgers and for diet drinks often draw on sexist ideas in a supposedly parodic way.

women and talk which would need to be unpacked before the phrase could be responded to (for example, that women's talk is trivial, that women engage in gossiping more than men, that two women talking together can be assumed to be gossiping, and so on). The question as it stands demands a 'yes' or 'no' answer and this is obviously problematic for those who would wish to take issue with the presuppositions.

Cameron (2006) has investigated the complaints about advertisements to the Advertising Standards Authority, a UK regulatory body which investigates and adjudicates on claims that an advertisement is offensive. Many advertisements work on verbal play, presupposition and inference, and because of this it is difficult to accuse them of being overtly sexist. Complaints to the ASA about particular advertising campaigns which were considered sexist by viewers were often not upheld, as the ASA:

> allowed the producers to exploit the defeasibility of the disputed propositions in a particular way; by suggesting that the complainants' interpretation was an arcane and to most people implausible one, reflecting the special sensitivities of a politicised minority. In my sample it is fairly common for this tactic to be deployed in cases where the complaint alleges sexism or homophobia, as opposed to bad taste or indecency. (Cameron, 2006: 41)

Thus, for Cameron, advertisers actively exploit the difficulty of complaining against sexism at the level of presuppositions or inference, because it can be argued that an interpretation that an advert is sexist is simply that – an individual interpretation, which would not be agreed on by the majority of viewers.

Eckert and McConnell-Ginet have also analysed the functioning of presuppositions. They comment that very often words such as 'director' presuppose a male referent and therefore when it is followed by the pronoun 'she', there may be a feeling of disjuncture (Eckert and McConnell-Ginet, 2003). McConnell-Ginet (2003) notes that when informing a colleague about a student who had childcare problems and who had therefore missed an examination, the colleague automatically assumed that the student was female and referred to her as 'she'. The student was indeed female, and therefore McConnell-Ginet felt that she could not draw attention to the assumption that the colleague had made, stating, 'I may well fail to point out that there was a presumptive leap made and thus may contribute . . . to sustaining the gendered division of labour that supports that leap' (McConnell-Ginet, 2003: 91). Eckert and McConnell-Ginet (2003: 192) have also noted that we often imply more than we mean and it is the implications of the words that are used which might be assumed to be based on sexist views. For example, they note that, when someone remarks that a woman is tall:

> someone might be conveying that she'll have a hard time finding a suitable boyfriend, drawing on non-linguistic assumptions about relative heights in heterosexual partnerings

and also taking it for granted that her finding a boyfriend is important. Covert or hidden messages like these often do more to create and sustain gender ideologies than the explicit messages that are overtly conveyed.

Hellinger and Bussmann (2001: 10) term this type of indirect sexism 'social gender' and argue that 'personal nouns are specified for social gender if the behaviour of the associated words can neither be explained by grammatical nor by lexical gender'. That is, social gender is the association of certain terms with stereotypical beliefs about gender. They give an illustration of social gender:

Many higher-status occupational terms such as lawyer, surgeon or scientist will fre-quently be pronominalised by the male-specific pronoun 'he' in contexts where referen-tial gender is either not known or irrelevant. On the other hand, low status occupational titles such as secretary, nurse or schoolteacher will often be followed by anaphoric 'she'.
(Hellinger and Bussmann, 2001: 11)

However, they are also aware that 'even for general human nouns such as "pedestrian", "consumer" or "patient", traditional practice prescribes the choice of "he" in neutral contexts' (Hellinger and Bussmann, 2001: 11). Braun (1997) has described this as the MAN principle (Male as Norm Principle); that is, if confronted by a genderless noun, you choose the masculine, unless there are stereotypes which make you choose the feminine. This type of presupposition of stereotypical beliefs about women is much more difficult to challenge than overt sexism.

5.3.   Conflicting messages

There are many texts and situations where mixed messages are given about gender and feminism. Because of feminist pressure and general changes in representational practices, many organisations have found it necessary to adopt certain changes in the way that they present themselves to the public: these are often superficial changes and they often conflict with other messages in texts which the organisation distributes. For example, in an advertisement for Dateline dating agency which I analysed (Mills, 1998), readers are asked to complete a questionnaire and describe themselves and their 'perfect partner' using non-sexist terms – Ms is included as an alternative to Mrs, and Miss is not used. Males and females are treated equally and there is no option of listing 'housewife' as an occupation. This could be seen as a feminist victory, in that it assumes that women are in paid employment rather than confined to the home. However, within the confines of the advertisement, women who are full-time carers can only describe themselves as 'unemployed' or 'not working'. It seems that 'unemployed' is meant to be used by men and women who are not employed at present and 'not working' describes women who are full-time carers. The only time that women can describe their work with children comes under the heading 'Interests' where 'children' and 'homemaking' are listed alongside other hobbies such as 'reading' and 'pets'. Thus, in such advertisements there is a conflict between egalitarian discourses that inform the changes which have been made in terms of the titles used for women and men, and the assumptions which underlie some of the ways in which women are represented. However, at the same time there are some profoundly sexist presuppositions about women and work which underlie this text.

5.4.   Scripts and metaphors

It is interesting also to examine the type of narrative pathways or scripts which are brought into play in new reports about women and men in the public sphere. In an article entitled 'Jilted Clara seeks suitor, Frenchman preferred', in the Business pages of the *Guardian* about Clara Furse, the London Stock Exchange chief executive, Edmond Warner chose to draw on an extended metaphor of failed relationships. The article describes the negotiations between the London Stock Exchange and the Deutsche Börse, when the Stock Exchange was considering taking over the German exchange and their offer was finally refused (Warner, 2005). The cartoon accompanying the article portrays Clara Furse as Juliet leaning out of a balcony awaiting her true love and crying because she has been spurned. The article itself draws on the language of spurned love, referring to the German exchange as a 'suitor' and, rather than seeing Furse and her board as being quite hard-headed in their negotiations, she is characterised as 'playing hard to get' and having 'only one eligible partner left'. Warner even goes on to argue that unless Furse tries to get another company 'to the altar', she will lose her job. The female executive of a very influential institution is thus portrayed as a spurned lover, whereas this type of vocabulary and script is not used to portray male chief executives in takeover negotiations. It is difficult to characterise this article as overtly sexist. However, we need to see that this is a type of institutionalised indirect sexism, where sexual or romantic scenarios or scripts are drawn on when referring to women in positions of institutional power.

5.5.   Collocation

In order to analyse the more complex way in which sexism operates at the moment I will examine the connotations of words associated with women and also the collocations of those words. Collocation, as I have indicated, is concerned with the company that words keep, so that for example a word like 'greenhouse' generally keeps company with the word 'gas'; when you hear the word 'greenhouse' in the context of debates about the environment, it sets up expectations that it will be followed by the word 'gas' and if that does not appear, the word which does appear takes on a marked quality.

Particularly in the media, there are a number of words which do not appear to be sexist in themselves but which collocate or are associated with a range of negative connotations and lexical fields of negative terms. For example, the word 'mum' is not in itself sexist but is generally used in situations where there is conflict over responsibility. For example, Clark has analysed the way the word 'mum' is interpreted in the following headline from the British right-wing *Sun* newspaper: 'Girl, 7, murdered as mum drinks in pub' (Clark, 1998). Particularly around issues of alcohol abuse, the word 'mum' is used to blame women in a way in which the word 'dad' is not. In addition, a news report in the local Sheffield newspaper, the *Star* (2004), about a woman who had been sent to jail on a part-time basis for trying to defraud the Social Services, referred to her as 'Part-time jail fraud mum'. The fact of this woman being a wife and mother are referred to repeatedly throughout the report but are not relevant to the crime she has committed. Thus, although the word 'mum' is not in itself sexist, in the media it is often used in situations where there is conflict over responsibility or where there is a convenient perception on the newspaper's part that there is a conflict between the person's actions and their roles as wife and mother. 'Divorcee', 'single mother', 'lone parent', 'working mother' and 'career woman' are also not sexist in themselves but collocate with words with negative connotations or are used in situations where problematic issues are discussed. 'Lone parent' is nearly always used in newspaper reports in relation to problems of drug abuse, council tax fraud, or lack of discipline in relation to children.

In many women's magazines, the words used to describe female celebrities are often negative. In particular, the words which collocate with discussions of celebrities' diets and weight are nearly all negative. As an example, on the cover of the British women's magazine *Closer*, which is largely concerned with gossip about female celebrities (June 2007), Victoria Beckham was pictured under the headline 'Punishing diets: Posh exhausted by melon and booze fad'. Despite the fact that the majority of the articles in the magazine scrutinise the weight of individual celebrities and judge them as too thin or too fat (three out of the five articles represented on the cover of this issue are concerned with body size and diets), this representation of Beckham's diet consists of words which generally have negative connotations: 'exhausted', 'fad', 'punishing'. 'Fad' here is particularly interesting, since it is magazines such as *Closer* which stress the importance of female celebrities maintaining a certain body shape.

Romaine (2001) examines the 1995 British National Corpus for the colloca-tions of 'spinster', and, whilst she finds that there are some fairly neutral co-occurrences such as '66 year old' and 'American', 'the majority of the words collocating with spinster have negative connotations. They include: gossipy, nervy, over-made up, ineffective, jealous, love/sex-starved, frustrated, whey faced' and so on (2001: 159). She argues that:

This example shows how the connotations of words do not arise from words themselves but from how they are used in context. The meanings of words are constructed and maintained by patterns of collocation. Collocations transmit cultural meanings and stereotypes which have built up over time. (Romaine, 2001: 160)

It might be argued that Romaine has chosen a word which seems to have very negative connotations, partly because it is a word which is generally seen to be outdated, but even with more neutral words there do seem to be collocational patterns. For example, Carroll and Kowitz (1994) found that certain adjectives tended to collocate with male-referent nouns ('rich', 'poor', 'brave', 'short', 'lazy', 'important', 'famous', 'pleased', 'happy') and others with female-referent nouns ('angry', 'beautiful', 'pretty', 'busy'). They also found that 'husband' occured much less frequently than 'wife' and in subject position rather than the object position occupied by 'wife'. This analysis of collocation and subject/object position is crucial in the way that women and men are represented and perceived. Thus, not only do these contexts have an indirect impact on the meaning of these terms, they also have a wider impact on other terms referring to women and men and on the way women and men are represented generally.

5.6.   Androcentric perspective

Many feminists have remarked upon the fact that there exist a great number of words in the English language which etymologically display a male perspective at work; 'vagina', for example, derives etymologically from the word meaning 'sheath' in Latin. 'Penetration' also suggests a male active and female passive perspective. The term 'foreplay' suggests that this stimulation is not a sexual act in its own right but is only engaged in as a prelude to penetrative sex. However, it should be noted that although terms like 'screwing' and 'fucking' historically have referred to a male-oriented perspective on sex, where the male is active and the female passive, that is not necessarily the case with these verbs now; women also tend to say that they have 'fucked' or 'screwed' or 'laid' someone, despite the masculine metaphor of 'screwing', and men also may refer to 'getting laid'.

Eckert and McConnell-Ginet note that reports of rape very often seem to have a male perspective. When they compared the representations in newspapers of rape cases where women teachers had raped male students and where males had raped female students, they found that the victims were described differently. The female victims were referred to as 'young women' and as 'students' whereas the male victims were referred to as 'boy' and the rape was referred to as 'child rape' rather than 'statutory rape'. This difference in the way these crimes are represented 'downplays male responsibility for cross-generational sexual contact' and 'highlights female responsibility' for encouraging the rape and being provocative (Eckert and McConnell-Ginet, 2003: 210–11).

We can find similar androcentric perspectives in recent reports in UK newspapers about the move to appoint women as bishops.[14] Generally in these news reports there is no explicit statement arguing that women cannot be appointed as bishops, or detailing what is at fault with women which would make them unsuited to be bishops, but implicit in their statements is that women are not fit to be bishops. Many articles refer to arguments about the apostolic succession being male, and suggest that some church leaders would rather leave the Church than accept women bishops. However, the campaigns in favour of women being appointed as bishops are often not reported and thus, the newspaper's perspective seems to collude with those church leaders. An example of this can be seen in a news report in the right-leaning British newspaper the *Sunday Times,* entitled 'Churchmen on brink of exodus over women bishops' (Morgan, 2005). The article is accompanied by a picture of Andrew Burnham, Bishop of Ebbsfleet, who, it is reported, would defect to the Roman Catholic Church if women bishops were appointed. His views are extensively quoted directly throughout the article, as are the views of Geoffrey Kirk, national secretary of Forward in Faith, and John Broadhurst, Bishop of Fulham, who all oppose the appointment of women bishops and argue for the setting up of a separate province within the Church of England or the Roman Catholic Church for those who cannot accept women bishops.

In this relatively short article, there is no mention that appointing women as bishops seems to be a logical step from having women priests (see Walsh, 2001). There is no discussion of the advantages of equal opportunities within the church hierarchy. There are no comments from women priests or from anyone who supports women bishops. Burnham is quoted directly, without any modifying evaluation, such as 'claimed'. Burnham, in fact, is portrayed as a victim of injustice, since it is he who is positioned in the recipient role/as the object: 'he would be forced to quit [the Church]'. Here, implicitly, it is the women who are campaigning to be allowed to be bishops who are 'forcing' him to leave the Church. Burnham's argument, as it is presented here, is that 'a woman bishop wouldn't be a bishop because a bishop is someone whose ministry is acceptable through the ages to all other bishops'. This carefully avoids accusations of sexism, as Burnham is not asserting that there is anything wrong with women *per se*, but simply that they cannot be bishops as women

---

[14] Women are able to become priests within the Protestant Church of England, but are not yet able to become bishops.

have not been bishops before. A further element in Burnham's argument is that appointing women bishops would devalue male bishops: 'bishops would no longer be what they say they are', since they would no longer belong to a united Church. Within this particular context, the term 'traditionalist' is used as a positive term, and the 'traditionalists' are represented as acted upon, since they 'face the prospect of serving in the church alongside women bishops or leaving' and they are being 'forced to leave'. The setting up of a separate province for those who could not accept women bishops is represented as a compromise and as a 'free' province. The bishops who would leave the Church are described as a 'haemorrhage, an exodus' as if this is something which they have not decided upon themselves and as if this is simply a result of a process enacted upon them. Whilst it is arguably they who are trying to disrupt the unity of the Church by suggesting that there should be a separate province for (male) bishops who cannot tolerate women bishops, they characterise the plans to appoint women bishops as something which would endanger the unity of the Church (Morgan, 2005: 10).[15] The newspaper report colludes with the views of this minority group of churchmen by representing the conflict entirely from their perspective. This constitutes a form of indirect sexism, since they simply represent the conflict over women bishops as if there were no other views on the subject. In texts such as this, the androcentrism of the text is not foregrounded and thus this type of indirect sexism is quite difficult to identify and contest.

6.   Challenging indirect sexism

Because, as I have shown throughout this book, indirect sexism is not overtly stated, but occurs at the level of presupposition, humour or irony, it can be difficult to challenge. Furthermore, there is a general instability within sexism which means that there are difficulties in interpreting utterances and texts as unequivocally sexist. Because of these factors, there is also an instability within anti-sexism itself. Anti-sexist campaigns have been destabilised in recent years because of the existence of 'political correctness'. As I noted in the previous chapter, many people feel that there is confusion or at least overlap between anti-sexism and 'political correctness'. It is necessary to distinguish anti-sexist practices from 'political correctness'. However, for anti-feminists, 'political correctness' is perceived to be the same as anti-sexism and consists of a real set of rules which should be challenged in the name of free speech (Matsuda et al., 1993). With indirect sexism, instead of assuming that each element of discrimination is in itself pernicious, theorists of race and sex discrimination have developed the notion of a 'chilly climate' to describe the way that a

---

[15] The fact that the newspaper does ultimately accept the fact that women will be made bishops by the Synod is, however, a positive sign.

discriminating environment is constructed through the systematic and continual use of a wide range of markers which signal to 'out' groups that they are not welcome or that they do not belong. Indirect sexism and indirect racism are difficult to challenge on an individual basis, but it is the cumulation of these elements which constitutes the creation of a chilly climate. Indirect sexism can only be countered by making apparent some of the presuppositions which are implicit or by making explicit the sexism underlying statements. In women's magazines, for example, letters from readers are often published which draw attention to the contradictions in the way that female celebrities are represented. One letter to the UK women's magazine *Now!* (a magazine which largely focuses on celebrities) was concerned with the way that a celebrity, Coleen McLoughlin, was represented in a previous issue. The letter states:

Every issue of *Now!* seems to have articles criticising celebrities for being either too fat or too thin. I had to use a magnifying glass to see Coleen McLoughlin's 'holiday tummy' in a picture recently. Come on, *Now!*, You're supposed to be on our side. I have a sneaking suspicion that thin is in and if you're not a size 10, you just don't cut it. (*Now!*, July 2007: 60)

It is only through the use of such metastatements about underlying sexism that indirect sexism can be exposed. The fact that there are so many comments by individual members of the public to newspapers and magazines about such instances of indirect sexism indicates that this type of sexism does not generally go uncontested and is resisted by many women.

6   Conclusions

Throughout this book, I have suggested ways in which we can analyse both overt and indirect sexism, despite the fact that sexism is a very complex, unstable phenomenon. Analysing sexism is made particularly complex because of the need, as Talbot puts it, to learn 'how to side-step the snarl word "PC" while continuing to tackle discrimination' (Talbot, 2007: 760). 'Political correctness' is not the only problem facing us in the analysis of sexism. Cameron (2006) asserts that because of the problem of working out intentionality, all that we can rely on is the hearer's or reader's interpretation in discussions of sexism. By contrast, I would argue that we have to assume an intentionality on the part of the speaker in order to make sense of utterances. However, it is clear that sexism is not simply ingrained in individual language items but manifests itself at the level of discourses and patterns in language use. These discourses may themselves be institutionalised, and this institutional sexism constitutes a resource that can be drawn on by people who wish to authorise their sexist beliefs.

1.   Public sensitivity to issues of sexism

Rather than being the concern solely of feminist linguists, sexism appears to be something which the general public are concerned about. The complexity of public sensitivity to language and sexism and the debates about 'political correctness' can be seen to have positive benefits as well as causing difficulties for feminists. As an example of the degree of sophistication which has been brought to the issue of representing women in language, I would like to consider the case of the reporting of the murder of five women in Ipswich, UK in 2006. In this murder case, the press foregrounded the fact that all were sex workers, by terming the murders 'prostitute murders' and continually focusing on the women's involvement in prostitution and drug-culture, the problems of prostitution, and debating whether prostitution should be legalised (BBC News On-line, December 2006). The public reacted quite vigorously to this focus on the occupation of the women who had been killed, by writing in to newspapers and to on-line newspaper chat forums, to challenge this continual focus on prostitution. Very swiftly, the BBC changed from using the word 'prostitute' to using the term 'sex worker' and opened a chatroom on the issue of whether 'tolerance zones' should be established to increase the safety of sex workers. In the discussion of this question, there was a string of comments about what sex workers should be called and whether in fact their occupation was a salient issue. For example, 'Jonas' posted a message which reads: 'Does anyone find it disturbing that the media refer to the dead or missing women as prostitutes first and women second? There is almost an intimation that they are a lower class of life' (BBC News, December 2006). A subsequent posting by 'Anne' reads: 'Having just listened to the news I could only wonder at how many times it was possible to use the word "prostitute" in one article. It seems that the occupations of the victims is being used to qualify the crime. After all the Yorkshire Ripper "only" killed prostitutes and it was only when he mistakenly killed "innocent" victims that the public started to demand action' (BBC News, December 2006). However, in a response clearly influenced by notions of 'political correctness', 'Tom' wrote: 'But they were prostitutes, or is this another word we're not allowed to use? If only carpenters had been targeted, then we would refer to carpenters. Identifying their occupation helps solve the crime, and will almost certainly save lives in future' (BBC News, December 2006). Responding to this, 'John' retorts that: 'Three young women have gone missing. Can you not just refer to them as "women", people with families and friends who are grieving, without the distasteful banner "PROSTITUTION"?' 'Disgusted of Mitcham' responds: 'I wonder if this story would be in the news at all if it weren't for all those tabloid editors who just love the opportunity to print the word "prostitute"' (BBC News, December 2006). From these comments in a BBC News chatroom, it is clear that questions of what names are given to women and whether these terms are positively evaluated or not is a key concern to many. The people in the chatroom debate the issue of how these women who have been murdered should be named (even though that was not the original topic of the chatroom string). What I take from this type of debate is the fact that anti-sexism was not just a campaign of feminists in the 1990s; the issue of how to represent women and what language should be used in relation to women is a live issue.

2.   Why analyse sexism

By drawing attention to the way language is used to represent women, we also draw attention to the general and specific discrimination against women. By analysing language, and describing the possibilities of changes in usage, we can signal to women and men that there are other ways of thinking and behaving; these sexist forms of representation can be changed. As Talbot puts it: 'Before change can even be wanted what appear to be natural aspects of the everyday lives of women and men have to be exposed as culturally produced and as disadvantageous to women . . . An important stage in emancipation is identifying mechanisms of oppression' (Talbot, 1998: 149). The study of language is therefore of utmost importance, for, as Talbot (1998: 150) argues: 'looking at language critically is a way of denaturalising it'. Gill comments:

Although the concept of sexism seems to be slightly unfashionable at the moment, it is important to retain the notion, because as Williamson argues: 'sexism isn't just a phenomenon, it's an idea – and once the word stops being used, the idea goes out of fashion. What then becomes passé isn't actually sexism, which is doing just fine, but the concept of sexism in advertising or anything else.' (Gill, 2007: 271)

We need to retain the concept of sexist language and, even though reform is difficult, we need to continually draw attention to it.

3.   Why reform matters

It is important that we continually debate what constitutes sexism and suggest ways of representing women which are more progressive. Hellinger and Pauwels (2007) survey the studies which have analysed the effects of sexist language or non-gender-inclusive language on visualisation. In an analysis of reforms of the German language, they show that, if generic pronouns are used, visualisation is overwhelmingly male. They argue that:

while the use of masculine generics was found to produce overwhelmingly more male-specific imagery, the various gender-inclusive alternatives produced quite unexpected results: only long nominal splitting (Bürger under Bürgerinnen 'citizens') appears to achieve a roughly symmetrical mental representation of female and male referents, while abbreviated splitting (Bürger/innen 'citizens') and neutral expressions (die wissenschaftlich Tätigen 'scientists') produced asymmetries of various degrees. (Hellinger and Pauwels, 2007: 672)

Thus, it is only when women are pointedly referred to that there seems to be roughly equivalent visualisation of women and men. Whilst such reforms of the language may appear clumsy or difficult to say, perhaps it is precisely their awkwardness which in fact draws the reader's or hearer's attention to women. In more 'neutral' forms, women's presence is erased. Hellinger and Pauwels (2007: 672) argue that: 'The on-going debate on (non) sexist language must be interpreted as part of the on-going political discourse over the equal participation of women in all public domains.' Thus, this debate is not solely about language.

People who oppose anti-discriminatory campaigns often characterise reform as impossible. But intervention in language is quite common; it is not just language reformers who do it. As Fairclough (2003) notes, bank accounts have been relexicalised as 'financial products'; Talbot (2007) notes that patients within the British National Health Service have been relabelled as 'customers'. In my own university, courses have been relexicalised as 'products'. Whilst these changes have been made to the language with little protest, Talbot comments, 'the significant difference is that "PC" is marked off as "political" while, from a liberal perspective, commodification and marketisation are not' (Talbot, 2007: 759). Perhaps, she argues, 'a key difference between covert neo-liberal manipulation and the "linguistic engineering" done by feminists and anti-racists is that the latter is done openly' (Talbot, 2007: 759).

4.   Should we accept sexism?

In recent discussion of 'hate speech' – that is, speech which is intended to incite violence against others – there has been an assumption that such speech should be banned. Indeed the British Labour government has tried to enact legislation which would mean that this type of speech is illegal. The government is largely concerned with speech which incites violence against a religious or ethnic minority. Although the proposed legislation is phrased in general terms it is quite clear to most that its main focus is on anti-Muslim sentiments which have led or may lead to racist attacks. The proposed Bill has been contested by a wide range of groups, partly because of the difficulty of defining 'hate speech' and of deciding whether in fact speech can incite violence. This issue has been widely debated in America where there have been campus regulations aimed at regulating speech, but most of those regulations have now been largely repealed because of the difficulty of enforcement and definition (Lakoff, 2000).

However, as I have argued in Chapter 3, some critics have suggested that rather than attempting to ban 'hate speech' we should accept it and see it as a symptom of clashes of interest within society which have to be acknowledged and dealt with. Perhaps the same is true of sexist language – it might be seen as an instance of clashes within society about women's position within the public sphere, rather than simply an expression of negative emotions about women in general. Whillock and Slayden (1995: ix) argue that:

The increase in expressions of hate . . . has been typically accounted for as the result of cultures clashing and merging . . . The implications of this 'crisis' model of hate are that hateful expressions are extra-societal phenomena: isolated instances of extreme, disruptive, illegitimate, irrational, antisocial behaviour . . . But seeing hate as an extreme expression that arises only in moments of cultural tension encourages us to ignore its role in the subtle negotiations that take place daily in complex modern society, indulging the comfortable notion that hate is a pathological practice of 'others'.

Although, of course, I do not agree that sexism should be simply accepted as part of an inevitable contest over resources, it has been the argument of this book that we need to see sexism as not just the expression of hatred for women, but rather we need to recognise the role both overt and indirect sexism play in the 'subtle negotiations that take place daily in complex modern society' (Whillock and Slayden, 1995: ix). Sexism seems to be a set of semi-authorised statements which people can draw on, play with, joke about and ironise. It is a complex phenomenon, not reducible to linguistic features alone, which is interpreted by different people in various ways depending on the context. Rather than assuming that women adopt an outraged approach *en masse* to the phenomenon of overt or indirect sexism, that they can recognise certain statements as sexist or that they even agree with feminist campaigns around sexist language, I have argued that a range of positions can be adopted in relation to sexism. Furthermore, we cannot assume that those women who do not recognise certain utterances or texts as sexist are simply the passive 'victims' of sexism. Many women find it relatively easy to respond to perceived sexism with humour, banter, mockery or aggression. Some women might want to use sexist terms themselves in a playful, ironising or assertive way. Whilst this position has the advantage of giving women a certain amount of interactional power, it may lead them to being seen as complicit with certain statements which are not necessarily in their political interests.

Some may argue that concentrating on sexist language is a waste of time as people will express sexist views in creative new ways whatever reforms are brought in. However, working on sexism and thinking about what constitutes sexism, how statements may or may not be interpreted or intended as sexist, seems to me a valid enterprise. As Holmes and Meyerhoff (2003: 14) argue:

There seems little point in our academic interests if they do not at some stage articulate with real world concerns and enable us and our readers to identify, for example, certain employment practices as unfair and ill informed, based more on stereotypes and prejudice than they are on people's actual behaviour in the real world. At some point, our research has to be able to travel out of the academy in order to draw attention to and challenge unquestioned practices that reify certain behaviours as being morally or aesthetically better than others. We should never cease to engage actively with and challenge assumptions about gender norms and loudly draw attention to the way power, privilege and social authority interact with and are naturalised as properties of independent social categories.

Holmes and Meyerhoff argue that what is necessary is an acceptance of the fact that we need as feminists to be able to look at the 'big picture' (to identify regularities and to make generalisations about sexism), as well as at the same time being aware of the way that sexism is something which is negotiated at a local level. However, this local level where we undertake our contextualised analyses cannot be analysed in isolation from an assessment of community of practice norms, which influence, and are, in turn, influenced by, local co-constructed norms of appropriateness and wider social norms. Thus, we need to analyse how individuals make sense of sexism at a local level, as well as trace the effects of wider social norms on the local level. What people consider appropriate at the local level contributes to the general norms of the society as a whole.

One aspect of sexism which should give us all hope is that, because women's status and confidence has changed so rapidly in recent years, direct/overt sexism at least is often greeted in conversation with derisive groans from women and men alike. Indirect sexism is unfortunately much more difficult to treat with derision, but it is a measure of how much sexism has been challenged by feminism that sexists have had to disguise their attitudes towards women. Furthermore, perhaps the fact that overt sexism is now seen as an ideological position which is neither a commonsense position nor necessarily supported by institutions has caused the greatest change in the way that sexism is used. As Janet Holmes observes in relation to New Zealand English, 'many New Zealanders have become aware that use of a form such as *Mrs* or using *chairman* as a generic, reflects an ideological position just as clearly as selecting forms such as *Ms* or *chairperson*' (Holmes, 2001: 118).

Holmes (2001: 131) argues that there have been significant changes in sexist usage with alternatives to sexist usage being adopted:

whilst changing the language will not in itself solve the problems of women's lack of power or improve their subordinate statuses in the wider society, . . . the provision of non-sexist options can contribute to the construction of a more positive female iden- tity. Similarly, avoiding sexist language and challenging sexist assumptions contributes indirectly to the construction of more positive images of women. Drawing attention to evidence of widespread male bias in conventional uses of language is a worthwhile activity in its own right. But it is also true that such changes can ultimately affect attitudes because in and of themselves they alter the status quo.

However, we need to be aware that arguing for changes to sexism alone will not bring about widespread changes, but anti-sexist campaigns should be seen as part of a call for wider changes in society. Litosseliti (2006: 21) argues that:

effective change has to come from both personal and institutional levels . . . a focus on language has to be part of a focus on gender inequality in general, and viewed in the context of wider social and institutional change. For example a change in the language used in rape reporting and court examination of rape victims . . . needs to materialise within the context of legal and social changes. Such changes would involve, most notably, a more realistic correlation between crime and convictions . . . changes would also involve the provision of better support for victims and the inclusion on the agenda of male rape. Our language regarding how rapists and their victims are perceived and treated can then reflect as well as help consolidate the legal, institutional and social developments in this area.

This is an important point, in that feminists need to campaign on general issues of inequality as well as continuing to campaign on issues of language usage. I remain convinced that, despite the slightly anachronistic feel to accusations of sexism, it is still important to challenge language which appears sexist, both at the individual, community of practice and institutional levels and at the level of the society or culture as a whole. As Lazar (2005: 6) claims:

analysis of discourse which shows up the workings of power that sustain oppressive social structures/relations is itself a form of analytical resistance and contributes to ongoing struggles of contestation and change.

By intervening in conversations and provoking discussion of sexism, writing to advertisers and bodies governing advertising practices, as well as ensuring that language guidelines for gender-fair usage are in place in institutions, women and men will be able to challenge stereotypical thinking about gender-relations.

To conclude, we need to see current sexism as constituting a distinct response to the challenge of women working in the public sphere and arguing for equality. This response takes two forms: overt sexism and indirect sexism. Overt sexism is a set of institutionalised linguistic practices which can be adopted or contested, which have been authorised in some sense in the past because of their association with institutions and because they have a history ('we have always used the generic "he" pronoun to refer to students and no-one misunderstands it'). Although these linguistic practices have been normalised in the past, they have now been called into question, so that now it is difficult to simply use them unquestioningly. Some people now find it uncomfortable to find the 'right' term when referring to a female chairing a meeting, and that discomfort is positive and productive as it is indicative of the changes which have been made in relation to the language used about women. Overt sexism, whilst still available as a resource, is largely stigmatised and women feel that they have the resources available to challenge it. The second type of sexism, which I have termed indirect sexism (just like 'political correctness'), is a response to the feminist critique of overt sexism. Indirect sexism is also a product of the way that some men have been working out their masculinity in relation to the challenges of feminism and also the notions of 'new man' and 'new lad'. This more 'subtle' type of sexism, as Lazar (2005) terms it, is occasioned by the ongoing disquiet amongst men about women's role in the workplace, in relationships and increases in women's power generally, and can be seen as a way of, at one and the same time, bringing sexist attitudes into play, displaying a sophisticated irony or humour in relation to sexism, whilst not taking responsibility for the sexism. Both of these types of sexism spring from the same insecurity around women's position within society, and institutions, whilst challenging overt sexism on the whole, continue to promulgate indirect sexism. It is this more complex form of sexism which needs to be thoroughly challenged. Feminist action is still of importance to ensure that this indirect, seemingly more playful type of sexism does not become part of the way that men define themselves more generally. It is essential that men can negotiate the norms of masculinity without needing to define themselves in stark contrast to the norms of femininity and without expressing contempt and even hatred for women. Part of a feminist vision for the future is of a less binary model of gender, where it will be possible, for example, for women in management positions to interact with others without having to define themselves according to masculine norms and where their presence is responded to neutrally, without their sex being their defining feature as a manager (Mullany, 2007). My aim, in discussing sexism, is to try to move forward to a: 'feminist humanist vision of a just society, in which gender does not predetermine or mediate our relationships with others, and our sense of who we are or might become' (Lazar, 2005: 6).

Sexism constantly calls attention to our sex and gender and forces us to mis-recognise ourselves, to see ourselves as others might see us, as over-emotional, as incompetent and as less important or powerful than men. This negative vision of women has to change even further than it has already changed, rather than relying on challenges to stereotypes and ironising.

Furthermore, as Fairclough (2003: 22) has argued, the way that we are referred to and come to see ourselves is important in material terms. It is not just a question of naming, but naming has consequences:

social practices are inherently reflexive – people interact, and at the same time they represent to themselves and each other what they do (sometimes drawing upon representations of what they do which come from other practices, including governmental and 'expert' practices). What they do is then shaped and reshaped by their representations of what they do ... changing discourses will, or may, lead to changes in other elements of social practices through processes of dialectical internalisation. For instance, if people can be persuaded to talk of 'partner' rather than 'the person I'm living with' or 'lover' (or even 'mistress'), or if people being 'sacked' is partly displaced in public discourse by organisations 'downsizing', there will (or may) be consequential changes in how non-marital relationships and economic restructuring are perceived, and how people act and react towards them.

Thus, calling for change at the level of the phrase or word is drawing attention to problems at the level of conceptualisation, at a discourse level, and at the level of social practices. Anti-sexist-language campaigns and activism are not concerned simply to change language, but to draw attention to ways of thinking and behaving which are anachronistic; these campaigns constitute a call for change at the level of material practice.

Bibliography

I have made a decision to represent all theorists whom I have referred to by using their initial in the bibliography rather than their first name. Castro (2007) argues that a feminist practice in relation to references might be that of feminisation, i.e. to refer to the first name of the theorist, making women academics visible. I have decided on a gender-neutralisation practice and have thus referred to all critics by initial alone and have avoided pronouns in the text which refer to the sex of the theorist, since in this way the professional status of the female critic is foregrounded rather than her sex.

Ainsworth, S. and Hardy, C. (2004) 'Critical Discourse Analysis and identity: why bother?' *Critical Discourse Studies*, 1/2, 225–59.

Althusser, L. (1984) *Essays on Ideology*, London, Verso.

Antaki, C. and Widdicombe, S. eds. (1998a) *Identities in Talk*, London, Sage.

(1998b) 'Identity as an achievement and as a tool', pp. 1–14, in Antaki, C. and Widdicombe, S. eds. *Identities in Talk*, London, Sage.

Armstrong, J. (1997) 'Homophobic slang as coercive discourse among college students', pp. 326–35, in Livia, A. and Hall, K. eds. *Queerly Phrased: Language, Gender and Sexuality*, Oxford University Press.

Banks, M. and Swift, A. (1987) *The Jokes on Us: Women in Comedy from Music Hall to the Present*, London, Pandora.

Baran, D. and Syska, O. (2000) 'Harsh words are women's words: the emergence of a new female speech style in Poland', paper presented to the International Gender and Language Association, Stanford University, California.

Bates, J. (2004) 'The men to watch', *Radio Times*, 19–25 June, 21.

Baxter, J. ed. (2006) *Speaking Out: The Female Voice in Public Contexts*, Basingstoke, Palgrave.

(2003) *Positioning Gender in Discourse: A Feminist Methodology*, Basingstoke, Palgrave.

Beaken, M. (1996) *The Making of Language*, Edinburgh University Press.

Bell, D., Binnie, J., Cream, J. and Valentine, G. (1994) 'All hyped up and no place to go', *Gender, Place and Culture*, 1/1, 31–48.

Benwell, B. ed. (2006) *Masculinity and Men's Lifestyle Magazines*, Oxford, Blackwell.

Benwell, B. and Stokoe, E. (2006) *Discourse and Identity*, Edinburgh University Press.

Bergvall, V., Bing, J. and Freed, A. eds. (1996) *Rethinking Language and Gender Research: Theory and Practice*, London, Longman.

Bing, J. (2004) 'Lesbian jokes: a reply to Christie Davies', *Humor*, 17/3, 323–8.

Bing, J. and Bergvall, J. (1996) 'The question of questions: beyond binary thinking', pp. 1–30, in Bergvall, V., Bing, J. and Freed, A. eds. *Rethinking Language and Gender Research: Theory and Practice*, London, Longman.

Bing, J. and Heller, D. (2003) 'How many lesbians does it take to screw in a light-bulb?'*Humor*, 16/2, 157–82.

Black, M. and Coward, R. (1981) 'Linguistic, social and sexual relations: a review of Dale Spender's *Man-Made Language*', *Screen Education*, 39, 69–85.

Bodine, A. (1998) 'Androcentrism in prescriptive grammar: singular "they", sex-definite "he", and "he or she", pp. 124–38, in Cameron, D. ed. *Feminist Critique of Language: A Reader*, 2nd edition, London, Routledge.

Bourdieu, P. (1991) *Language and Symbolic Power*, Cambridge, Polity Press.

Bradby, B. (1990) 'Do-talk and don't talk: the division of subject in girl-group music', pp. 341–68, in Frith, S. and Goodwin, S. eds. *On Record: A Rock and Pop Reader*, London, Routledge.

Braid, M. (2001) 'Cruella of prime time', *Independent*, 10 March, 5.

Bramson, J. (2006) 'Beyond political correctness', HPR On-line: http://hprsite. squarespace.com/beyond-political-correctness/.

Braun, F. (1997) 'Making men out of people: the MAN principle in translating genderless forms', pp. 3–30, in Kotthoff, H. and Wodak, R. eds. *Communicating Gender in Context*, Amsterdam, John Benjamins.

Braun, V. (1999) 'Public talk about "private parts"', *Feminism and Psychology*, 9/4, 515–22.

Braun, V. and Kitzinger, C. (1999) 'Snatch, hole, or honey-pot? Semantic categories and the problems of non-specificity in female genital slang', discussion paper, Loughborough University.

Brooks, A. (1997) *Postfeminisms: Feminist Cultural Theory and Cultural Forms*, London, Routledge.

Bucholtz, M. (2000) 'Geek feminism', paper presented to the International Gender and Language Association, Stanford University, California.

(1999) 'Why be normal? Language and identity practices in a community of nerd girls', *Language in Society*, 28/2, 203–25.

(1996) 'Black feminist theory and African American women's linguistic practice', pp. 267–90, in Bergvall, V., Bing, J. and Freed, A. eds. *Rethinking Language and Gender Research: Theory and Practice*, London, Longman.

Burton, D. (1982) 'Through glass darkly; through dark glasses', pp. 195–214, in Carter, R. ed. *Language and Literature: An Introductory Reader in Stylistics*, London, Allen and Unwin.

Butler, J. (1997) *Excitable Speech: A Politics of the Performative*, London, Routledge.

(1993) *Bodies that Matter: On the Discursive Limits of Sex*, London, Routledge.

(1990) *Gender Trouble: Feminism and the Subversion of Identity*, London, Routledge.

Caldas-Coulthard, C. (1995) 'Man in the news: the misrepresentation of women speaking in news-as-narrative discourse', pp. 226–40, in Mills, S. ed. *Language and Gender: Interdisciplinary Perspectives*, Harlow, Longman.

Cameron, D. (2007) *The Myth of Mars and Venus*, Oxford University Press.

(2006) *Language and Sexual Politics*, London, Routledge.

(2000) *Good to Talk? Living and Working in a Communication Culture*, London, Sage.

ed. (1998a) *The Feminist Critique of Language: A Reader*, 2nd edition, London, Routledge.

(1998b) '"Is there any ketchup, Vera?": gender, power and pragmatics', *Discourse and Society*, 9/4, 435–55.

(1998c) 'Lost in translation: non-sexist language', pp. 155–63, in Cameron, D. ed. *The Feminist Critique of Language: A Reader*, London, Routledge.

(1997) 'Performing gender identity: young men's talk and the construction of heterosexual masculinity', pp. 86–107, in Johnson, S. and Meinhoff, U. eds. *Language and Masculinity*, Oxford, Blackwell.

(1995) *Verbal Hygiene*, London, Routledge.

(1994) 'Words, words, words: the power of language', pp. 15–34, in Dunant, S. ed. *The War of the Words: The Political Correctness Debate*, London, Virago.

(1990) *The Feminist Critique of Language: A Reader*, 1st edition, London, Routledge.

Cameron, D. and Kulick, D. (2003) *Language and Sexuality*, Cambridge University Press.

Cameron, D., McAlinden, F. and O'Leary, K. (1988) 'Lakoff in context: the social and linguistic functions of tag questions', pp. 13–26, in Coates, J. and Cameron, D. eds. *Women in their Speech Communities*, Harlow, Longman.

Carroll, D. and Kowitz, J. (1994) 'Using concordance techniques to study gender stereotyping in ELT textbooks', pp. 73–83, in Sunderland, J. ed. *Exploring Gender Questions and Implications for English Language Education*, Hemel Hempstead, Prentice Hall.

Cashmore, E. (2006) 'Sticks and stones', *Independent*, 11 June.

Castro, V. (2007) 'Feminism, gender and translation', paper presented to the Sheffield Hallam University Linguistic Research Seminar.

Chan, G. (1992) 'Gender, roles and power in dyadic conversation', pp. 57–67, in Hall, K., Bucholtz, M. and Moonwomon, B. eds. *Locating Power*, Berkeley, University of California.

Chang, J. (2006) 'Keeping it real: interpreting hip hop', *College English*, 68/5, 545–57.

Chouliaraki, L. and Fairclough, N. (1999) *Discourse in Late Modernity*, Edinburgh University Press.

Christie, C. (2001) *Gender and Language: Towards a Feminist Pragmatics*, Edinburgh University Press.

Clark, K. (1998) 'The linguistics of blame: representations of women in the *Sun*'s reporting of crimes of sexual violence', pp. 183–97, in Cameron, D. ed. *The Feminist Critique of Language: A Reader*, 2nd edition, London, Routledge.

Coates, J. (2003) *Men Talk*, Oxford, Blackwell.

(1996) *Women Talk*, Oxford, Blackwell.

Coates, J. and Cameron, D. eds. (1988) *Women in their Speech Communities*, Harlow, Longman.

Cooper, R. (1984) 'The avoidance of androcentric generics', *International Journal of Social Language*, 50, 5–20.

Crawford, M. (1995) *Talking Difference: On Gender and Language*, London, Sage.

Crawford, M. and Chaffin, R. (1986) 'The readers' construction of meaning', pp. 3–30, in Flynn, E. and Schweickart, P. eds. *Gender and Reading*, Baltimore, MD, Johns Hopkins University Press.

Daly, M. (1981) *Gyn/ecology*, London, Women's Press.

Davies, C. (2004) 'Lesbian jokes: some methodological problems', *Humor*, 17/3, 311–21.

Day, D. (1998) 'Being ascribed and resisting membership of an ethnic group', pp. 151–69, in Antaki, C. and Widdicombe, S. eds. *Identities in Talk*, London, Sage.

De Klerk, V. (1997) 'The role of expletives in the construction of masculinity', pp. 144–59, in Johnson, S. and Meinhof, U. eds. *Language and Masculinity*, Oxford, Blackwell.

Deutscher, G. (2005) *The Unfolding of Language*: *An Evolutionary Tour of Mankind's Greatest Invention*, New York, Metropolitan Books.

Diamond, J. (1996) *Status and Power in Verbal Interaction: A Study of Discourse in a Close-knit Social Network*, Amsterdam and Philadelphia, John Benjamins.

Donald, S. ed. (n.d.) *The Joy of Sexism*, London, John Broon Publishing.

Doyle, M. (1994) *The A–Z of Non-sexist Language*, London, Women's Press.

Dunant, S. ed. (1994) *The War of the Words: The Political Correctness Debate*, London, Virago.

Duranti, A. and Goodwin, C. eds. (1992) *Rethinking Context: Language as an Interactive Phenomenon*, Cambridge University Press.

Eckert, P. (2000) *Linguistic Variation as Social Practice*, Oxford, Blackwell.

Eckert, P. and McConnell-Ginet, S. (2006) 'Putting communities of practice in their place', *Gender and Language*, 1/1, 27–38.

(2003) *Language and Gender*, Cambridge University Press.

(1999) 'New generalisations and explanations in language and gender research', *Language in Society*, 28/2, 185–203.

(1998) 'Communities of practice: where language, gender and power all live', pp. 484–94, in Coates, J. ed. *Language and Gender: A Reader*, Oxford, Blackwell.

Edley, N. and Wetherell, M. (1997) 'Jockeying for position: the construction of masculine identities', *Discourse and Society*, 8/2, 203–17.

Edwards, D. (1998) 'The relevant thing about her: social identity categories in use', pp. 15–33, in Antaki, C. and Widdicombe, S. eds. *Identities in Talk*, London, Sage.

Eelen, G. (2001) *Critique of Politeness Theories*, Manchester, St Jeromes Press.

Ehrlich, S. (2001) *Representing Rape: Language and Sexual Consent*, London and New York, Routledge.

(1999) 'Communities of practice, gender and the representation of sexual assault', *Language in Society*, 28/2, 239–57.

Ehrlich, S. and King, R. (1996) 'Consensual sex or sexual harassment: negotiating meaning', pp. 153–73, in Bergvall, V. *et al.* eds. *Rethinking Language and Gender Research: Theory and Practice*, London, Longman.

(1998) 'Gender based language reform and the social construction of meaning', pp. 164–79, in Cameron, D. ed. *The Feminist Critique of Language: A Reader*, London, Routledge.

Elgin, S. (1988) *A First Dictionary and Grammar of Laaden*, Madison, WI, Society for the Furtherance and Study of Fantasy and Science Fiction.

Fairclough, N. (2003) '"Political correctness": the politics of culture and language', *Discourse and Society*, 14/1, 17–28.

(2000) *New Labour, New Language,* London, Routledge.

(1995) *Critical Discourse Analysis: The Critical Study of Language*, Harlow, Longman.

(1992) *Discourse and Social Change*, London, Polity.

(1989) *Language and Power*, Harlow, Longman.

Foley, W. (1997) *Anthropological Linguistics*, Oxford, Blackwell.

Foucault, M. (1981) 'The order of discourse', pp. 48–79, in Young, R. ed. *Untying the Text: A Poststructuralist Reader*, London, Routledge and Kegan Paul.

(1978) *History of Sexuality: An Introduction*, vol. I, Harmondsworth, Penguin.

(1972) *Archaeology of Knowledge*, trans. Sheridan Smith, A.M., London, Tavistock.

Frank, F. and Treichler, P. (1989) *Language Gender and Professional Writing*, New York, MLA.

Frankenberg, R. (1993) *White Women, Race Matters: The Social Construction of Whiteness*, London, Routledge.

Freed, A. (1999) 'Communities of practice and pregnant women: is there a connection?', *Language in Society*, 28/2, 257–71.

(1996) 'Language and gender research in an experimental setting', pp. 54–76, in Bergvall, V., Bing, J. and Freed, A. eds. *Rethinking Language and Gender Research: Theory and Practice*, London, Longman.

Fuss, D. (1989) *Essentially Speaking: Feminism Nature and Difference*, London, Routledge.

Gilbert, S. and Gubar, S. (1988) *The War of the Worlds*, vol. I, New Haven, CT, Yale University Press.

Gill, R. (2007) *Gender and the Media*, London, Polity.

Gillis, S., Howie, G. and Munford, R. eds. (2004) *Third Wave Feminism: A Critical Exploration*, London, Palgrave.

Goldberg, D. (1993) *Racist Culture: Philosophy and the Politics of Meaning*, Oxford, Blackwell.

Goodwin, C. and Duranti, A. (1992) 'Rethinking context: an introduction', pp. 1–43, in Duranti, A. and Goodwin, C. eds. *Rethinking Context: Language as an Interactive Phenomenon*, Cambridge University Press.

Goodwin, C. and Harness Goodwin, M. (1992) 'Assessments and the construction of context', pp. 147–91, in Duranti, A. and Goodwin, C. eds. *Rethinking Context: Language as an Interactive Phenomenon,* Cambridge University Press.

Gormley, S. (2008) 'Third Wave feminist critical discourse analysis of chick lit', PhD thesis, Sheffield Hallam University.

Graham, A. (1975/2006) 'The making of a non-sexist dictionary', pp. 135–7, in Sunderland, J. *Language and Gender: An Advanced Resource Book*, London, Routledge.

Greater Manchester Police (2001a) *Mind our Language*, www.gmp.police.uk/language.

(2001b) *Reporting a Hate Crime*, www.gmp.police.uk/working-with/pages.

(2001c) *The Stephen Lawrence Inquiry*, www.gmp.police.uk/inquiry.

Greater Manchester Police Appropriate Language Working Group (2000) *The Power of Language: A Practical Guide to the Use of Language*, www.gmp.police.uk/language.

Grey, F. (1994) *Women and Laughter*, London, Macmillan.

Hachimi, A. (2001) 'Shifting sands: language and gender in Moroccan Arabic', pp. 27–51, in Hellinger, M. and Bussmann, H. eds. *Gender Across Languages: The*

Linguistic Representation of Women and Men, vol. 1, Amsterdam and Philadelphia, John Benjamins.

Halberstam, J. (1998) *Female Masculinity*, London, Routledge.

Hall, K., Bucholtz, M. and Moonwomon, B. eds. (1992) *Locating Power: Proceedings of the Second Berkeley Women and Language Conference*, vol. I, Berkeley, CA, Berkeley Women and Language Group, University of California.

Haugen, J. (2000) 'Unladylike divas: the gender performances of female gangsta rappers', paper presented to the International Gender and Language Association, Stanford University, California.

Hellinger, M. (2006) 'Why Merkel is not enough: on the representation of fe/male politicians in German newspapers', paper presented to the International Gender and Language Association, Valencia, Spain.

(2001) 'English-gender in a global language', pp. 105–13, in Hellinger, M. and Bussmann, H. eds. *Gender Across Languages: The Linguistic Representation of Women and Men,* vol. I, Amsterdam and Philadelphia, John Benjamins.

(1998) 'Gender across languages: international perspectives on language variation and change', pp. 211–20, in Wertheim, S., Bailey, A. and Corston-Oliver, M. eds. *Engendering Communication,* Berkeley, CA, Berkeley Women and Language Group, University of California.

Hellinger, M. and Bussmann, H. eds. (2001) *Gender Across Languages: The Linguistic Representation of Women and Men,* vol. I, Amsterdam and Philadelphia, John Benjamins.

Hellinger, M. and Pauwels, A. (2007) 'Language and sexism', pp. 651–81, in Hellinger, M. and Pauwels, A. eds. *Handbook of Language and Communication: Diversity and Change*, Berlin and New York, Mouton de Gruyter.

Henley, N. (1995) 'Ethnicity and gender issues in language', pp. 361–96, in Landrine, H. ed. *Bringing Cultural Diversity to Feminist Psychology*, Washington, DC, American Psychological Association.

Hewitt, R. (1997) '"Box-out" and "Taxing"', pp. 27–47, in Johnson, S. and Meinhof, U. eds. *Language and Masculinity*, Oxford, Blackwell.

Heywood, L. and Drake, J. 2002 *Third Wave Agenda: Being Feminist, Doing Feminism,* Minneapolis and London, University of Minnesota Press.

Hodges, L. (2004) 'Fighting talk', *Independent,* 1 April, 6.

Holland, S. (2002) 'Challenges to femininity', PhD thesis, Sheffield Hallam University.

Holmes, J. (2001) 'A corpus based view of gender in New Zealand English', pp. 115–36, in Hellinger, M. and Bussmann, H. eds. *Gender Across Languages: The Linguistic Representation of Women and Men,* vol. I, Amsterdam and Philadelphia, John Benjamins.

(1995) *Women, Men and Politeness*, London, Longman.

Holmes, J. and Meyerhoff, M. eds. (2003) *The Handbook of Language and Gender*, Oxford, Blackwell.

(1999) 'The community of practice: theories and methodologies in language and gender research', *Language in Society*, 28/2, 173–85.

Holmes, J. and Stubbe, M. (2003) '"Feminine" workplaces: stereotype and reality', pp. 573–600, in Holmes, J. and Meyerhoff, M. eds. *The Handbook of Language and Gender*, Oxford, Blackwell.

Hughes, K. (2001) 'Caring and sharing', *Observer on Sunday*, July, 2.

Jackson, P. (1994) 'Black male: advertising and the cultural politics of masculinity', *Gender, Place and Culture*, 1/1, 49–59.

Johnson, S., Culpeper, J. and Suhr, S. (2003) 'From "politically correct councillors" to "Blairite nonsense": discourse of "political correctness" in three British newspapers', *Discourse and Society*, 14/1, 29–47.

Johnson, S. and Meinhof, U. eds. (1997) *Language and Masculinity*, Oxford, Blackwell.

Johnson, S. and Suhr, S. (2003) 'From "political correctness" to "politische Korrektheit": discourses of "PC" in the German newspaper *Die Welt*', *Discourse and Society*, 14/1, 49–69.

Joyce, P. ed. (1995) *Class*, Oxford University Press.

Kaplan, E. Ann (2002) 'Plenary paper: 9/11 and feminist theory', paper presented to the Third Wave Feminism conference, Exeter University.

Kellett, P. (1995) 'Acts of power, control and resistance: narrative accounts of convicted rapists', pp. 142–56, in Whillock, R. and Slayden, D. eds. *Hate Speech*, London, Sage.

Kendall, G. and Wickham, G. (1999) *Using Foucault's Methods*, London, Sage.

Kendall, S. and Tannen, D. (1997) 'Gender and language in the workplace', pp. 81–106, in Wodak, R. *Gender and Discourse*, London, Sage.

Kitzinger, C. and Thomas, A. (1995) 'Sexual harassment: a discursive approach', pp. 32–49, in Wilkinson, S. and Kitzinger, C. eds. *Feminism and Discourse*, London, Sage.

Kramarae, C. and Treichler, P. (1985) *A Feminist Dictionary*, London, Pandora.

Kulick, D. (2000) 'Gay and lesbian language', paper presented to the International Gender and Language Association, Stanford University, California.

Labov, W. (1972) *Language in the Inner City*, Philadelphia, University of Pennsylvania Press.

Lakoff, G. (1987) *Women, Fire and Dangerous Things: What Categories Reveal about the Mind*, Chicago University Press.

Lakoff, R. (2000) *The Language Wars*, Berkeley, University of California Press.

(1990) *Talking Power: The Politics of Language*, New York, Basic Books.

(1975) *Language and Woman's Place*, New York, Harper and Row.

(1975/2006) 'On the "generic" *he*', pp. 97–8, in Sunderland, J. *Language and Gender: An Advanced Resource Book*, London, Routledge.

Lazar, M. (2005) *Feminist Critical Discourse Analysis: Gender, Power and Ideology in Discourse*, London, Palgrave Macmillan.

Leap, W. (1997) 'Performative affect in three gay English texts', pp. 310–34, in Livia, A. and Hall, K. eds. *Queerly Phrased: Language, Gender and Sexuality*, Oxford University Press.

(1995) *Beyond the Lavender Lexicon: Authenticity, Imagination and Appropriation in Lesbian and Gay Languages*, Amsterdam, Gordon and Breach.

Leech, G. (1983) *Principles of Pragmatics*, Harlow, Longman.

Levy, A. (2005) *Female Chauvinist Pig: Women and the Rise of Raunch Culture*, New York and London, Free Press.

Lewis, R. and Mills, S. eds. (2004) *Post-colonial Feminist Theory: A Reader*, Edinburgh University Press.

Liladhar, J. (2000) 'Making, unmaking and making femininity', PhD thesis, Sheffield Hallam University.

Litosseliti, L. (2006) *Gender and Language: Theory and Practice*, London, Hodder Arnold.

Litosseliti, L. and Sunderland, J. eds. (2002) *Gender Identity and Discourse Analysis*, Amsterdam and Philadelphia, John Benjamins.

Livia, A. and Hall, K. (1997a) '"It's a girl": bringing performativity back to linguistics', pp. 3–21, in Livia, A. and Hall, K. eds. *Queerly Phrased: Language, Gender and Sexuality*, Oxford University Press.

   eds. (1997b) *Queerly Phrased: Language, Gender and Sexuality*, Oxford University Press.

Lovell, T. (2000) 'Thinking feminism with and against Bourdieu', *Feminist Theory*, 1/1, 11–32.

Lovering, K. (1995) 'The bleeding body: adolescents talk about menstruation', pp. 10–32, in Wilkinson, S. and Kitzinger, C. eds. *Feminism and Discourse*, London, Sage.

McClintock, A. (1995) *Imperial Leather: Race, Gender and Sexuality in the Imperial Contest*, London, Routledge.

McConnell-Ginet, S. (2003) '"What's in a name?" Social labelling and gender practices', in Holmes, J. and Meyerhoff, M. eds. *The Handbook of Language and Gender*, Oxford, Blackwell.

McCrum, R., Cran, W. and MacNeil, R. (1986) *The Story of English*, London, Faber.

McElhinny, B. (1998) '"I don't smile much anymore": affect, gender and the discourse of Pittsburgh Police Officers', pp. 309–27, in Coates, J. ed. *Language and Gender: A Reader*, Oxford, Blackwell.

MacKinnon, C. (1993) *Only Words*, Cambridge, MA, Harvard University Press.

Manke, M. (1997) *Classroom Power Relations: Understanding Student Teacher Interaction*, London, Lawrence Erlbaum Associates.

Matsuda, M., Lawrence, C., Delgado, R. and Grenshaw, K. eds. (1993) *Words that Wound: Critical Race Theory, Assaultive Speech and the First Amendment*, Boulder and San Francisco, Westview Press.

Midgley, S. (2004) 'A child of the 1960s', *Independent*, 1 April, 11.

Miller, C. and Swift, K. (1982/1989) *The Handbook of Non-Sexist Writing*, London, Women's Press.

Miller, E. (1995) 'Inside the switchboard of desire', pp. 30–42, in Leap, W. ed. *Beyond the Lavender Lexicon: Authenticity, Imagination and Appropriation in Lesbian and Gay Languages*, Amsterdam, Gordon and Breach.

Mills, J. (1989) *Womanwords*, Harlow, Longman.

Mills, S. (2006) 'Institutionalised contempt', paper presented to the Feminisms conference, Sheffield Hallam University.

   (2004a) *Discourse*, 2nd edition, London, Routledge.

   (2004b) 'Third Wave feminist linguistics and the analysis of sexism', *Discourse Analysis On-Line*, www.shu.ac.uk/daol.

   (2003a) 'Caught between sexism, anti-sexism and "political correctness": feminist women's negotiations with naming practices', *Discourse and Society*, 14/1, 87–110.

   (2003b) *Gender and Politeness*, Cambridge University Press.

   (2002) 'Rethinking politeness, impoliteness and gender identity', in Litosseliti, L. and Sunderland, J. eds. *Gender Identity and Discourse Analysis*, Amsterdam, John Benjamins.

(1999) 'Discourse competence: or how to theorise strong women speakers', pp. 81–99, in Hendricks, C. and Oliver, K. eds. *Language and Liberation: Feminism, Philosophy and Language*, New York, State of New York University Press.

(1998) 'Post-feminist text analysis', *Language and Literature*, 7/3, 234–52.

(1996a) 'Knowing y/our place', pp. 241–60, reprinted in Weber, J. ed. *The Stylistics Reader*, London, Routledge.

(1996b) 'Powerful talk', discussion paper, Loughborough University.

(1995a) 'Discontinuity and post-colonial discourse', *Ariel: A Review of International English Literature*, 26/3, 73–89.

(1995b) *Feminist Stylistics*, London, Routledge.

ed. (1994) *Gendering the Reader*, New York and London, Harvester Wheatsheaf.

Minh-ha, T. (1989) *Woman Native Other: Writing Postcoloniality and Feminism*, Bloomington, Indiana University Press.

Mohanty, C. (1984) 'Under Western eyes: feminist scholarship and colonial discourse', *Boundary* 2/3, 333–58.

Montgomery, M. (1999) 'Speaking sincerely: public reactions to the death of Diana', *Language and Literature*, 8/1, 5–33.

Morgan, C. (2005) 'Churchmen on brink of exodus over women bishops', *Sunday Times*, 10 July, 10.

Morrish, E. (1997) 'Falling short of God's ideal: public discourse about lesbians and gays', pp. 335–49, in Livia, A. and Hall, K. eds. *Queerly Phrased: Language, Gender and Sexuality*, Oxford University Press.

Muir, J. K. (1995) 'Hating for life: rhetorical extremism and abortion clinic violence', pp. 157–85, in Whillock, R. and Slayden, D. eds. *Hate Speech*, London, Sage.

Mullany, L. (2007) *Gendered Discourse in the Professional Workplace*, Basingstoke, Palgrave.

Nichols, P. (1998) 'Black women in the rural South: conservative and innovative', pp. 55–63, in Coates, J. ed. *Language and Gender: A Reader*, Oxford, Blackwell.

O'Barr, W. and Atkins, B. (1980) '"Women's language" or "powerless language"?', pp. 93–110, in McConnell-Ginet, S., Borker, R. and Furman, N. eds. *Women and Language in Literature and Society*, New York, Praeger.

Ochs, E. (1992) 'Indexing gender', pp. 335–59, in Duranti, A. and Goodwin, C. eds. *Rethinking Context: Language as an Interactive Phenomenon*, Cambridge University Press.

Ogbar, J. (2005) 'Review of *Nuthin' but a "G" Thang*: the culture and commerce of gangsta rap', *Journal of American History,* 92/3: 1072–3.

Page, R. (2005) *Literary and Linguistic Approaches to Feminist Narratology*, London, Palgrave.

Pauwels, A. (2003) 'Linguistic sexism and feminist linguistic activism', pp. 550–70, in Holmes, J. and Meyerhoff, M. eds. *The Handbook of Language and Gender*, Oxford, Blackwell.

(2001) 'Spreading the feminist word: the case of the new courtesy title *Ms* in Australian English', pp. 137–51, in Hellinger, M. and Bussmann, H. eds. *Gender Across Languages: The Linguistic Representation of Women and Men,* vol. I, Amsterdam and Philadelphia, John Benjamins.

(1998) *Women Changing Language*, London, Longman.

Pilkington, J. (1998) '"Don't try and make out that I'm nice!" The different strategies women and men use when gossiping', pp. 254–69, in Coates, J. ed. *Language and Gender: A Reader*, Oxford, Blackwell.

Potter, J. (1996) *Representing Reality: Discourse, Rhetoric and Social Construction*, London, Sage.

Queen, R. (1997) 'I don't speak Spritch: locating lesbian language', pp. 233–42, in Livia, A. and Hall, K. eds. *Queerly Phrased: Language, Gender and Sexuality*, Oxford University Press.

Quinn, E. (2000) '"Who's the Mack?" The performativity and politics of the pimp figure in gangsta rap', *Journal of American Studies*, 34/1, 115–36.

Rajagopalan, K. (2004) 'On being critical', *Critical Discourse Studies*, 1/2, 261–4.

Romaine, S. (2001) 'A corpus-based view of gender in British and American English', pp. 154–75, in Hellinger, M. and Bussmann, H. eds. *Gender Across Languages: The Linguistic Representation of Women and Men*, vol. I, Amsterdam and Philadelphia, John Benjamins.

Sadiqi, F. (2003) *Women, Men and Language in Morocco*, Leiden and Boston, Brill.

Schegloff, E. (1997) 'Whose text? Whose context?', *Discourse and Society*, 8/2, 165–85.

Schultz, M. (1990) 'The semantic derogation of women', pp. 134–48, in Cameron, D. ed. *The Feminist Critique of Language: A Reader*, 1st edition, London, Routledge.

Schwarz, J. (2003/2006) 'Quantifying non-sexist usage: the case of Ms.', pp. 142–8, in Sunderland, J. ed. *Language and Gender: An Advanced Resource Book*, London, Routledge.

Shaw, S. (2002) 'Language and gender in the House of Commons', PhD thesis, University of London.

Simpson, P. (2004) *Stylistics*, London, Routledge.

Sinclair, J. (1987) *Collins Cobuild English Language Dictionary*, London and Glasgow, Collins.

Skeggs, B. (1997) *Formations of Class and Gender: Becoming Respectable*, London, Sage.

Smith, S. (2004) 'The women to watch', *Radio Times*, 19–25 June, 21.

Smith, S. (1995) 'There's such a thing as free speech – it's a good thing too', pp. 224–64, in Whillock, R. and Slayden, D. eds. *Hate Speech*, London, Sage.

Spencer-Oatey, H. ed. (2000) *Culturally Speaking: Managing Rapport through Talk Across Cultures*, London, Continuum.

Spender, D. (1980) *Man Made Language*, London, Routledge.

Sperber, D. and Wilson, D. (1986) *Relevance: Communication and Cognition*, Oxford, Blackwell.

Spivak, G. (1990) *The Post-colonial Critic: Interviews, Strategies, Dialogues*, ed. Harasym, S., London, Routledge.

Stephens, V. (2005) 'Pop goes the rapper: a close reading of Eminem's genderphobia', *Popular Music*, 24/1, 21–36.

Stone, A. (2004) 'On the genealogy of women: a defence of anti-essentialism', pp. 85–96, in Gillis, S., Howie, G. and Munford, R. eds. *Third Wave Feminism: A Critical Exploration*, London, Palgrave.

Stryker, S. (2002) 'Plenary paper: transgendered identity and feminism', paper presented to the Third Wave Feminism conference, Exeter University.

Suhr, S. and Johnson, S. (2003) 'Revisiting PC: introduction to special issue on political correctness', *Discourse and Society*, 14/1, 5–16.

Sunderland, J. (2007) 'Contradictions in gendered discourses: feminist readings of sexist jokes?' *Gender and Language*, 1/2, 207–28.

ed. (2006) *Language and Gender: An Advanced Resource Book*, London, Routledge.

(2005) '"We're boys miss!": finding gendered identities and looking for gendering of identities in the foreign language classroom', pp. 160–79, in Mills, S. ed. *Language and Gender: Interdisciplinary Perspectives*, Harlow, Longman.

(2004) *Gendered Discourses*, London, Palgrave Macmillan.

Swann, J. (2002) 'Yes, but is it gender?', pp. 43–67, in Litosseliti, L. and Sunderland, J. eds. *Gender Identity and Discourse Analysis*, Amsterdam and Philadelphia, John Benjamins.

Talbot, M. (2007) 'Political correctness and freedom of speech', pp. 751–64, in Hellinger, M. and Pauwels, A. eds. *Handbook of Language and Communication: Diversity and Change*, Berlin and New York, Mouton de Gruyter.

(2003) 'Gender stereotypes: reproduction and challenge', pp. 468–86, in Holmes, J. and Meyerhoff, M. eds. *The Handbook of Language and Gender*, Oxford, Blackwell.

(1998) *Language and Gender: An Introduction*, London, Polity.

Talbot, M., Atkinson, K. and Atkinson, D. (2003) *Language and Power in the Modern World*, Edinburgh University Press.

Tannen, D. (1991) *You Just Don't Understand: Women and Men in Conversation*, London, Virago.

Taylor, T. (1992) *Mutual Misunderstanding: Scepticism and the Theorising of Language and Interpretation*, London, Routledge.

Thornborrow, J. (2002) *Power Talk: Language and Interaction in Institutional Discourse*, Harlow, Longman.

(1994) 'The woman, the man and the Filofax: gender positions in advertising', pp. 128–51, in Mills, S. ed. *Gendering the Reader*, Hemel Hempstead, Harvester Wheatsheaf.

Toolan, M. (2003) 'Le politiquement correct dans le monde français', *Discourse and Society*, 14/1, 69–86.

(1996) *Total Speech: An Integrational Linguistic Approach to Language*, Durham and London, Duke University Press.

Trades Union Congress (1998) *Words Can Never Hurt Me: A TUC Briefing on Avoiding Language which May Be Offensive to Disabled People*, London, TUC.

Troemel-Ploetz, S. (1998) 'Selling the apolitical', pp. 446–58, in Coates, J. ed. *Language and Gender: A Reader*, Oxford, Blackwell.

Van Dijk, T. (1995) 'Elite discourse and the reproduction of racism', in Whillock, R. and Slayden, D. eds. *Hate Speech*, London, Sage.

Vetterling-Braggin, M. ed. (1981) *Sexist Language*, New York, Littlefield Adams.

Volosinov, V. (1973) *Marxism and the Philosophy of Language*, trans. Matejka, L. and Titunik, I., New York, Seminar Press.

Walsh, C. (2001) *Gender and Discourse: Language and Power in Politics, the Church and Organisations*, Harlow, Longman/Pearson.

Wareing, S. (1994) 'And then he kissed her: the reclamation of female characters to submissive roles in contemporary fiction', pp. 117–36, in Wales, K. ed. *Feminist Linguistics in Literary Criticism*, Woodbridge, Boydell and Brewer.

Warner, E. (2005) 'Jilted Clara seeks suitor, Frenchman preferred', *Guardian*, 12 March, 30.

Webster, W. (1990) *Not a Man to Match Her*, London, Women's Press.

Wenger, E. (1998) *Communities of Practice*, Cambridge University Press.

Wetherell, M. and Potter, J. (1992) *Mapping the Language of Racism: Discourse and the Legitimisation of Exploitation*, Hemel Hempstead, Harvester Wheatsheaf.

Whelehan, I. (2000) *Overloaded: Popular Culture and the Future of Feminism*, London, Women's Press.

Whillock, D. (1995) 'Symbolism and the representation of hate in visual discourse', pp. 122–41, in Whillock, R. and Slayden, D. eds. *Hate Speech*, London, Sage.

Whillock, R. (1995) 'The use of hate as a stratagem for achieving political and social goals', pp. 28–54, in Whillock, R. and Slayden, D. eds. *Hate Speech*, London, Sage.

Whillock, R. and Slayden, D. eds. (1995) *Hate Speech*, London, Sage.

White, M. (2006) 'From Callaghan era to last days of Blair – Labour's great survivor', *Guardian*, 6 May, 4.

Wodak, R. (1998) *Disorders of Discourse*, Harlow, Longman.

Wodak, R. and Meyer, M. eds. (2001) *Methods of Critical Discourse Analysis*, London, Sage.

Wright, D. (2007) 'Disability discourse and women's writing', MPhil thesis, Sheffield Hallam University.

Wright, S. and Hay, J. (2000) 'Fred and Wilma: a phonological conspiracy', paper presented to the International Gender and Language Association, Stanford University, California.

Zwicky, A. (1997) 'Two lavender issues for linguists', pp. 21–35, in Livia, A. and Hall, K. eds. *Queerly Phrased: Language, Gender and Sexuality*, Oxford University Press.

Zylinska, J. (2006) 'Guns n' rappers: moral panics and the ethics of cultural studies', *Culture Machine,* http://culturemachine. tees.ac.uk/Cmach/Backissues/j006/article.

Index